Relationship Development Intervention with Children,
Adolescents and Adults

Companion volume

Relationship Development Intervention with Young Children
Social and Emotional Development Activities for Asperger Syndrome,
Autism, PDD and NLD
Steven E. Gutstein and Rachelle K. Sheely
ISBN 1 84310 714 7

of related interest

Asperger's Syndrome
A Guide for Parents and Professionals
Tony Attwood
Foreword by Lorna Wing
ISBN 1 85302 577 1

Pretending to be Normal
Living with Asperger's Syndrome
Liane Holliday Willey
Foreword by Tony Attwood
ISBN 1 85302 749 9

Relationship Development Intervention with Children, Adolescents and Adults

Social and Emotional Development Activities for Asperger Syndrome, Autism, PDD and NLD

Steven E. Gutstein and Rachelle K. Sheely

Jessica Kingsley Publishers
London and Philadelphia

The right of Steven E. Gutstein and Rachelle K. Sheely to be identified as authors of this work has been asserted by them in accordance with the Copyright, Designs and Patents Act 1988.

First published in the United Kingdom in 2002
by Jessica Kingsley Publishers Ltd
116 Pentonville Road
London N1 9JB, England

and

325 Chestnut Street
Philadelphia, PA 19106, USA
www.jkp.com

Copyright © 2002 Steven E. Gutstein and Rachelle K. Sheely

Library of Congress Cataloging in Publication Data
A CIP catalog record for this book is available from the Library of Congress

British Library Cataloguing in Publication Data
A CIP catalogue record for this book is available from the British Library

ISBN 1 84310 717 1

Printed and Bound in Great Britain
by Athenaeum Press, Gateshead, Tyne and Wear

"Friendship is unnecessary, like philosophy, like art... It has no survival value; rather it is one of those things that give value to survival."

C.S. Lewis

This book is dedicated to Oliver Lapin who blessed us by sharing his experiences with us for a too-brief time.

Contents

Activities

I

Introduction

Remove our emotional bonds with family, colleagues and friends and few of us would want to go on living. On a personal level we cherish relationships but, as a society, we sometimes do not appreciate their precious and fragile nature. We take for granted the capacity to make and keep friends. We laud those who show empathy and compassion, but we expend few resources and little time to ensure their development. As a result, we leave behind those born without the innate talent for making emotional connections. Some people believe that persons in the Autism Spectrum do not need friends, allies and lovers. They talk about the disorder as if those who suffer from it were aliens from another planet, but people with Asperger Syndrome, Pervasive Development Disorder (PDD), Autism and Non-Verbal Learning Disabilities (NLD) are human beings. One thing we all agree on is that the desire and need for emotion-based relationships is universal to the human species. We cannot deprive them of our most fundamental reason for being.

This is the second volume in a two-set collection of therapeutic activities for relationship development and it contains exercises for older children, adolescents and adults. Our work is especially useful for persons with Asperger Syndrome, PDD, Autism and NLD, but the activities in this book are equally applicable to anyone, regardless of diagnosis. We have provided over 150 activities and exercises ranging over the entire gamut of social and emotional development. The exercises presented in this book are based upon our six level, 24-stage Relationship Development Intervention (RDI) model. A prior book by Steven Gutstein, *Autism / Aspergers: Solving the Relationship Puzzle*, describes the theory and intervention model.

Producing these manuals has been the equivalent of writing a complete textbook for relationship skills. In the mathematical field our endeavor would be akin to publishing two volumes that ranged from simple addition to complex calculus. We are often asked why we use a developmental model. Why not just address age-appropriate social skills and not worry about things that have been missed in the past? Our response is to ask the person if they would recommend teaching calculus to a student who happened to be of college age, even if the student had never learned addition and subtraction. Or, what if we were teaching literature to a high school student and tried to assign an age-appropriate novel? Would this be a good idea if the student were so severely dyslexic, he could not decode the words on the page, let alone understand them? When we employ a mathematical or literary analogy, people quickly recognize the absurdity of such an endeavor. But, when it comes to friendship and relationship development, people lacking the fundamentals of relationship development continue to be taught advanced social skills. Relationships, like mathematics or reading, depend upon a foundation of many skills built one upon the other. You cannot do higher math until you've mastered the more basic skills. True friendships are like complex calculus, or complex literature. You cannot open a text to advanced friendship and expect much success if you have not mastered the earlier chapters on more basic forms of relationships.

How to use this book

Exercises in this book are designed for older children and adolescents. Adults who wish to use the exercises can do so with very few modifications. Younger children, who have completed exercises in the companion volume, can use the activities in Levels III and IV to continue with their development. We do not expect children to be ready for Level V until at least the age of seven. Level VI addresses those skills that are developmentally appropriate for individuals of young teenage years and above. If you are working with a child and are unsure of which of the books to choose, you can use the Relationship Development Questionnaire in Appendix A to help determine the best starting point.

We have included many objectives to help you plan and evaluate your program. An important aspect of our system is the ability to easily evaluate progress by tracking the specific objectives that have been mastered. These objectives are listed in Appendix C. Each one is related to a specific exercise, or series of exercises in one or both of the manuals. This means that you will always know why you are doing an activity.

Appendix C provides a cross-referenced index of activities and objectives. Most activities are presented in developmental progression. If you wish, you can move in a systematic fashion from one objective to the next, by progressing through the activities in the order they are presented.

If you would prefer to work on specific topic areas, rather than following the progression we have laid out, we provide a topic index of activities in Appendix D. Here you can choose a topic such as Conversation, or Emotional Regulation and find activities corresponding to it, listed in developmental order. As RDI is a developmental program, we believe it is helpful to begin working at the correct stage for each person. It is more important not to start too high than it is to begin too low. At The Connections Center, in Houston, we always begin our work by administering the Relationship Development Assessment (RDA) – a two-hour-long series of sample activities that we observe, videotape and carefully rate. We have begun training clinicians in different areas of the USA to use the RDA. Keep checking our website to see if there is anyone trained in your area: *www.connectionscenter.com*.

What if you cannot access a clinician who administers the RDA? Does this mean you should not go on with the program? Of course you should! Fill out the Relationship Development Questionnaire in Appendix A. Then read the descriptions and objectives for each stage. Try out the exercises for the stage that seem to best represent the developmental level of the person you are planning to work with (including yourself!). Make sure you have not skipped any critical developmental steps. For example, it astonishes us to see how many "High Functioning" persons come to us with deficits in basic Social Referencing, a skill we address in Stage 2 of our 24-stage model. Do not bypass these foundation skills in a rush to get to more age-appropriate exercises.

Who should use this book?

Parents

Parents can implement most of the exercises in the early stages. We have written this book to take the mystery out of social development. Many activity instructions are provided in a step-by-step manner that should not require a professional. By Stage 8, when peer partners are needed, we do recommend finding a suitable therapist, or other Coach, and carefully matching peers based on their level of progress. Most of our activities can be performed in a small group setting by Stage 10.

Adolescents and Adults

Adolescents and adults who wish to use the book themselves should have no trouble using many of the exercises that focus on thinking, self-development and emotion regulation. Of course you will need suitable partners if you wish to work on interaction activities.

Teachers and Special Educators

Teachers and Special Educators should enjoy using this manual. The RDI Program is designed for easy implementation in school settings. In fact we use it at The Monarch School, our own therapeutic day school with children that range in age from early childhood through high-school. Most of the exercises in this volume can and should be used in school settings with all students, whether they have specific disabilities or not. These volumes should make developing an Individualized Educational Plan – an IEP – a much simpler process, as the program provides clear objectives, which are connected to specific exercises and activities. While earlier activities should be performed with a Coach, once the person has reached Stage 4, and has acquired basic Apprenticeship skills, there is no reason why the activities cannot be done in small groups. Just keep in mind that until Stage 7, the Coach will still be the center of attention.

Therapists

Therapists should also greatly benefit from using these manuals. Our activities are already in use by therapists in various disciplines throughout the USA and Canada. An added benefit for clinic and managed care providers is the clear objectives that help obtain insurance coverage and demonstrate the effective utilization of resources.

Using the website as a companion

Although this is a self-contained manual, our website, *www.connectionscenter.com*, can be used as a companion to the book. It should serve as a major support to implement RDI. On the site you will find ways to contact clinicians from different areas who have been trained in our evaluation method – the RDA. We also list professionals whom we have trained to serve as Relationship Coaches, using the RDI model. Our message board allows parents and professionals to exchange tips and ideas for new and modified activities. It also provides a place where people from the same area can find one another to set up dyads and groups of partners at a similar stage. On the site you will find links to purchase all of the materials and supplies needed for the program. Finally, we are in the midst of videotaping and producing most of the RDI activities. Activity CDs and DVDs will be available for order on the site. All purchasers will receive a free limited time subscription to view videotaped segments of many of the activities described in the book. They will also have free, unlimited access to the activities archive and to the activities exchange message area.

What is the end product of RDI?

As you implement our program, you will notice significant changes. The person you are working with will be more fun to be with. She will smile and laugh more. She will dramatically increase the amount of time she spends looking at other people in a meaningful way – not just making eye contact, but also trying to figure out how you feel and think. She will appear more "alive" and natural and show more enthusiasm and joy. In the months and years to follow, you should expect to see the following social changes:

- Other people will feel that they are being seen as a real person and not an object.

- Communication and humor will become less scripted and more creative.

- There will be more invitations from peers and a much greater amount of peer acceptance.

- She will become a good collaborator and a valued team member.

- She will make contributions to others' lives.

- She will be much more fun to teach.

- She will make true friends who genuinely appreciate her.

- Her actions will be governed less by scripts and rules and more by your needs and feelings.

Thinking and information processing will change as well:

- She will act in a more flexible manner and be more accepting of change and transitions.

- She will be more curious about discovering new features of her world.

- She will be more creative in her communication, play and problem solving.

- She will consider several alternative solutions to problems.

- She will think in terms of "gray" areas, not just in "right or wrong, black and white" terms.

- She will seek out and value others' perspectives and opinions.

- She will be more aware of her unique identity.

Who is RDI for?

We are frequently asked if one age group, one disorder, or people at a certain level of severity are suitable for RDI. The answer is that RDI is a very broad-ranging program. About the only people who would not benefit from RDI are those for whom we must first address aggressive, oppositional or non-compliant behaviors.

- RDI activities are designed for the entire range of Asperger Syndrome, PDD, Autism and NLD with exercises suitable for all types of people.

- The program can and should be used with persons who are not AS or Autistic but who have relationship development problems, such as Attention Deficit Hyperactivity Disorder (ADHD), Tourette Syndrome and learning disabilities.

- Activities are presented which can be useful for persons from age two onward.

Where did RDI come from?

I [Steve] spent over twenty years studying relationships as a child, marital and family therapist, academic researcher and program developer. After years of working intensively with people in the Autism Spectrum, Rachelle and I grew dissatisfied with the limited results we obtained using the methods that were available. We believed that many people in the Autism Spectrum were capable of participating as true partners in authentic emotional relationships, if only we provided a means for them to learn about and experience them in a gradual, systematic way. For the past ten years we have been developing and refining our assessment and intervention methods based upon this belief.

In the next chapter we will discuss the essential skills of friendship and how relationship skills are different from other social skills. The third chapter provides you with information about how to get started in our program. Beginning with Level 1: Novice, we describe activities for the six levels of our program. Each Level section introduces and covers the activities for that level.

2
Relationships

In preparing this book, we reviewed the extensive research on friendship. We distilled our findings into ten skill areas representing the qualities of people who are successful in finding and maintaining friends. These skills progressively build upon one another over a period of many years. The skill areas are: Enjoyment, Referencing, Reciprocity, Repair, Co-Creation, We-go, Social Memories, Maintenance, Alliance and Acceptance. As you progress through our exercises you might find it helpful to return to this section and use it as a reference for the areas you are addressing. Below, we provide a brief description of each area:

Enjoyment

Friends must be enjoyable, exciting companions. Persons with enthusiasm and an upbeat mood are valued, even if they have other deficits or limitations. Friends strive to find ways to make positive emotional connections with their peers. The nature of this connection changes developmentally, with collaborative play giving way to conversations involving humor, shared interests, emotions and problem solving about relationships.

Referencing

Being a friend means that the feelings, ideas and actions of social companions become a primary reference point for determining our behavior. What our friends do matters to us a great deal and we are constantly "referencing" them. In its earliest stages, "referencing" involves basing your actions on the immediate emotional reactions of your social partners. Referencing rapidly moves to the "inside" world and becomes a continual discovery of the minds of our social partners. Good friends develop mental "reference maps" of the interests, favorite activities, strengths and weaknesses of their pals.

Reciprocity

Friends must "pull their own weight." Reciprocal, "give-and-take" relationships begin when young children learn to become equal partners in order to maintain the shared meaning and enjoyment of their social encounters. At a later stage, reciprocity becomes focused on mutual appreciation and support. The person who is responsive to a friend's needs and interests has the right to expect responsiveness in return. Good friends expect that at times they will choose to give up doing something they want to do in order to satisfy the strong desire of a friend.

Repair

Friends must be able to manage disagreements and resolve conflicts without doing permanent damage. Individuals who disagree more than they agree are unlikely to become friends, but you cannot have unrealistic expectations of friends and friendships. Many people encounter difficulties because they expect their friends never to disappoint them, to know everything about them, or to be their friend exclusively. Hurt feelings and disappointments are an unavoidable part of close friendships. The person who is unwilling, or unable, to forgive others or seek to "repair" his relationships will have difficulty forming close friendships. A friend must be able to separate the intentions of an act from its consequences and be ready to understand that the motivations of friends are sometimes not clearly demonstrated by their actions. Finally, a friend must be willing and able to look within himself and that he is responsible for causing some of the difficulties that inevitably occur.

Improvisation and Co-Creation

One of the major payoffs of a friendship is the enjoyment we feel when we find off-beat or novel ways to share our perceptions and ideas in off-beat or novel ways that produce our own unique products. Others may not appreciate our "inside" jokes. But they bring us to our knees with laughter every time.

We-go

Being a friend means that you experience yourself as an essential part of greater unit than just yourself. Friendship implies the concept of a "We-go" – a group Ego that allows friends to accomplish things that they could never do alone.

Social Memories

Successful and stimulating experiences contribute to a sense of shared history, joint fate and a perception of investment in the relationship. Friends jointly record Social Memories that become the essential glue that cements friendships together. Memories of sharing joy and overcoming adversity remain with the friendship forever and serve to rekindle it in times of adversity, or after periods of inactivity.

Maintenance

One of the hallmarks of friendship is the desire to commit free time to one another in the absence of pressures or external rewards to do so. Good friends think about each other, even when they are apart. They keep in contact on a regular basis. They maintain this contact just to stay connected, without other agendas or ulterior motives.

Alliance

Friends rely on one another. Keeping confidences, sticking up for someone and being honest, are all behaviors which encourage close friendships. A person who violates confidences, acts disloyally with a friend when others are around, or engages in deception is perceived as unreliable. As children get older they judge friends based upon consistency between their words and their deeds. You must be willing and able to help your friends when they are in need, not just when it is convenient for you to do so.

Acceptance

People are at ease with their friends because they feel liked and accepted by someone who is familiar with their strengths and their weaknesses, their charming and their irritating qualities. When you succeed at difficult endeavors, your friends are expected to recognize these achievements with congratulations and to express admiration. By contrast, failures and negative events provide equally important opportunities for functioning as a source of support, with displays of acceptance, affection, caring and concern. Friends are called upon to provide help, advice, comfort and emotional support. Criticism must also be rendered tactfully, but only when it is needed.

Relationship Skills

Reading these, you may have noticed that many of the skills involved in being a good friend differ from typical social skills that you may have practiced or read about. We are used to thinking of social skills as specific behaviors, such as making eye contact, waiting your turn, smiling, shaking hands and asking polite questions. In fact, these behaviors are types of social skills, but learning them does not lead to friendships. They are more about getting what you need and fitting into society. Scientists refer to them as "Instrumental Skills" because, when we employ them, we tend to use people like instruments to get our needs met. When people use the term "Social Skills," most of them are really thinking about Instrumental Skills, but the set of attributes that leads to friendship does not fall into the instrumental category.

Instead of learning a repertoire of behaviors, a person wishing to develop real friendships must learn a new way to observe his social environment. He must rapidly process the critical emotional information he sees and hears and use that information as the critical reference point for determining his actions. Only then will he be able to apply the appropriate behavior to the interaction and experience both success and pleasure. "Relationship Skills" are a second type of social interaction. Both Instrumental and Relationship Skills are important, but only Relationship Skills lead to friendships. Instrumental Skills are applicable to situations where social contact is pursued as a means to an end. Relationship Skills have a very different purpose. They are used to create and deepen emotional connections between people, share excitement and joy, collaborate for novel problem solving, reach shared goals and cooperate in joint creative efforts. The following diagram provides a simple illustration of this distinction:

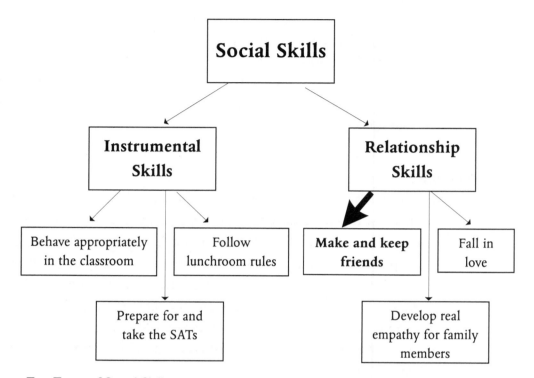

Two Types of Social Skills

Relationships teach us the importance of considering multiple perspectives and viewpoints. They demonstrate the validity of multiple ways of thinking, feeling, problem solving and behaving. Through our relationship encounters, we see the world through another's eyes and notice that it is not identical to our own. Relationships teach us to think relatively. In a relationship things are not absolute. Actions are useful or not, depending upon how they affect our level of coordination. Rather than pushing a button or following a script, we have to constantly evaluate and re-evaluate the state of the relationship and make ongoing adjustments.

Instrumental and Relationship Skills require very different learning methods. This fundamental difference is the reason we developed our RDI Program. It is also why many of the exercises in this book may appear different than other approaches you have heard about or tried.

When we teach Instrumental Skills, we work with memorized scripts that are employed in a specific manner in order to reach a desired endpoint. We teach people to recognize the proper context in which to perform a particular script. These social stories or scripts are best learned in natural environments, so that you will recognize the context and connect the script with the specific setting. They are best taught through direct instruction, social stories, behavioral shaping and modeling. The partners we choose for learning Instrumental Skills are typically more competent people. Often we will assign a more capable buddy to serve as a role model. The curriculum for Instrumental Skills involves learning a set of rules and expecting that everyone will follow them. The progression of learning entails the gradual accumulation of a larger repertoire of discrete scripts for as many settings as possible. Skills are selected based upon the age of the person and the daily settings he must encounter. The main objective is to help the person cope with the day-to-day problems and situations that he faces.

Relationship Skills cannot rely on pre-selected scripts. The actions we take in a relationship depend heavily upon what our partner is doing at that instant. The "right" action is only determined by "referencing" the actions and reactions of our social partners and these change from moment to moment. Relationships require constant regulation and balancing because they involve the ongoing introduction of novelty. We have to ensure that the amount of variation introduced is not so great that the interaction degenerates into confusion and chaos. But, if there is too little novelty and creativity, the encounter becomes stilted and boring. Success in relationships requires learning to continually monitor and regulate a balance between variation and creativity on the one hand and predictability and structure on the other. It is like an ongoing juggling act – we try to add as many balls as possible without dropping any of them.

Relationship competence requires a careful, systematic layering of skills. They must be taught with increasing complexity and carefully added as the person gains new levels of understanding and mastery. Each step we take in constructing relationship competence serves as the scaffolding for the next step in a carefully crafted manner.

Learning to rapidly observe and process the relationship between a social partner's actions and your own, is a highly complex endeavor. Learning this new form of information processing requires the full attention of people who are not innately talented, for example, individuals in the Autism Spectrum. These "coordination" skills must first be learned and mastered in simple one-on-one environments, where there are no distractions or other demands placed upon the person. Initially, the best teachers are adults whom we refer to as "Coaches." They act as both guides and participants. Coaches lead the person on a gradual path of learning where they develop skills to help them manage increasingly complex environments as a more equal partner. When the person is ready to work with a peer, it is best to find someone who is at the same level of development. More competent partners tend to delay the development of regulation and referencing skills that the less able person needs for relationship competence. The more able partner tends to do all of the "Relationship Balancing." Even the best juggler may add too many balls or become distracted for a moment and the same is true with relationships. No matter how skilled we are, relationships are always becoming disconnected and so participants must learn to monitor for breakdowns and quickly effect repairs. They will not do this if more competent partners are taking care of problems for them.

3

Using the activities

RDI is an invitational model. You will not be coercing or bribing. Rather, as a guide, you will invite the person to let you lead him to new and exciting means of involvement with the world. You will introduce new things to see, hear and touch and new ways to move, play and speak. You are a guide to an unfamiliar but potentially thrilling (or terrifying) world.

Relationships are self-motivating and inherently reinforcing. When we engage in encounters with friends and loved ones, we feel an immediate increase in excitement and joy, or a sudden decrease in anxiety or distress. Unfortunately, the people that this book addresses do not initially obtain the same degree of satisfaction from their interactions. Throughout our program, you will notice that we work hard to provide samples of the potential payoffs in enjoyment and competence that can be obtained from social encounters. As quickly as possible we want the person to observe his social world because he is curious and excited about what he might see and hear around him rather than for any material reward. We want him to be thinking, "Let me see what is going on. It might be interesting and fun."

Anyone who learns to be a good friend will almost certainly know how to be a good son, daughter, sister, brother, father, team-mate, husband and co-worker. Relationship skills are almost all interchangeable. Friendship skills are to have the same attributes that make a good family member, boy scout and team-mate. You cannot learn to be a good friend without being good at these other relationships as well.

Information for Coaches

If you are a parent, or "helping professional," this section is for you. We want you to become a trusted guide to the social world. We hope to teach you how to add small bits of novelty, mixed with predictable elements, in such a way that they are exciting rather than disturbing. You will be acting in a type of partnership, but one that will initially be quite unequal. It does not make sense to allow a person who is learning disabled in relationships to be in the lead, with you, the more expert guide, following behind. That would be like expecting a person with severe dyslexia to discover how to overcome his handicap by himself. You will take as many elements as possible from what the person provides and integrate them into your activities and phrases, but you will decide which elements to chose.

You must not only guide, you must also pace. Pacing means carefully observing and matching the person's need for movement, action and language. It means incorporating her words, phrases and even some of her activities, as long as they do not interfere with your guidance. It means carefully determining how quickly you can add new exercises, modify existing ones and chain them all together. It means determining how many times you can repeat an activity before she grows bored. All of these things create a greater sense of meaning and familiarity and in turn allow you to add more excitement and novelty.

We have chosen the term "Coach" to describe your role. The term can apply whether you are a parent, teacher, therapist, or other involved person. The designation of the word "Coach" moves us away from a medical "pathology" model. Coaching requires careful observation. It also requires a different style of communication. You will slow down your speech, use fewer words, and amplify and exaggerate your non-verbal communication. You are also going to become skilled at walking a tightrope of guiding and pacing, always trying to stay right at the edge of the person's competence; the point of maximum learning potential. Your objective is to introduce continual, pleasant surprises. This is akin to going to an amusement park, where a ride leaves you pleasantly startled and wanting to immediately ride again. You will inevitably make mistakes. Even our most trained clinicians err on the side of either too much variation or predictability. The key is to learn from your mistakes and rapidly modify the balance.

Pay careful attention to changes in your role as you move through the different stages and levels. You should begin as a highly directive (but hopefully fun) guide. In the beginning you may have to invite a Novice – the term we use for someone at the first level of the program – in physical ways. You may turn his head, not to force him to make eye contact, but to show him where an exciting face is so that he can enjoy it. However, you should not continue to turn his head to "make him" look. That is coercive and he may develop an aversion to looking. Instead, you can make a loud noise that startles him into looking, but you should not continue to startle just for the sake of upsetting him. Over time your role will shift. By the close of Level II you will have become an activity partner. By the close of Level III you will have begun to move into the role of a facilitator; no longer the center of attention, but still an important resource to peer partners engaged in their joint efforts. The changes are gradual and subtle, but critical nonetheless.

The relationship curriculum

The RDI curriculum is composed of six levels – Novice, Apprentice, Challenger, Voyager, Explorer and Partner – and 24 stages. Each level has four stages. Each of the six levels represents a dramatic developmental shift in the central focus of relationships. As we move up the levels, the number and complexity of skills necessary for success increases exponentially. The following chapters begin with brief summaries of stages and levels. For those of you not familiar with the RDI system we present a brief outline of the six levels below:

Level I: Novice

Level I is structured around teaching the pre-requisites for becoming a good Apprentice in Level II. As such, it sets the stage for all future guidance. The first goal is to make sure you, the Coach, are the center of attention when the two of you are together. The next is to develop the skills of Social Referencing; literally using other people as primary reference points. The third goal focuses on the person learning to accept having his or her behavior regulated by the Coach, so that he or she can go on to learn the skills of coordinating actions with social partners.

Level II: Apprentice

Our second level introduces the responsibilities of shared regulation and communication repair. We also emphasize the importance of learning to enjoy variation and rapid transition. At the end of Level II we begin working with carefully matched peer partners whom we refer to as "dyads."

Level III: Challenger

This middle level introduces Challengers to the enjoyment of Improvisation and Co-Creation. In this level we introduce activities designed to provide the experience of what it means to have a "We-go" – a group Ego that gives us the ability to accomplish things we could never imagine achieving on our own. By the close of Level III, we may begin working in small groups.

Level IV: Voyager

This pivotal level celebrates the movement of relationships to the world of perceptions and subjective experience. Here, the Voyager is introduced to different perspectives and the use of imagination to enhance his joint voyage through the world. In Level IV, Voyagers come to grips with a world that is not defined by absolutes. It is a world where your point of view, the way you uniquely interpret your world, is just as important as what you actually see and hear.

Level V: Explorer

In Level V the topic of relationships again transforms, this time to the inner world of ideas, interests, beliefs and emotional reactions. Conversation takes on a whole new richness and depth as partners try to share each other's inner worlds. The person is now capable of exploring his, and others' pasts and futures, and to put himself in another's shoes – an important step in developing empathy.

Level VI: Partner

Our final Level focuses on the types of partnerships that we develop for lifelong relationships. Partners re-examine their relationships with family and groups in a new, more sophisticated light. They develop a coherent sense of Personal Identity and they seek out more mature friendships based on trust and personal disclosure.

An overview of activities

By just skimming through the activities in this volume, it may appear as if we have covered the "terrain" and left no relationship stone unturned. Nothing could be farther from the truth. While the breadth of the program appears huge compared with a typical text on social skills or emotional development, there is much more work to be done. Most of the exercises we present are models or are representative of many others that stand behind them. A number of additional activities are suggested or described in the "Variations" section of each activity. We also encourage you to develop your own variations.

The exercises are laid out in what we hope is a user-friendly manner. Each one begins by identifying "Activity Highlights" – a quick way of identifying the main theme of the exercise. This is followed by a brief summary which provides a more in-depth overview and rationale as well as tying the activity to those that come before and after it. The next sections are the "nuts and bolts" of the activity. "Participants" describes the optimal number of persons who should be involved. Typically Stage 7 is an ideal time to expand the social unit and include a matched peer partner. "Getting Ready" describes the materials and preparation needed. "Coaching Instructions" are just that; step-by-step directions for implementing the activity. Following this, the "Variations" section describes or suggests activities that we feel would be excellent extensions and/or complements of the "main attraction." The final section, "Obstacles/Opportunities," contains critical points to look out for in both positive and potentially negative domains.

In the initial levels, a typical practice period will include several different activities. The length of practice periods and number of activities within a period is related to the person's attention span and need for variety. We prefer that you consider using more frequent, brief periods of 30 minutes to an hour, rather than fewer, longer ones. The exercises are designed for repeated practice and many require a good number of hours to complete. Some activities will take months to reach a level of proficiency and others weeks. How long an activity takes to master depends upon the person you are working with and the time you have allotted for practice. We urge you not to rush! We recognize that this requires a high level of commitment, but we have found that there is simply no quick and easy way to learn relationship skills.

Of course, you are free to use whichever activities you wish in whatever order you wish to use them. We have no objections to your skipping any exercises you find unappealing, or that address objectives you believe have already been mastered. However, we do caution you against using activities that may be significantly above the person's developmental level as this can lead to a frustrating experience for everyone.

The activities are presented in order of their level and stage. For those who choose not to follow the RDI model, Appendix D provides a handy reference of activities listed by commonly understood topic areas.

For those in schools and other professional settings where objectives must be clearly specified prior to authorization of intervention, Appendix C provides an index of activities that corresponds with each objective. You can pick your target objectives and immediately reference the exercises that correspond to each.

Friendships require many skills not usually thought of as "social." Therefore, our curriculum encompasses a number of non-social objectives including flexible thinking, rapid attention shifting, reflection, planning, forethought, preparation, emotion regulation, improvisation, creativity, mistake management and problem solving. Along with these, friendships also require more familiar social skills. Among these are reciprocal conversation, collaboration, and teamwork, all of which are amply covered in this book.

Tips for Relationship Coaches

Before we move on to the activities, we want to briefly outline some of the basic principles of being an RDI Coach. We hope you will return to this section frequently and use it as a reference point for your work.

Focus on competence

We cannot emphasize how important it is to teach persons in the Autism Spectrum, and others with relationship disorders, that they can be active, capable participants in the relationship process. Feelings of competence and mastery are just as reinforcing as joy and excitement. When people know they can "pull their own weight" and act as equal partners, it dramatically increases their motivation. This is a good reason to begin working at a simple stage, where the person can more quickly achieve mastery. This is also a reason to match peers carefully when the time is right, rather than placing someone with more severe deficits with a more competent peer, a scenario that is bound to create a feeling of incompetence in the less able.

Work towards equal partnership

Persons in the Autism Spectrum learn best when they are matched with peers who have the same tempo and need for slow-paced, sequenced learning and carefulness as they do. Evenly matching peers increases the likelihood that each person will perceive the need to act as a partner in order to regulate their activity. We find that matching persons with equal development and then placing them together in "dyads" and groups to help each other learn, leads to the development of intensely powerful emotional bonds. The history of struggling and succeeding together as equals creates an experience of "We-go" that is unmatched by any other.

In a similar vein, we ask that you do not prematurely worry about larger groups. Groups are often used because they are cheaper to conduct. That does not mean they are effective. In the first three levels of development, relationships are best learned in one-on-one relationships.

Spotlight

As you use the activities, you must learn to make sure that you keep the focus trained on your non-verbal communication. We call this "spotlighting." Emotions are communicated primarily through the visual medium so you need to learn to limit your language and also emphasize your facial expressions, voice inflection and movement.

Keep it simple

Relationship skills have to be developed in a careful, systematic progression, with one set of skills serving as the scaffolding to support the next level of complexity. In the beginning you will need to keep the environment simple. You will also need to keep your objectives simple, and make sure that you are only working on one thing at a time. You will also need to simplify activities and begin with exercises where objects do not compete for attention, thus leaving the person's focus free to concentrate on learning a new way of perceiving and thinking.

Create a space for RDI

When we talk about "space," we are referring to both the physical and mental dimensions. You cannot limit relationship skills to a specific time in the day. There should be a "lab" time; a period when you get to practice and modify activities. However, if you cannot generalize the skills into the rest of the day, they will just fade away. On the other hand, make sure that your efforts do not become all work and no play. Watch out for burnout. This is a marathon not a sprint and these activities must be genuinely fun for everyone. If it seems like work, this is a sign you may be doing something wrong.

Balance enjoyment with responsibility

Try to keep things fun and lively, but do not allow too much variation and novelty before the person can function as a partner in regulating the interaction. We always make sure that those we work with can be a regulating partner before we allow them to improvise and participate with us in adding new elements to activities. Remember: "regulation" before "creation!"

Make sure skills are meaningful

As you move through the exercises, you will notice that we take great pains to ensure that there is some value and meaning for every skill being taught. You may use external reinforcement to teach skills that have little intrinsic payoff, but do not be surprised if the skills are not used outside the specific setting where they were taught. Years ago, we taught social skills without much consideration for developmental readiness and meaning. We successfully taught complex skills such as joint attention, but found that they were never used outside the treatment setting.

Find the edge of development and stay there

Many people with relationship disorders are placed in social settings where they wind up doing too much work for too little payoff. None of us will retain the motivation to do something when we receive little benefit and especially when we feel incompetent. We do not want to put people in situations of intense frustration and incompetence. We try to find the boundary area that allows for both understanding and independence under the tutelage of a Coach, because that is the spot where the most excitement lies. The correct stage to work on is one that is not so low that it is boring but equally not so high as to be overwhelming.

As you journey through the following pages, we want you to remember the most important principle of RDI, which we refer to as "Joyful Collaboration." When developing relationships it is critical that everyone experiences a great deal of joy. Furthermore, the source of joy must be seen as the product of a unique collaboration. The participant must perceive that joy emanates not from a game or toy, but from sharing a special experience with a social partner. If you keep the concept of Joyful Collaboration in mind, the following activities will reward you as they come to life for you and your participant.

LEVEL I: NOVICE

Introduction

Summary

The goal of Level I is to develop a core relationship between Novice and Coach. We begin the RDI Program by working on the skills of being a good Apprentice – literally one who recognizes that he is in need of guidance by a Master. In Stage 1, the face and gestures of the Coach become the center of attention. The Novice learns in Stage 2 to use non-verbal information – the Coach's reactions and expressions – as a critical reference point for his own behavior. Stage 3 provides Novices with a primer on following the guiding actions of the Coach. Stage 4 introduces the experience of coordinating actions with another person. The data crucial for this is derived from comparing one's actions with those of a partner to determine the best way to create and maintain a connection. This is a new form of perception and information processing which will be crucial for the remainder of their lives.

Level I skills are like the foundation of a house and as such are essential support for the entire structure. Yet because they are hidden underneath more sophisticated skills in typical relationship encounters, there is often a tendency to rush through, or bypass, these critical skills, especially when working with older or more verbal persons. However, we have found time and time again, that insufficient practice at Level I has resulted in dead-ends in development later on.

We are often asked if there are any precursors to beginning RDI. Our answer to this is that while our activities in Stage 1 are geared for a very basic level, they cannot be successful with a Novice who is unwilling to comply with instructions, or one who is highly defiant. These Novices are candidates for behavioral approaches that emphasize compliance and the acceptance of direction and instruction, hopefully using positive reinforcement approaches. While not essential, it is also helpful if the Novice has some experience with structured teaching approaches and has learned to follow at least a simple activity schedule.

Participants

Coach and Novice are the sole participants in Level I. In our opinion the Novice is a person who is not yet ready to manage a relationship with peers, nor can she handle interaction with more than one person. In Level I the Coach is doing almost all of the work involved in maintaining the relationship. Initially it is important to have a single, main Coach who becomes the center of the Novice's attention, but as we move to the end of Stage 1, we are already interested in expanding the list of persons who qualify as a Coach.

Settings

The first few activities of Stage 1 are designed to teach you both to change your style of communication. Later activities are designed as specific exercises to be conducted within controlled settings. In Level I many Novices may be highly distractible and we do not want to constantly compete for attention with objects and noise, so we try to limit potential visual and auditory distractions. The degree to which we set up a minimal stimulation environment as our intervention setting is wholly dependent upon the distractibility of the Novice. Sometimes we have to begin in an almost completely bare room whereas other Novices may only require a careful consideration of objects that serve as competitors for their attention.

Language

Language in Level I is used to enhance facial referencing and not distract from, or compete with it. Vocalization is used for the enhancement of excitement, the direct attention to our faces and to celebrate our simple successes. Ritualized song segments, often repeated "chants," set phrases and silly words are used for their relationship-binding and enhancement elements. We often take phrases that the Novice enjoys and repeat them, with slight changes in emphasis or rhythm and find that this significantly increases their fun. We may pick up on stereotypical language, modify it and then add it contextually to the activity we are setting up. For example, one of our young children was repetitively saying, "Blue bubbles" during a marbles activity. We turned this into "Bubbles please, bubbles please," and then "Big blue bubbles please." The following is a short list of how language is used in Level I:

- Repeat a common phrase. First very slowly and then very rapidly.

- Purposely fail to complete an often-repeated phrase or sentence and observe as the Novice completes it.

- Pause at a crucial word in a frequently used phrase and allow the Novice to fill it in.

- Add or substitute just one word to increase the silliness of a phrase but still leave the phrase recognizable.

- Language used for celebration:
    - We did it!
    - That was great!
    - Good work!

- Yeah!
- Give me five!
- Wow!
- Cool!
- That's funny!
- That's silly!

Coaching Points

- Remain firmly in charge of the structure of all activities. Novices are allowed to introduce only small amounts of variation.

- During the initial stages of intervention, we usually combine a number of Stage 1 and 2 activities in a ritualized, but fast-pace practice period.

- Stage 1 may take a great deal of energy. If you are a parent trying to do the work yourself, consider finding students and other helpers to relieve you.

- Carefully observe and make a list of language, objects and other elements to determine which enhance, which distract and which are neutral as agents to focus the Novice's attention onto you.

- It is critical for activities to be exciting and to produce happiness. They should never be practiced when you, or the Novice, is tired or in a bad mood.

- Prepare to be very exaggerated and dramatic with your face, gestures and voice tone. You must use continual variation of voice tone, pitch, volume and phrasing in exciting, enjoyable ways.

- Take a short break about every ten minutes to evaluate spontaneous referencing and initiation skills.

- Watch out for a tendency for the Novice to try to control the interaction.

- Watch out for the Novice being entertained by your actions rather than sharing the enjoyment with you through face-to-face emotion sharing.

- Don't project how you are feeling onto the Novice. Because you think you are sharing the same experience doesn't mean he is. If the Novice tries to do the activity by himself without you, it means that he has not learned that you are a crucial part of his enjoyment.

- Referencing should increase dramatically in the first 30 hours of practice.

- There is no need to teach eye contact as a discrete skill. When we work in RDI, Novices learn to gaze at our faces not because we provide some external reward, but because they are curious about our expressions and eager to share our emotions.

STAGE 1: ATTEND

Goals and Objectives

The activities in Stage 1 are designed to create sufficient motivation, so that henceforth the Novice will orient to Coaches as the center of attention, without any prompting or external reinforcement. The main objective of this stage is to eliminate or drastically reduce the need to cue, or prompt the Novice in order to get his attention. When the Novice is focusing on your face and actions, it is much simpler to invite her to participate in increasingly more exciting and enjoyable activities.

Activity Summary

The stage begins with activities that provide guidelines on how to conduct communication with someone at Level I. The first four exercises train you to simplify and amplify the communication environment. You will learn to use fewer words and to use your words more meaningfully and powerfully. You will work on reducing the amount of energy spent prompting the person to respond. You will "spice-up" your communication with unexpected actions and sounds. Finally, you will learn to spotlight and amplify your expressions, in order to magnify the importance of non-verbal facial communication.

Following these initial activities, we move on to exercises that emphasize excitement and fun. Curiosity and a desire to share enjoyment will hopefully replace verbal prompting and external reinforcement as the major reason why the person pays attention to you. We typically observe significant increases in facial expression and emotional communication, due to this new motivation. We also expect increases in the number of shared smiles, amount of laughter, appreciative communications, and requests to initiate and continue enjoyable activities. If you complete the activities we have presented but find that you need more before moving on, you can consult our companion book aimed at younger children – *Relationship Development Intervention with Young Children*, which provides a more extensive repertoire of Stage 1 exercises.

Critical Tips

- Limit verbal communication and spotlight your facial communication.

- Communicate verbally only when the Novice is watching your face.

- Use "indirect" cues when the Novice is not paying attention to your communication.

- Emphasize the excitement and fun of interacting over the demand for interaction.

- Observe carefully to determine the correct length and pacing of an activity.

- Observe carefully to determine objects that interfere with social attention.

- Remain clearly in control of activities.

- Introduce sufficient unpredictability in your actions so that the Novice is motivated to continue monitoring your actions and whereabouts.

- Take frequent breaks so that you can rest and provide an opportunity for the Novice to communicate with you.

My Words are Important

ACTIVITY HIGHLIGHTS
○ Developing attentiveness to communication

○ Learning to value your words

○ How to speak so you are listened to

Summary:

How often do you become frustrated because you have to repeat yourself over and over again? Many Novices in the Autism Spectrum do not listen well. They are easily distracted and require the speaker to repeat himself and do all the work of making sure that the communication is received. In this exercise, we emphasize, in a subtle way, that both the speaker and listener have responsibilities during communication.

In this exercise, Novices learn to use indirect cues to increase their attention to the speaker. It is important for them not to rely on prompts ("Pay Attention! Look at me! Are you listening!"), to know when to pay attention. Such direct prompts result in increased "prompt dependence;" always waiting for someone to provide a cue to listen, before shifting attention to the communicator. The indirect prompts we use in this activity do not create the same type of dependency. The Novice perceives himself as voluntarily choosing to take an orienting action, rather than being requested or told to do so. The perception of voluntary action leaves him less prompt dependent and more likely to pay attention in the future, without any cues or prompts. The emphasis on developing voluntary action is a theme that you will find in all of our exercises.

You will notice that the first activities in this initial stage do not fall under the heading of "exercises." Rather they encourage you to make changes in your communication style. Think of these activities as new communication habits we would like you to develop.

Participants:

This exercise requires participation from all of the significant persons in the environment.

Getting Ready:

Remember that this is not an activity to reserve for a specific time or place. It is an ongoing method of communication that you should employ, until the Novice pays attention to your communication without prompts.

Coaching Instructions:

Do not provide any formal explanation. You will be observing and gauging your actions based upon whether the Novice is listening carefully and visually observing you when you speak. There are three basic steps in this exercise:

☐ STEP 1   DELIBERATE SPEECH

The first step requires that everyone communicating with the Novice slow their rate of speech and, when they do speak, they should leave more deliberate pauses between words and sentences. This will take extensive practice and feedback. Do not underestimate the importance of changing your language style, even for very verbal Novices. By speaking slower and with clearer enunciation, you increase the value of each of the words spoken and you also make it simpler for them to process the information.

☐ STEP 2   BALANCING

The next step is to keep your communication in "balance." "Balancing" your communication has two elements. First, try not to use more words in any utterance than the Novice uses. This means that if he normally speaks in two or three word phrases, you should also keep your own phrases at this length. If the Novice is completely non-verbal, you should use very short phrases. The second part of balance entails not adding further words until the Novice provides a meaningful response the first set of words that you have spoken. Don't continually repeat yourself and don't add more information if your initial information has been ignored. If we are aiming to make our words valuable to the listener, it is important that we do not continue to provide more words, if initial words are not attended to. If you do, it will devalue your words.

☐ STEP 3   SPOTLIGHTING

The third step is to insert "spotlighting" elements into your speech. These are indirect but powerful signals that some important information which requires attention is being presented . Spotlighting helps the Novice perceive the words you choose to stand out. Spotlighting is much more effective than "cueing" in creating generalization and the perception that the Novice has "chosen" to focus attention. You will need to experiment with what alterations in your speech pattern produce the most effective "spotlights" and have the most impact on attention. You may insert a deep breath, a sigh, or a "stutter" when coming to a critical point in a sentence. You may get "stuck" on one word, repeating it, as if stuttering for about five seconds or so. Stuttering at critical moments usually results in a gaze shift and rapidly increased focus. If a stutter on its own does not work, we will often make a significant shift in voice volume to accompany the stutter.

Variations:

Other options for providing indirect cues include, changing voice tone, slowing down your rate of speech, pausing, coughing and clearing your throat.

Obstacles/Opportunities:

Occasionally, someone with autism appears oblivious to these methods. They may monitor their communication environment so poorly that they do not even notice your highly emphasized, indirect prompts. Initially, they will require a behavior modification approach in order to learn to how respond to direct prompts. Then, this exercise should be applied as a second step.

I Lost my Voice

ACTIVITY HIGHLIGHTS

° Develop attentiveness to facial expressions

° Increase the importance of non-verbal communication

Summary:

This activity is similar to "My Words are Important" in that it emphasizes that other people's communication should be the focus of the Novice's attention. The difference is that now we emphasize the need to pay attention to faces, rather than words. Many highly verbal people attend to much of the language directed at them, but are oblivious to the non-verbal communication that accompanies the words. They continue to communicate while looking away, walking away and even out of sight of others. They devalue non-verbal communication and unwittingly train us to do likewise when we are with them. Unfortunately, research tells us that over seventy per cent of a speaker's intent is communicated through non-verbal channels. This exercise is a critical training experience for anyone wishing to be a Coach.

Participants:

Once again, we will need the cooperation of all the important persons in the environment.

Getting Ready:

This activity requires that the Novice seek out your non-verbal communication for fun, excitement and needed information. If the Novice can simply choose another person in the immediate vicinity to talk to, your efforts will be futile. Make sure you explain to others that the intent of this activity is not to give the Novice "the silent treatment" or to create a negative experience. We are not recommending that anyone ignore the Novice, or not pay attention to his speech, rather, we are requesting that everyone de-emphasize their own verbal responses and rely instead on rich and clearly exaggerated non-verbal responses.

Decide upon a period of time in which you will act as if you have lost your voice. Make sure that nobody else "fills in" for you at that time and that your speaking loss occurs at times when communication is important to the Novice. This includes making sure you have some periods of time with the Novice in areas where you have removed any competing objects that would distract him, such as computers or video games. The exercise will not accomplish much if the Novice does not even realize that something is different. If you believe he will understand, explain that you are losing your voice as an exercise. You have been instructed to only use your face and your body to communicate. You can invite the Novice to play along with you and pretend that he or she has lost his or her voice as well.

Coaching Instructions:

When you are ready to stop responding verbally, maintain an inviting expression. Stay very involved. Be highly responsive to his communication attempts. Use lots of pointing, gesturing and amplified facial expressions. Stay very emotionally animated. Invite the Novice to interact in exciting ways when possible. Do not spend time watching TV, or playing games that do not require any speech. Finally, make sure you do not allow anyone to become a "substitute" communicator for you.

Variations:

This is an excellent activity for home and small classroom settings. We also employ several similar important variations. One is called "I Lost my Hearing!" In this exercise you can speak, but explain that you must pretend not to be able to hear the Novice, who must then find non-verbal ways to communicate with you. You can tell him that you are allowed to lip-read and so he will have to find your face in order for you to "see" his words.

Obstacles/Opportunities:

Like the previous exercise, this activity will not be effective with a Novice who does not have a strong need to communicate with you. If this is the case, you should first employ a behavior modification "shaping" approach to develop the desire to communicate. We do not believe this activity should be continued if it causes undue upset. However, initial protests are common and should not deter you from persisting.

LEVEL I, STAGE I, ACTIVITY 3

Unexpected Sounds and Actions

ACTIVITY HIGHLIGHTS
° Maintain attention to speakers
° Staying focused during interaction

Summary:

Trying to talk to someone who "drifts away" after you begin speaking is just as irritating as having to prompt him to pay attention in the first place. We include this activity to address the problem some Novices have of initially orienting to people they interact with, but then quickly becoming distracted and not maintaining their attention. The simple premise of this exercise is that some Novices do not stay focused on the speaker because they lose interest, or are distracted by something in their environment that has more novelty. They may randomly focus on some object, return to some prior activity, or simply "tune out" the speaker.

Participants:

This exercise is not as dependent upon the cooperation of everyone in the environment. However, the more people who engage in it the better!

Getting Ready:

This is another activity that cannot be done effectively in a specific time period. You have to be ready to take unexpected actions whenever you observe there is difficulty in maintaining the Novice's attention while you are communicating. We once again feel the need to provide an important caution: if you want the Novice to pay better attention to your words, you must learn to use fewer of them and to talk with much more emphasis and deliberation with the words you do use. If you do not make your words valuable, do not expect them to be valued. Remember, the way we increase the worth of any commodity is to make it more precious to the consumer!

Coaching Instructions:

First, decide on which unexpected actions you are going to use. We have provided a sample list at the end of the exercise description (feel free to add your own). You will need to be a good observer during this exercise. Watch for signs that the Novice is not paying close attention to you. As soon as you see his or her attention flagging, stop what you are saying and take one of your unexpected actions. Then observe the result. It is important to keep a positive, enthusiastic attitude and expression during this activity. Actions should be dramatic. They can be "startling" without being frightening or threatening.

Variations:

Unexpected actions are a great way to add "spice" to activities that have started to become "stale" but still contain skills that we would like to practice. Some Novices fail to maintain their gaze on those speaking to them, but assume that when it is their turn to talk all eyes will be upon them. For them, a truly unexpected action is to suddenly turn away in the middle of their attempts to communicate. Of course, you should only do this if you believe the Novice will notice and attempt to get you to shift your gaze back to them.

Obstacles/Opportunities:

Once again, we want to be careful to distinguish between actions that might surprise or even startle, and those that are truly upsetting.

Unexpected Actions:

- ○ Looming in close while talking and/or walking.
- ○ Placing a meaningless word in the middle of a sentence.
- ○ Grabbing your head with your hands dramatically, while opening your mouth silently in an expression of great surprise.
- ○ Moving from whisper to shout and back to whisper in the course of a sentence.

- Taking off your shoe and placing it on your head (or a similar type of action).
- Taking out a handkerchief and placing it over your face or as a barrier between you and the Novice while you are talking.
- Suddenly falling down in the middle of a sentence.

LEVEL I, STAGE I, ACTIVITY 4

Fast-Paced Activities

ACTIVITY HIGHLIGHTS
- Enjoying fast-paced social interaction
- Referencing for shared excitement and joy
- Rapid attention shifting from objects to social partners
- Eye–Hand coordination

Summary:

Now we focus on activities that provide a great deal of excitement, while at the same time teach the Novice to rapidly shift focus. These activities also allow the Novice to function as a more active participant in creating the action. "Hot Potato/Trade Me/Overload" is the first activity we introduce that has several different elements – rapid passing, trading, and "bombarding," combined into a single activity. In addition, "Trade Me" practices rapid attention shifting. While we have chosen a combination of three activities, there are countless more. The key factor is that the activity be fast-paced, easy to do, require the Novice to rapidly shift gaze from object to person and involve no objects that would distract from the social focus.

Participants:

Coach and one or two Novices

Getting Ready:

For "Hot Potato/Trade Me/Overload" choose the objects you will use for the "potato" as well as for trading. We prefer soft balls as "potatoes" and small soft stuffed animals for trading. You can trade any small object that is soft and moderately interesting to the Novice. Initially, try not to use any object that will distract them. Place the "potatoes" and trading objects in a box from which you can easily retrieve them as needed.

Coaching Instructions:

This activity has three steps:

☐ STEP 1

This activity begins by teaching the Novice a rapid passing game. The objective of the "hot potato" part of the activity is to establish a rapid pace. Pretend, with exaggerated voice and gestures that you have "hot" object in your hand. Pass the object over to the Novice while indicating that they are to pretend it is hot and quickly pass it back, so as not to be burned. Keep at this until you can maintain a rapid back-and-forth exciting pace that can last several minutes.

☐ STEP 2

After a few minutes, when the excited, rapid pace is established, switch to the second part of the activity. Instead of passing one of the "potatoes," quickly reach into the box in which your passing objects have been stored, take out a new object, use it as the "potato" and pass it to the Novice. Do not let her pass it back. Quickly remove a second object for yourself. Now, immediately say, "Trade me," and exchange the objects. If the Novice balks, take the object from her and quickly make the trade. Then increase your pace even more. Discard your object and quickly take a third object from the box. Rapidly make another trade. Continue in this fashion for several minutes.

☐ STEP 3

Now the game shifts to "Overload." Begin taking soft objects out of the box and rapidly passing them to the Novice. Do not give her time to examine any, or give them back to you. Rather keep taking balls and soft objects and "piling" them onto her lap, while laughing and inviting her to laugh with you. Of course the key is to "overload" the Novice so that she does not focus on any one particular object.

Variations:

Tessa Sandlin, a teacher at The Monarch School plays a game called "Hot Potato with Referencing." In this game a small group forms a circle and begins rolling a ball to each other rapidly. Then the rules shift. You can only roll a ball to a group member if you gaze at them and they smile at you. When this gets too easy, she introduces more balls with the same rules. As you might imagine, there are an infinite number of fast-paced activities that will yield similar results. Remember to be careful about introducing objects that will distract them from the human interaction.

Obstacles/Opportunities:

This is a great opportunity to determine whether a rapid pace increases the Novice's ability to shift focus and not become "stuck" with any one object. Make sure to keep the pace of "Trade Me" rapid, so that the Novice does not have sufficient time to get involved with any one object. Even though we emphasize the rapidity of the pace, observe carefully, in order to determine the optimum pace for each person.

LEVEL I, STAGE I, ACTIVITY 5

Beanbag Medley

ACTIVITY HIGHLIGHTS
° Rapid attention shifting
° Sustained excitement
° Active social participation

Summary:

For this exercise we use beanbag chairs to reinforce rapid referencing and attention shifting. Here we present four fast-paced activities that almost all Novices love to play again and again. The only caveat is to be careful which you play with a Novice who has problems with aggression.

Participants:

Coach and Novice.

Getting Ready:

All you need are about eight beanbag chairs and a dozen soft balls that can be thrown without causing damage or hurting anyone. You will need to clear out a room of all furniture to play "Beanbag Dodge" and "Beanbag War."

Coaching Instructions:

There are four activities in this exercise:

■ **ACTIVITY 1   BEANBAG ISLANDS**

Spread out the beanbags leaving spaces of varying sizes between them. The activity involves moving from island to island in order to reach a destination of safety. This may entail climbing a bit onto a table or platform. If you think it will make the game more exciting, talk fearfully about the sharks in the water that will eat you both if you do not stay on the beanbags. Explain that only you can see the sharks coming. Now, suddenly lose your voice. The Novice can only tell when the sharks are coming by looking at the scared expression on your face and then following your gaze and pointing. Start at any beanbag and make sure that you and the Novice always stay together.

■ **ACTIVITY 2   BEANBAG FORT**

There are two ways to conduct this activity. The first version entails each of you selecting one beanbag that acts like a moveable shield. In the second version, you both construct larger "Beanbag Forts." Either way, when ready, you begin "bombarding" each other with harmless balls. Periodically peek out from your fort and try and move yourself or your pile of beanbags closer and closer to the Novice, without saying a word or uttering a sound. When you peek out, do so with a really "sneaky" expression on your face.

■ **ACTIVITY 3   BEANBAG DODGE**

This is our beanbag chair equivalent of "Dodge Ball." Use a masking tape to designate a centerline which neither of you can cross. Begin by trying to hit the Novice with beanbags (remember to throw them softly). The Novice has to "dodge" them and avoid being hit. She cannot throw any of her own. You can play this with as many beanbags as you would like. The key is to use many "feints" where you pretend to throw the beanbag but do not. Try to catch the Novice off guard. Only your face will give away whether you are going to throw the beanbag or not. Make sure the Novice knows she has to keep moving and dodging if she doesn't want to get hit. Frequently reverse roles and become the "dodger" while the Novice assumes the role of "thrower."

■ **ACTIVITY 4   FALLING TOGETHER**

You and the Novice stand directly in front of the pile of beanbags, facing each other with your sides to the beanbags. You should be holding hands, unless this is unpleasant for the Novice. Count to three together and fall together onto the beanbags. The cadence of the counting should be completely controlled by you. Once you have landed, take a few seconds for shared laughter and, depending on the person, tickling or a similar action. A "high five" after landing together is an option.

Variations:

You will find that the rapid pace of these activities can quickly wear you out. Take frequent breaks and vary these activities with less aerobic ones. If the Novice can keep her excitement from overflowing you can get rid of any taped lines and play a "free-for-all" version of "Beanbag Dodge" we call "Beanbag War." By now we believe that you can begin to generate your own beanbag chair activities.

Obstacles/Opportunities:

Do not do any of these activities to win or score points. This is just fun and not competition. If the Novice insists upon making them competitive, stop them immediately.

STAGE 2: REFERENCE

Goals and Objectives

As the title implies, the activities in Stage 2 are geared to increase the Novice's use of other people as their primary reference point for interacting with the world. In Stage 1 we worked on building up referencing for enjoyment and excitement. Now, we develop new reasons to spend time and effort observing the social world. Excitement is a necessary but not sufficient reason to reference the social world on a constant basis. Other people must be perceived as important to the Novice, even when they are not entertaining them. In Stage 2, we teach Novices that, through referencing, they have the ability to decrease their distress and anxiety and increase their understanding of the world. If they watch your face and your body, you can lead them to exciting discoveries about their world as well as helping them avoid dangers.

Activity Summary

In this stage, we learn that if we are not monitoring what people around us are doing, we cannot predict or anticipate what is going to happen next. Many Stage 2 activities provide the Novice with the awareness that he needs to keep track of others, even as they continually move around. They also learn that another crucial reason to visually stay in touch with their Coach's face is that it provides important information about the safety of the environment and the acceptability of their actions, including the potential consequences of taking or persisting in some action.

One of the critical skills in Stage 2 is rapid attention shifting. Rapid shifting is necessary in situations where we are involved in some task or activity, but still wish to monitor what is happening around us in our social world. When we learn to rapidly shift attention from objects to persons, we are more likely to continue referencing in more complex, everyday settings.

By the close of Stage 2, Novices have taken a much more active role in the communication process. Rather than passively glancing at your face for information, they learn to "actively" reference, by inquiring more about their environments. They also become aware that they are senders of information. At the close of this stage they learn that their own faces are reference points for others and that they are a powerful source of effective communication.

Critical Tips

- Learn to distinguish between referencing facial expressions and making eye contact.

- Limit verbal communication to develop facial referencing.

- Make sure your face is a powerful reference point. Exaggerate your facial expressions!

- Provide constant reasons why the Novice should reference your face.

- Be careful to observe the amount of unconscious prompting you engage in.

- Spend sufficient time and energy for the Novice to master rapid gaze shifting, including shifting from a non-social activity to referencing your face.

- Be careful not to engage in any activities that become competitive or goal driven.

Sneaky Pete

2

ACTIVITY HIGHLIGHTS

° Monitoring the social environment, while engaged in an interesting solo activity
° Rapid attention shifting from objects to persons
° Increased vigilance

Summary:

Some Novices become so focused on an activity of interest they tune out everyone and everything else. This makes any attempt to make a transition or interrupt them a nightmare. "Sneaky Pete" works on the ability to maintain divided attention, even when you are involved in something very engaging. We hope that the "game-like" nature of the activity makes attention shifting a positive experience that can be practiced repeatedly.

Participants:

Coach and Novice.

Getting Ready:

Find an activity that the Novice will become moderately involved in. As our goal is success, we don't want to begin by choosing a favorite activity. Avoid anything he is absolutely obsessed with, or that is completely novel.

Coaching Instructions:

Warn the Novice that you will be playing a game, where you are a "Sneaky Pete" and that your job is to try and sneak up on him. The Novice has the power to freeze you with his eyes and make you go back to the starting position. But, if he fails to catch you with his eyes, you get to go up to him and do a "sneaky trick," some slightly annoying action, such as taking one piece of the materials that he is working on. Make sure the action is only mildly annoying and not likely to elicit a meltdown! Now have the Novice sit at a table and place the chosen activity materials in front of him. Stand behind the Novice so that he will have his back to you while he is working. Wait until you believe he is fully focused on the activity. Then gradually sneak up on him. Depending upon his ability, you can be as sneaky as you need to be, even "camouflaging" yourself behind furniture and "moving" beanbag chairs. If the Novice is particularly insensitive, be noisier and more obvious in your approach. If you need to, you can even use some "unexpected action" like a noise, a fake fall, or phrase, to orient the Novice that you are approaching. You can even use an ever-increasing drumbeat, which stays soft and steady when you are standing still, but gets louder and faster as you approach him.

Variations:

Try reversing roles, when you believe the Novice is ready. If you want to increase the excitement and do not mind getting a bit wet, provide both of you with small water pistols. Instead of freezing you with his eyes, the Novice gets to squirt you and of course, if you make it all the way, you get to squirt him. Make sure the Novice knows he is not allowed to leave the chair where he is sitting. This is not a game of chase.

Obstacles/Opportunities:

Make sure that you do not choose a "sneaky" activity that the Novice actually enjoys. Otherwise you might find yourself playing a different version of the game, where the Novice deliberately averts his gaze, so you can successfully sneak up on him.

LEVEL 1, STAGE 2, ACTIVITY 7

Follow my Eyes to the Prize

ACTIVITY HIGHLIGHTS
° Following the eye gaze of social partners
° Using non-verbal cues for problem solving

Summary:

People often talk about the importance of "eye contact." However, we believe that merely teaching someone to stare at other people's eyes leads to a social "dead-end." Our emphasis is to teach Novices the payoffs that accrue from watching the eyes, faces and bodies of social partners. This activity teaches one key function of watching another's eyes – they can often lead you to some very interesting things!

Participants:

Coach and Novice.

Getting Ready:

You will need six beanbag chairs or similar objects that you can hide small objects beneath. You will also require two chairs and several small objects that might be interesting to the Novice. Place the beanbag chairs around the room.

Coaching Instructions:

The activity has two steps:

☐ STEP 1

Explain to the Novice that her job is to find a hidden object. Show her the object and explain that she should then leave the room. When she returns, she needs to sit on the chair next to you. Explain that she will only have one chance to look for the object and that the clue to the object's location can only be found on your face. While the Novice is out of the room, place an object under a beanbag chair.

☐ STEP 2

The Novice now returns to the room and sits in a side-by-side position next to you. Tell her not to begin searching until you indicate it is time to get up. In a highly exaggerated manner, look at the Novice, smile broadly and then shift your gaze to the beanbag chair under which the object is hidden. Do not stick out your neck or move your body in such a way that provides additional information. Signal to the Novice to begin searching. If the Novice is unable to follow your gaze and begins to search in another location, immediately stop her and return. This time point to the correct beanbag and then signal her to begin searching. Keep working on this exercise until the Novice can easily follow your gaze to the indicated object. After this is accomplished, try and hide various objects in many different places and repeat the exercise. Once she is able to find the prizes easily, reverse roles and have the Novice hide objects, gaze toward their hiding place and indicate where you should look for them.

Variations:

Modify this activity to become "Follow my Face to the Prize." In this variation you do not gaze at the object's location. Only your degree of smiling and frowning provides information to the Novice about how close or far she is to the object. The broader your smile, the "warmer" he is to the prize. The broader the frown, the "colder" she is becoming. We also enjoy playing "Follow the Sound of my Voice." Without any words, use your voice volume and tone to indicate if the Novice is "hot" or "cold" while she is searching.

Obstacles/Opportunities:

If the Novice does not visually reference, you will need to spend time teaching her to understand the meaning of pointing and to follow your pointing to an object that is a little way off. Remember to begin by pointing to objects that are very close and then gradually increase the distance.

LEVEL 1, STAGE 2, ACTIVITY 8

Locked Box

ACTIVITY HIGHLIGHTS
° Referencing the non-verbal communication of others
° Relying on facial gestures to solve problems
° Managing a series of choices to reach a goal

Summary:

Everyone enjoys a good mystery and finding a hidden key certainly qualifies as one. This is a good activity for those older Novices who need a degree of stimulation and challenge to stay attentive. It is also excellent for those disorganized individuals who need practice in following a sequence of actions to reach a goal. The initial setup is a bit complex, but after the first time, it is a breeze!

Participants:

Coach and Novice.

Getting Ready:

You will need three chairs, several tables, nine cups, three simple puzzles each clearly depicting a different animal, three photos or pictures, each with an image corresponding to one of the puzzles, a small "surprise" reward and a box that can be locked with a key. Place the reward inside the box and lock it, then tape the key behind one of the three pictures. Remove one piece from the puzzle that corresponds to the picture behind which the key is hidden. Disassemble all three puzzles and place them in three piles in a row, about one foot apart from each other. Make sure that all the puzzle pieces are turned over onto their "gray" side, so that they do not reveal anything about the puzzle. Place the three pictures in a row on one wall. Take the puzzle piece you have removed and place it under one of three cups that are placed in a line on a table. Place two more sets of three cups each on two different tables, but do not put anything under them. Place a chair at one end of the room and use masking tape to tape three lines. Each line should lead from the chair, to one of the three tables.

Coaching Instructions:

There are five steps to this activity:

☐ STEP 1

Tell the Novice that this is a treasure hunt. Show her the locked box and tell her that there is a "treasure" inside, but unfortunately, the key is hidden. Explain that the Novice has to find the key to obtain the treasure and that the only way to find the key is to follow the trail and get all the clues. Now, seat the Novice in the chair.

☐ STEP 2

Show the Novice the three lines of masking tape leading in different directions from the chair where the Novice is seated. Show her that each taped line leads to a table containing three cups. Before doing anything else, make sure to emphasize several times that once the Novice starts on one road, or makes a choice, she cannot go back. The only way for her to determine which is the right choice is to carefully watch your face. You are not allowed to give any verbal cues, or to point. You can only communicate whether the Novice is getting "warmer" or "colder" by the degree of your smile or frown. Now tell the Novice that she can use her non-verbal pointing, gestures, facial expressions and any part of her body to communicate with you and find out which path is the correct one. Any time the Novice makes an incorrect choice she must stop and return to the very beginning.

☐ STEP 3

If the Novice takes the correct path, she arrives at the next stage, which is a table containing three cups. Make sure she is seated in a chair facing the three cups. Sit right beside her. Tell her that the clue is under one of the cups, however, she is only allowed to lift up one cup. The right cup can again only be determined from observing your non-verbal responses to her non-verbal inquiries. Remember, obvious facial cues like head nods and head shaking are not allowed on your part.

☐ STEP 4

If the Novice lifts up the correct cup, she will find a puzzle piece under it. Now, point to the area of the room that contains the three disassembled puzzles. Tell the Novice that two of the puzzles are complete but one is missing a piece. Then explain that the Novice has the missing piece and that if she can put together the puzzle with the missing piece she will get the last clue. However, first she has to choose which puzzle to work on without getting up from her chair. The only way to figure out which puzzle is the correct one, is to ask you, without using any words, and then look at your face.

☐ STEP 5

If the Novice chooses correctly, she can then move to the table with the correct puzzle, sit down and assemble the puzzle. Now, show the Novice the area on the wall containing the three photos or pictures of animals corresponding to the puzzles. Tell her that there is a key under one of them but that she can only choose one. The animal on the puzzle provides the clue this time, not you. When the Novice finds the key, she can open the surprise box and obtain the small reward that is inside.

Variations:

Once you set the game up, you can play many more "rounds" by varying the placement of the puzzle piece, adding different stages, or varying the stages. Feel free to construct your own treasure hunts and mysteries. You can also modify "Locked Box" by requiring the Novice to listen for the degree of your intonation to obtain the clue to which way to go. A higher tone would indicate that she is "closer" and a lower voice would indicate an incorrect guess. Still another variation is to set up an outdoor maze and have the Novice communicate with you non-verbally in order to find her way out.

Obstacles/Opportunities:

Remember to simplify, or add complexity to the activity, depending upon the Novice's reaction to elements of the activity. If she is unable to read your degree of smiling or frowning, make the activity easier by using head nods and headshakes.

LEVEL 1, STAGE 2, ACTIVITY 9

Was it Right or Wrong?

ACTIVITY HIGHLIGHTS

° Using social referencing to solve complex problems
° Shifting strategies based on feedback from others
° Improved visual organization

Summary:

This activity combines the rapid referencing of facial expressions, with the ability to shift sets rapidly – a cornerstone of executive functioning. "Was it Right or Wrong?" is inspired by a test of executive functioning, called the Wisconsin Card Sorting Test. In this activity the Novice is faced with a pattern matching problem, where the only way to determine the correct pattern is to reference your facial expressions.

Participants:

Coach and Novice.

Getting Ready:

You will need anywhere between nine and twenty-seven cards depending upon the ability of the Novice to manage and organize information. Cards should vary in color (red, yellow, green), shape (circle, square, triangle) and size (large, medium, small). Sit across a table from the Novice. Place as many of the cards in front of the Novice as you believe he can handle.

Coaching Instructions:

This activity contains two steps:

☐ STEP 1

Explain that you are going to play a card sorting game. To win the game, the Novice has to match different patterns, but the only way he will know which is the right pattern will be by looking at your face.

☐ STEP 2

Choose a card and then turn over the first card so that the Novice can see it. Then spread out the remaining cards so that he can see them all easily. The Novice now has to place the "correct" card on top of your first card. He has to decide whether to match your card by color, shape, or size. The only way he can tell which is correct is by observing your facial expressions. You can smile or frown after the Novice has made his choice and placed one of the cards on top of your cards. If the Novice chooses incorrectly make sure that after you frown, you remove the card and place it back in its original position. Reference the pattern chart provided at the end of the description of this exercise, to determine which pattern you should be "playing" at any time in the game.

Variations:

After you have used the reference chart that we have provided, create more variations of your own. See how complex you can make the game without frustrating the Novice. While we suggest using smiles and frowns as "clues," an obvious progression is to use more sophisticated non-verbal expressions as well. You can substitute different emotional expressions as the Novice learns them. For example, an "angry" expression means "no" and a "proud" expression means "yes." You can use any type of patterns to do this activity. If the Novice becomes proficient you can use combinations of attributes like "small circles" or "red triangles" if you wish.

Obstacles/Opportunities:

This activity may be too difficult for a Novice with severe visual organizational problems and you are free to simplify it, using fewer cards and fewer variations. On the other hand it is a wonderful exercise for developing sequential tracking and "working" memory skills.

Pattern Chart:
- Same Color
- Same Color
- Same Color
- Same Shape
- Same Shape
- Same Size
- Same Size
- Same Size
- Same Size
- Same Size
- Same Color
- Same Shape

(Repeat the pattern)

STAGE 3: REGULATE

Goals and Objectives

With attention and referencing established, Novices are now ready to learn the "nuts and bolts" of Apprenticeship. Stage 3 covers the essential elements that prepare the Novice for becoming a good relationship student. The goal of Stage 3 is the establishment of a regulating relationship between Novice and Coach. The Novice learns to reference his Coach to determine how, where and when to act, in order to become more proficient in interacting with his world. Towards the close of Stage 3 we expect that schedules and other regulating information provided by the Coach will also serve as important reference points for the Novice's actions, along with the expressions and reactions of the Coach.

Activity Summary

Initial activities focus on the elements of establishing an Apprentice–Master relationship. The Novice learns to function as an assistant, accepting a limited role provided by you to aid him in whatever activity you are engaged in. Gradually he is given his own parallel activity and works on matching his actions with yours. Next, you move into a "guiding" function, where he is required to actively reference you to determine what he should be doing and how he should be working. Along with your guidance of their proper actions, Novices learn to accept your guidance to determine the proper speed and quality for their work efforts. Stage 3 ends with an exercise focusing on the essential skills of making activity transitions and understanding basic emotional expressions.

Critical Tips

- Carefully transition the Novice from an assistant to a parallel role.

- Do not allow the Novice to insert his own activity variations yet.

- Remember to teach the concept of "good enough" but not perfect work.

- Attention shifting will become more difficult and still continue to require practice.

- Practice talking to yourself about your own actions – "Self Narrating" – using just a few words, every time you are with the Novice.

- Teach transitions slowly and carefully.

Transition

ACTIVITY HIGHLIGHTS

° Accepting changes in routine

° Accepting insertion of new elements into a schedule of activities

° Transitioning from one activity to another

° Stopping an activity without protest, even when it is not completed

Summary:

This activity prepares Novices for the constant changes and transitions that occur in all relationship encounters. In this exercise we focus on four basic types of transitions: following an activity schedule where Novices move seamlessly from one activity to another, inserting and omitting elements of an activity, inserting and omitting activities in a schedule and finally stopping one activity midstream and moving on to another without coming back to complete the first.

Participants:

Coach and Novice.

Getting Ready:

Before beginning this activity, provide Novices with some experience in understanding and following simple daily activity schedules. Choose schedules that are suited to the developmental level of the Novice. The TEACCH program of the University of North Carolina, directed by Dr Gary Mesibov, presents excellent guidelines for constructing and using various kinds of individualized activity schedules (*www.teacch.com*). When ready, you should prepare two appropriate activity schedules. They do not need to be daily schedules, they just need to be long enough to sequence five or six activities within the designated time period. Make sure the activities are affixed to the schedule with Velcro, so you can either remove them altogether or move them around when needed. You will need to create two activity schedules. These should have an identical format but contain completely different activities. You should also construct a "finished" chart, where you can place mastered activities and a "future" chart where you can keep activities to be added to schedules at a future date. Use Velcro as backing for each of the activities, so that you can easily move them from one place in the sequence to another and from one chart to another.

Coaching Instructions:

This activity has eight steps:

☐ STEP 1

Novices learn to use an activity schedule that you have prepared. The schedule should simply outline the activities for a period of time in either pictorial or written form. Make sure the activities are not ones that easily distract the Novice. There is no need to include a time factor in the schedule. A simple sequence of activities, indicating where he or she should go when he or she has "finished" with an activity prior is sufficient.

☐ STEP 2

Create a second schedule; using the same format as the first, that contains the same number of completely different activities. Teach the Novice to use this "B" schedule.

☐ STEP 3

Now you are going to teach the Novice to use the two schedules on alternate days. Explain that now there is an "A" schedule and a "B" schedule. The Novice will alternate using them. Begin alternating the two schedules on a regular basis. Make sure the Novice can easily note which schedule is being used by placing a large moveable arrow above the schedule assigned to the day. When teaching the Novice to do the activities, make sure to clearly define what "finished" is for each, in a manner that the Novice can understand.

☐ STEP 4

Return to schedule "A." Stand in front of it with the Novice, remove two activities and transfer their position in the schedule. Continue to make transfers on a regular basis, until the Novice has no difficulty with them.

☐ STEP 5

Affix five alternating "A" and "B" schedules to the wall in a left-to-right fashion, to represent the five weekdays. Place the large, downward pointing arrow right over the schedule to indicate which one you are using on that day. After one or two weeks, bring the Novice over to the schedules and change their order, so that there are two "A" days, followed by two "B" days and so on. After the Novice has success, make more changes in schedule alternation.

☐ STEP 6

After the Novice can transition fluidly from "A" to "B" and has finished at least one activity to your specification in each schedule, place the two schedules side by side. Both you and the Novice should be standing in front of the schedules. Choose an activity from the "A" schedule that has been completed. Remove the activity and place it on a "finished" chart on the wall. Now go to the "future" schedule. Remove one activity and place it in the empty space on the "A" schedule. Do the same thing at a later time with the "B" schedule.

☐ STEP 7

When ready, choose an item from the "A" schedule that is not yet finished and remove it. Go to the "future" schedule and remove one activity. Insert the activity in its place. Now go to the "B" schedule and remove one activity that has been finished. Put the finished activity on the "finished" chart. Fill the space in on the "B" schedule with the unfinished "A" schedule activity you just removed.

☐ STEP 8

Now make sure that an identical activity is placed on both schedules. Next to the activity name, provide a short description (or picture) of how the activity should be "finished." Make sure that the description of "finished" in the "A" version of the activity is completely different than in the "B" version. The "A" activity is to be considered finished at a later stage of completion than its "B" version. For example, the "A" version of a puzzle will define finished as putting all the pieces together. The "B" version will specify in advance that the Novice is finished when he places five pieces correctly in the puzzle. Now make the "A" version finish at the same point as the "B" version. Keep varying this.

Variations

You can help the Novice adjust to unforeseen schedule changes and postponements using the same method. Draw a monthly "events" calendar on a large whiteboard. Place all the important events on the calendar. If any of these events has to be delayed or postponed demonstrate this on the whiteboard by circling the activity with a marker on the date it was originally to take place, writing in the events at the new date and time, and drawing a line to signify the movement of the activity from one date to another. Finally, erase the original activity and the connecting lines, after the Novice demonstrates he understands the transition. You can also do this with last-minute daily activity time changes.

Obstacles/Opportunities:

The variation presented above is a great way of helping Novices who become fixated on events and require that they occur exactly when and in the manner they anticipate. While this will not satisfy everyone, many "melt-downs" occur because the Novice cannot readily grasp that the expected event has not disappeared, it has simply moved to a new location in time.

LEVEL I, STAGE 3, ACTIVITY 11

Incomplete Completion

ACTIVITY HIGHLIGHTS
° Learning to define activity completion through social referencing
° Learning that being "finished" is a relative and not absolute term

Summary:

Many of our Novices define the completion of an activity by their own standards, rather than the requirements of the settings they are in or people they are with. Others are completely "bound" by the elements of the activity and cannot stop until it is precisely completed in the exact same manner each time. The goal of this activity is to help Novices learn to define being either temporarily or permanently finished, by the standards of their Coach. Referencing others to determine "completion" and eventually deriving a consensual definition of completion that meets our mutual needs and desires becomes a critical step in forming flexible relationships of all kinds.

Participants:

Coach and Novice.

Getting Ready:

Novices who have difficulty leaving activities that are not completed to their rigid standards, should first practice and master the "transition" activity prior to attempting this exercise.

Coaching Instructions:

There are five steps in this exercise:

☐ STEP 1   HOW MUCH IS ENOUGH?

In this activity Novices practice "filling" cups with water. Mark a "finish" point very near the top of three cups. Now request that the Novice fill the cups with water, making sure that he carefully observes the finish line on each cup. Now bring out three more cups whose finish lines are at the halfway point. Instruct the Novice to fill these cups, once again using the finish line for a reference "stopping" point. Next, bring out three more cups with the finish line drawn about one third of the way up and repeat the exercise. Bring out a final set of cups with no finish lines and request the Novice to fill them up. Now ask the Novice which of the cups are "finished." Make sure to point out that they are all finished, even though there is a different amount of water in each one.

☐ STEP 2   HOW TALL IS TALL ENOUGH?

Instruct the Novice that you are going to build some towers for jumping off. Explain that they have to be tall enough for a person to jump off and then ask the Novice how tall he thinks the towers need to be. Now, have the Novice build a tower with small blocks. Tell him to stop when it is about one foot high. When he reaches the designated point tell him that this is tall enough. Put a very small toy person on top of the tower. Now use bigger blocks and make a tower twice as big and place a larger toy person on top. Finally use the biggest blocks you have and make the tower as big as possible with the largest available toy person on top.

☐ STEP 3   A HOUSE WITH NO ROOF

Now tell the Novice that you will be building a house out of blocks. What is special about this house is that it will have no roof. Proceed to build the house with blocks. Include a floor and walls and declare it finished.

☐ STEP 4   INCOMPLETE PUZZLE

Tell the Novice that you are going to work together on a jigsaw puzzle. You will be in charge of the stopping point. Warn the Novice that some of the pieces are missing. Try this with varying "missing" pieces. Next, tell the Novice that you will do some more jigsaw puzzles, where no pieces are missing. However, we are going

3

to be "finished" before all the pieces are in place. Tell the Novice on each trial what the stopping point will be.

☐ STEP 5   INCOMPLETE COMPLETIONS WITHOUT PREPARATION

Now warn the Novice that he will no longer be receiving preparatory warnings about what constitutes "finished" prior to starting an activity with you. In the initial trials you will provide briefer and briefer warnings such as, "We'll be finished in two more puzzle pieces." After the Novice adjusts to this, you will practice communicating that you are "finished" without providing any warning.

Variations:

We can think of an infinite number of ways that you can reinforce the subjective nature of "good enough" as well as the concept that sometimes "finished" is a relationship term and not an absolute one. For example, declare a "one sock" day on a particular Sunday morning when you don't have anywhere to go and everyone in the family puts on just one sock. We know you will come up with many of your own creations.

Obstacles/Opportunities:

We do not have to emphasize that some of our Novices will balk if we move too quickly in this exercise, but the good news is that even the most rigid of Novices will gradually "loosen up" if we work slowly and gradually through all of the steps outlined above.

LEVEL I, STAGE 3, ACTIVITY 12

Do What I Do, Not What I Say

ACTIVITY HIGHLIGHTS

- ° Favoring non-verbal over verbal communication
- ° Focusing on relevant communication
- ° Managing discrepant information

Summary:

In this exercise we add a new dimension to social referencing. In real life, observing other people often takes place in noisy, complex environments where discrepant "noise" may compete for attention with critical information. In this version of "Simon Says," we teach the Novice to zero in on non-verbal communication, even when it is different from the verbal communication. This exercise is especially suitable for highly verbal Novices, as they tend to over-rely on language to the detriment of visual, non-verbal cues.

Participants:

Coach and Novice.

Getting Ready:

It is helpful if the Novice already knows how to play "Simon Says."

Coaching Instructions:

This exercise has two steps:

☐ STEP 1

Make sure that the Novice knows how to match your simple movements. Play a simple game where you say and, at the same time, non-verbally indicate what action you want the Novice to take. In this version both your words and actions will match. You can use the sample instructions below, or make up your own.

☐ STEP 2

Once the Novice demonstrates proficiency with the simple matching activity, it is time to make it more challenging. Warn the Novice that now you will be telling her one thing with your body and a different thing with your words. Provide some sample items for practice. Remind the Novice to, "Watch my actions and do not pay attention to my words." Now begin providing discrepant information. If the Novice has difficulty, stop and remind her once again to only pay attention to your body and not to your words. Work as slowly as you need to. If the Novice is having difficulty, provide a small pause between your words and actions and gradually decrease the pause until you are presenting both channels of information simultaneously.

Variations:

A natural variation is to modify the game in just the opposite manner. Now the Novice should only pay attention to your words and disregard your body. Of course the game is only interesting if the Novice has to keep looking at you while she is playing.

Obstacles/Opportunities:

Some Novices will not yet be ready to "separate" out the two channels of communication. If so, slow down the activity, make the two channels appear sequentially instead of simultaneously, or skip the activity. This activity does, however, provide a wonderful opportunity for Novices to learn to manage simultaneous information.

STAGE 4: COORDINATE

Goals and Objectives

The final stage of Level I exposes Novices to the basic elements of coordinated actions. Coordinating your movement with another person is the prototype for all future relationship skills. It requires ongoing awareness of your partner's actions in relation to your own. This is often the first time that the person may have experienced the excitement of acting alongside a social partner, operating together as a single, synchronized unit.

Activity Summary

Activities in Stage 4 cover the entire gamut of synchronized activity. Early exercises focus on simple coordinated movements, including sequential and simultaneous action. We take a brief detour in an important exercise, where the Novice is exposed to the concepts of "connection" and "disconnection." A final exercise practices remaining coordinated, not in action, but within the framework of rhyming words.

Critical Tips

- Remember to celebrate your small successes.

- Resist the temptation to allow the Novice to add his own variations to activities.

- Add excitement by introducing "world records" to some of the repetitive activities in this stage.

- You may work with more than one Novice at a time in this stage. However, no matter how large your group, you not the other participants are still the center of attention. This should begin to drastically change in Stage 7!

LEVEL 1, STAGE 4, ACTIVITY 13

Role Actions

ACTIVITY HIGHLIGHTS
° Coordinating two different roles with a social partner
° Working together, to reach a common goal

Summary:

Role activities require fluid turn-taking and coordinated movement. They also require partners to each take on a different "job" or role and make sure both roles stay coordinated with each other. The two roles have to fit together like a lock and key in order for the activity to succeed. We describe two simple role activities in this exercise; "Architect–Parts Department" ("builder–giver") and "Cups and Marbles."

Participants:

Coach and Novice.

Getting Ready:

You will need a set of Blocks and Marbles (these can be purchased from our website), a long table, a number of small plastic cups and several dozen marbles.

Coaching Instructions:

There are two different activities:

■ **ACTIVITY 1   ARCHITECT–PARTS DEPARTMENT**

Explain that you are going to be building together using the Blocks and Marbles set. But each of you will have a different job. The Novice's first job is to run the "Parts Department." Unlike in his previous limited "assistant" role, now he must decide which block to give you. Your job is to act as the "Architect." You receive the block and place it on the structure as you see fit. The Architect is not allowed to select a block. The Parts Department is not allowed to participate in the actual construction. Practice this for a while and then reverse roles.

■ **ACTIVITY 2   CUPS AND MARBLES**

In this simple activity, one role consists of placing a number of plastic cups on a long table, while the complementary role consists of placing one marble in each cup. The "Cup Placer" stands directly in front of the "Marble Dropper." As quickly as possible, he places a cup on the table and then moves to the side, in position to place the next cup and providing space for the Dropper to approach and drop in one marble. He cannot place an additional cup until the Dropper completes his action. After you become proficient, see if you can increase your speed and set a "world record."

Variations:

We are sure you can think of dozens of complementary activities to practice. Remember to replicate these activities later with peer dyads.

Obstacles/Opportunities:

This is a great opportunity for Novices to increase awareness of their body position in relation to another person. If they are the Placer they have to move onto the next position, leaving sufficient room for the Dropper. If a Novice has severe visual organizational difficulties the "placing" task may be quite difficult. If this is the case, try placing grids on the table to indicate where each cup should be placed.

LEVEL 1, STAGE 4, ACTIVITY 14

Two-Ball Toss

ACTIVITY HIGHLIGHTS
° Careful referencing of partner's actions
° Competence and mastery

Summary:

Playing "Catch" with two balls thrown and caught simultaneously by two partners, requires constant observation and synchronized actions. You and the Novice must work together for this activity to be successful. Because it is difficult, accomplishment signals a boost in self-esteem and sense of team accomplishment.

Participants:

Coach and Novice.

Getting Ready:

You will need two identical balls and two parallel taped lines. Lines are drawn with a distance between them that would be appropriate for a game of catch.

Coaching Instructions:

Begin by finding a distance where you can throw a ball back and forth ten times without dropping it. Place your taped lines at that distance. Explain to the Novice that you are both going to count and then, together, throw your balls to each other and try to catch them. The more catches you make the better. Count to three together. After each count the Novice should shift gaze from the ball to your face. Say, "One," then hesitate until the Novice looks at you. Continue counting and hesitating. At "Three" wait for the gaze shift and then say "Throw!" There should be excitement on your face and in your voice as you throw the ball simultaneously to each other. Continue in this manner until there is consistent mastery. Then move a few steps backwards and try from this distance.

Variations:

If you wish, you can add variations such as moving together while throwing, and varying underhand and overhand throws. You can also substitute many different kinds of balls.

Obstacles/Opportunities:

For a reason that is not especially clear, some Novices occasionally greatly enjoy behaviors that work against success. Make sure that these are not reinforced. Also, be careful not to allow the Novice to introduce variations in this stage. After a while you can create a wonderful sense of "We-go" by having your team successfully beat the "world record" for "Two-Ball Toss."

LEVEL 1, STAGE 4, ACTIVITY 15

Ropes

ACTIVITY HIGHLIGHTS
° Coordinating stop-and-go and hard-and-gentle actions with a partner
° Developing self-regulation

Summary:

This activity focuses on the Novice learning to synchronize actions with a partner in a simple activity. It requires the Novice to evaluate her partner's actions in relation to her own in a much more fluid relationship in order to achieve success. The first activity involves a sequential "first-me-then-you" coordination of actions. Following this, the Novice is required to increase the fluidity of her actions as Novice and Coach move to more simultaneous motion. The final exercise involves learning to move at two speeds, "fast" and "slow," and to practice strong and gentle actions with a partner. The rope provides clear and immediate feedback. Novices learn what it feels like, in a kinesthetic sense, to match their actions.

Participants:

Coach and Novice.

Getting Ready:

You will need a strong rope with plastic handles on each end that can be firmly grasped and do not easily slip. Ideally you should purchase a rope with handles that can be adjusted at different points on the rope, so you can practice from farther and farther apart. If you would like to purchase this item, there are details on our website. Make sure that if needed, the Novice has a "spotter" to check her fall, and/or cushions to land on if she does fall.

Coaching Instructions:

This exercise has four steps:

☐ STEP 1

Both partners remain standing on taped lines, facing each other. Begin with a simple turn-taking movement activity – the Novice pulls and the Coach pulls. Take the rope with two handles and teach the Novice how to firmly grasp her handle and gently pull without either leaving her assigned spot or pulling the rope out of your grasp. At this stage you are practicing a smooth back and forth movement where you each pull and allow yourself to be pulled in a gentle and comfortable motion. You should function as the "caller" and say, "Pull" when it is either partner's turn. The activity should rapidly become a fluid back and forth exercise.

☐ STEP 2

Now practice both "strong" and "gentle" pulls, still working in a back and forth manner. Make sure the "strong" pulls are not so strong as to result in either partner losing her balance, or grip on the rope.

☐ STEP 3

Now practice pulling hard at the same time and experience how you remain in balance.

☐ STEP 4

Finally, practice pulling gently at the same time while staying in balance with one another.

Variations:

Vary the activity by adding "stop-and-start" elements as well as pauses in the rhythm. You can use as an alternative a piece of exercise equipment known as a "rubber band" with two handles that provides a bit more elasticity. As another variation, you can tell the Novice to pull hard while you pull gently and illustrate the effects of a mismatch. Just make sure you do it safely.

Obstacles/Opportunities:

This is a good activity for Novices who tend not to know their own strength and might be too rough with objects, pets or people. Remember to repeat this activity in Stage 8, when you form peer dyads.

LEVEL 1, STAGE 4, ACTIVITY 16

Drums

ACTIVITY HIGHLIGHTS

° Coordinating loud and soft actions with a partner

° Coordinating a combination of elements

Summary:

This exercise introduces action coordination using auditory, in place of kinesthetic feedback. Novices learn to synchronize loud and soft sounds with a partner. This exercise also teaches Novices to coordinate a combination of elements practiced together. By the way, we love to use drums in a number of activities and we think they are well worth the purchase price.

Participants:

Coach and Novice.

Getting Ready:

Provide a drum each for yourself and the Novice and make sure he can use it without too much effort.

Coaching Instructions:

The activity has six steps. You will drum together in all steps:

☐ STEP 1

Teach the Novice to "stop" and "go" along with you whenever you cue him. You should shout, "Go!" and then bang vigorously. Smile at the Novice just as you are ready to say "Stop" so that he has a non-verbal cue.

☐ STEP 2

Teach the Novice to bang his drum along with you while you vary speeds from fast to slow.

☐ STEP 3

Combine elements so that the Novice is practicing "stop/go" along with "fast/slow" in a fluid manner along with you.

☐ STEP 4

Beginning with a simple straightforward progression, hit your drum loudly once and wait for the Novice to repeat. Practice "loud" drumming for a time. Next hit the drum softly while saying, "Soft, soft." Practice soft drumming together while continuing the repeat the word, "soft."

☐ STEP 5

When you are sure the Novice can distinguish loud and soft, begin drumming together and announce shifts from loud to soft, both with words and with your own drumming. The Novice is required to rapidly shift along with you and play at the same volume you are playing. As proficiency increases, increase the number of shifts from loud to soft and omit verbal announcements.

☐ STEP 6

Combining elements: Once this pattern has been established, you should begin to provide simple rhythms of, "stop/go, fast/slow and loud/soft," keeping in mind that before any patterns are introduced, the Novice must first visually reference. Here are sample patterns to work on:

> Start/stop and loud/soft
>
> Start/stop and fast/slow
>
> Start/stop, fast/slow, loud/soft

Variations:

Return to the rope activity and add a "fast/slow" variation to the back and forth movement. You may also want to practice this activity with "speech" as the "instrument." While you are shifting from "loud" to "soft" talking, you can provide appropriate contextual cues such as "Talk loudly, I am far away," or "Talk softly we are in church."

Obstacles/Opportunities:

Resist the temptation to allow Novices to add their own variations to this exercise. It is tempting to turn this into an improvisational session, but if the Novice is truly at this stage, he is not yet ready to conduct the type of behavioral regulation needed to make a more improvised activity work. We will get to practice plenty of improvised music in later activities.

LEVEL 1, STAGE 4, ACTIVITY 17

Patterns

ACTIVITY HIGHLIGHTS
° Learning to coordinate patterns
° Using a music keyboard together

Summary:

Now we move to a new type of coordination, that of matching simple patterns. Our Novices love using music keyboards and we find many uses for them throughout the program. In this first appearance we limit our actions to playing with one finger and only on the black keys. This increases the chance that the music we make together will be melodic and pleasing.

Participants:

Coach and Novice.

Getting Ready:

You can use a piano, or, ideally, a music keyboard with various stops. Coach and Novice sit side by side, facing the keyboard, with the Coach seated on the left. The numerous settings on the keyboard are covered for now.

Coaching Instructions:

This activity has three simple steps:

☐ STEP 1

Tell the Novice that you are going to make music together. You will use only the pointer finger on each hand and play on only the black keys. Take enough time to model and guide the Novice so that you are sure he understands the limits of the activity.

☐ STEP 2

Now play a very slow, simple, repetitive rhythm. Vary use of the pointer finger of each hand with each note you play. Play a black key with the left hand, then the right hand and then the left. Each note should be held for the same amount of time. Make sure to correctly position the Novice's hands on the black keys, one octave above your own. When you are finished playing your pattern, nod at the Novice and instruct him to nod back when he is ready to play on his black keys. The Novice has to match the pattern that you have just played on the lower keys.

☐ STEP 3

Now play a slightly faster and longer repetitive pattern. The Novice should join in when you invite him to do so with a nod. Once again, he joins in by replicating the pattern you have established. The piece is "finished" when you nod again.

Variations:

You can use drums or any other instrument. We also recommend that you work on matching patterns in a number of different media, including drawing and movement.

Obstacles/Opportunities:

When we first began experimenting with piano duets, some Novices who were rarely impulsive or easily distracted became so on this instrument. They delighted in playing full hand crashing noises and the louder the banging the more enjoyable the instrument became. If the activity is introduced carefully, this should not be a problem.

Rhyming Phrases

4

ACTIVITY HIGHLIGHTS

° Learning to be playful with words

° Being creative with word combinations

° Introduction to poetic rhyming

Summary:

This is a great activity to help those Novices who have learned to use language in a rote or overly rigid manner. Typical children are used to playing with words – creating every manner of nonsense combination as a normal activity. In this exercise you begin with rhyming words and progress to any sort of nonsense combination you desire.

Participants:

Coach and Novice. Return to do this again later with peer partners.

Getting Ready:

Construct at least forty rhyming phrases cards and divide them into two sets. Make up a number of "connecting" word cards from the list below. You will use them to add to your rhyming words and make them even funnier.

Coaching Instructions:

Each of you gets one set of identical rhyming phrase cards. Explain that you are going to play a game of rhyming phrases. Make sure the Novice understands that the point of this exercise is to put together phrases that sound good but that do not mean anything. They need to be nonsense but fun. You can demonstrate until you are sure she understands. You each take turns "playing" one card and then putting your cards together to make a ridiculous phrase. Use the necessary "connecting" words to make the phrases sound better. Make sure to put the two phrases together with amplified facial expressions and intonations. When you have been successful with two phrases, try to string together more of them.

Variations:

Make up your own rhyming phrase lists and put them together. We cannot emphasize enough the importance of developing a playful, creative approach to language development. It is an excellent means of helping the Novice to feel competent with language and avoid a stilted, scripted style of talking.

Obstacles/Opportunities:

Some Novices will object to connecting words that are not "supposed" to be together. If this occurs, make sure to emphasize that you are deliberately trying to connect words that do not mean anything. You can take turns and play two versions – one in which you put words together that are meaningful and the other where the words are nonsense.

Rhyming Word Samples:

Flat tire	Top bricks	Fire house	Big bed
Quagmire	Quick picks	Grey mouse	Burning red
Cat fire	Mouse clicks	Tire bounce	Horse's head
Big liar	Needle pricks	Psychotic spouse	Dig up the dead
Live wire	Cool tricks	Cat pounce	Heavy lead
I admire	Chopsticks	Head louse	Paper shred
Mad liar	Finger licks	Expired cows	Well read

Connecting Words:

A, and, It's, so, then, eat.

Example:

In a quagmire, the horse's head started a cat fire with heavy lead. However, chopsticks, after finger licks caused expired cows to burn down the fire house.

LEVEL 1, STAGE 4, ACTIVITY 19

First Conversations

ACTIVITY HIGHLIGHTS
° Introducing reciprocal conversation
° Maintaining connected topics

Summary:

Many Novices do not understand the importance of staying within a single theme. They jump from one topic to another, without regard for their partner's interests or prior statements. This is an exercise in beginning to maintain the coordination of topics within themes. Later we will present more sophisticated activities, but this is a great start.

Participants:

Novice and Coach. Repeat later with peer partners.

Getting Ready:

Choose five or six themes and make eight "topic cards" for each of the themes that you choose. Each topic card should contain a statement that is clearly related to a specific theme area. Also make a pile of ten cards with the word "Connection" written on them and ten more saying, "Disconnection." If the Novice cannot read, the topic cards can be pictures and you can use a connected and disconnected symbol.

Coaching Instructions:

There are three steps in this activity:

☐ STEP 1

First make sure that the Novice learns the basic concept of keeping topics connected. Demonstrate connections and disconnections in topics as much as you need. When you are ready, lay out the different topic cards on a table face up but in a random order. Practice making simple connected topics and then practice making disconnections and pointing them out.

☐ STEP 2

Now lay out the different topic cards (as many as you think the Novice can handle) in a random order on the table. Leave one half of the table clear to play the game.

You pick the first theme card and place it at the top of the table. Tell the Novice to find a connecting card with the same topic as you have "played." See how many connections you can make together. Each time you run out of connections start a new theme row. If you or the Novice plays a card that is not connected, you have to begin the row all over again.

☐ STEP 3

When the Novice has become skilled at making connections, it is time to practice disconnections. Now play by picking from the "Connection/Disconnection" deck. When either of you picks a "Disconnection" card, you must purposely pick a topic card that is not connected to the other cards in a row. Otherwise the row is taken apart.

Variations:

As a slightly more advanced activity, make up topic cards that can be equally divided into questions and answers. Now add cards with the phrase "Connected Question," "Disconnected Question," "Connected Answer" and "Disconnected Answer" on them. Now play the game in Step 3 with the additional variable of questions and answers.

Obstacles/Opportunities:

Some Novices have more difficulty learning the initial connection/disconnection distinction. If this is the case, use shorter sentences, and even one-word descriptions, to make the task simpler.

LEVEL II: APPRENTICE

Introduction

Summary

The move to the Apprentice Level signifies that Novices are ready to become "Co-Regulators." The major goal of Level II is to teach people to take responsibility for maintaining the coordination of their actions with social partners. By the final stage, Apprentices are required to do half of the work of keeping their interactions regulated, without resorting to rules or scripts to do so. By accomplishing this, they demonstrate they are ready to introduce variation and novelty and become "Co-Creators" as well, the major focus of Level III. In Level II physical actions are still emphasized. Movement is the way we learn to coordinate actions with social partners. A game that epitomizes Level II is "Hide and Seek." By the way, a very interesting element of this game is that when a typical child is "found," she produces the biggest smile of the entire game, even though from an instrumental point of view she has lost the game.

Participants

Level II sees the introduction of peer partners in our activities. We often begin with partner combinations in Stage 7. Peers are carefully matched so that they are approximately equal in the stages they have mastered. It is important that each peer knows that their partner will not do the work for them.

Settings

We still carefully restrict the settings in which we practice activities. However, typically by this stage, while we still have to carefully limit objects, we are not as concerned by every aspect of visual distraction.

Getting Ready

We cannot over-emphasize the importance of making sure that all Level I skills are in place before moving on to Level II.

Language

In Level II, language is used to teach enactment, to communicate the need for regulatory actions ("slow down"), to enhance joint effort – "We did it" – and to communicate encouragement of the partner. Language also begins to be used for purposes of regulation and repair. We may verbally check to make sure our partner is ready. Language may also be used to express confusion and to verbally take repair actions such as saying, "I'm sorry," when you throw a ball too high or too hard.

Language used for Encouragement, Regulation and Repair

Encouragement

- We can do it
- You can do it

Regulation and Repair

- Are you ready?
- I'm ready
- Start
- Stop
- Faster?
- Slower?
- Slow down
- Harder
- Softer
- Wait
- Come on
- Your turn
- I'm not ready
- Do it again
- Try again
- Change time!
- Watch out!

- I got it
- I can't hear you
- Did you get it?
- Do you understand?
- I'm confused
- What?
- What did you say?
- Now?
- Do you like it?
- Where are you?
- Here I am!
- Uh oh!
- Oh no
- We missed
- Try again
- Say it again
- Sorry!

Coaching Points

- A key concept in this level is that change occurs in small, manageable degrees.

- Allow the child to gradually introduce more variation into joint activities.

- Continue to carefully monitor your use of language.

- Similarly, carefully monitor your pacing during activities. Always sacrifice speed for coordination.

- In Stage 6, try to create dyads that combine two, well-matched children.

- When you add any type of complexity, always revert back to earlier mastered activities.

- Be on the lookout for a need to win becoming more important than sharing joy and excitement.

STAGE 5: VARIATION

Goals and Objectives

Most people with relationship disorders perceive change as a black-and-white, on-and-off phenomenon. They do not understand that relationships exist in shades of gray. Most of our time consists of determining whether to walk a little faster or touch a bit more gently. In Stage 5, we expose Apprentices to the fact that, in the relationship world, change occurs constantly in very small degrees, rather than in on/off segments.

Activity Summary

The Apprentice first has to become consciously aware of small changes in her own and others' actions. We begin with a very simple illustration of how of a simple change occurs by degrees. Next, we move onto learning to coordinate small changes in a number of different areas. Apprentices learn to throw balls, beat drums and walk alongside a partner, while adapting to variations introduced by the Coach. In the latter part of the stage we explore change as a subjective experience. Apprentices learn that emotions such as happiness come in degrees, which are determined by our own unique experience and reaction to events. We investigate the perception that we are too close or too far from one another. Finally, encourage the Apprentices to examine the changes in themselves that have occurred over time as we explore with them the concept of "improvement." In Stage 5 we continue to use very simple exercises. We are engaged in breaking complex things apart and working on just one element of coordination at a time.

Critical Tips

- Be careful to watch for Apprentices who are too focused on "winning" or perfection.

- Try not to emphasize speed of completion as an important factor.

- Use visual communication if language is limited.

- Stay in control of the activities.

- Make sure to practice walking side by side on an everyday basis, with the Apprentice taking more and more responsibility for keeping himself at your side.

LEVEL II, STAGE 5, ACTIVITY 20

Ball Toss Variations

ACTIVITY HIGHLIGHTS
° Rapid adaptation to change
° Enjoying activity variations

Summary:

Novelty is the "spice" of relationships. Our goal in this stage is not for Apprentices to endure variations in their activities, but to genuinely enjoy them and desire more. We accomplish this by introducing variations in small, understandable segments. We also use already mastered activities, so the Apprentice is not struggling to learn a new skill at the same time as she is learning to adapt to novelty. In this exercise we return to the two-ball toss activity and "spice it up" by adding variations.

Participants:

Coach and Apprentice.

Getting Ready:

You will need two balls of a size to accommodate the Apprentice's motor needs and some masking tape. Use the tape to mark out a one-foot center square, bordered on opposite sides by lined intervals, four, eight and ten or twelve feet apart. This should leave four possible starting points for the activity, if the perimeter of the central square is included.

Coaching Instructions:

This activity has three steps:

☐ STEP 1

Find the distance at which the Apprentice will most easily be successful in throwing and catching the ball. Once you have determined the optimal distance, find the right speed. Using one ball, determine the fastest speed with which you are able to throw the ball back and forth without either Coach or Apprentice dropping it.

☐ STEP 2

Once speed and distance are optimal, introduce simple variations. Continue to regulate the flow of motion while instructing the Apprentice to throw faster, slower, bounce the ball one time, etc.

☐ STEP 3

Once the Apprentice adjusts to your variations, add the second ball. Add as many variations as the Apprentice will enjoy. We have included sample variations below.

Obstacles/Opportunities:

Apprentices can become overwhelmed by the pace of this activity if not carefully monitored. This can result in controlling behavior or a refusal to play. Most

Apprentices will respond well to a break in the activity, followed by decreased expectations and a slower pace.

Sample Variation:

- Vary one- and two-ball toss.
- Roll the ball.
- Bounce it a different number of times.
- Alternate hard and gentle throws.
- Throw while moving.
- Throw from different spots.
- Vary the release count and signals.
- Catch the balls in baskets, rather than with your hands.
- Stand on platforms and play.
- Throw the balls to each other through an upright hula-hoop.
- Throw two balls to knock down a tower of blocks together.

LEVEL II, STAGE 5, ACTIVITY 21

Rhythm Changes

ACTIVITY HIGHLIGHTS

- Using keyboard and drums to create gradually varying rhythms
- Adapting to small changes

Summary:

In this activity we provide the Apprentice with the experience of maintaining the coordination of actions while you adapt to subtle shifts. "Rhythm Changes" uses drums and a music keyboard to provide auditory feedback.

Participants:

Coach and Apprentice.

Getting Ready:

You will need a set of two drums and an electric music keyboard. You will most likely have used these in prior exercises and will find much use for them again in future activities. The Apprentice should by now be skilled at using drums and keyboard.

Coaching Instructions:

This exercise has four steps:

☐ STEP 1   DRUM FASTER AND SLOWER

Practice matching gradually faster and slower drumbeats. Start with a steady slow beat and have the Apprentice join in. It is always fun to add some kind of "chant" while you are drumming. The nature of the chant will vary according to the age and interest of the Apprentice. Increase the speed of drumming and chanting in gradual increments, pre-announcing each change carefully, "A little faster." When you approach a rapid speed, begin to decrease speed in gradual increments, again pre-announcing each change, "A little slower!"

☐ STEP 2   DRUM LOUDER AND SOFTER

Now repeat the same procedure, but this time increase the volume until you reach a very loud noise and then gradually decrease it until you barely hear your beat.

☐ STEP 3   KEYBOARD HIGHER AND LOWER

Now move to the keyboard. Teach the Apprentice to play a rising scale ("C, D, E, F, G") using only one finger (unless she is already proficient on the keyboard). Play the scale alongside the Apprentice, one octave higher or lower. Make sure she is playing along with you and matching your notes as they gradually get higher and lower.

☐ STEP 4   KEYBOARD FASTER AND SLOWER

This step is very similar to "Faster and Slower" on drums. However now you will play a scale both "up" and "down" ("C, D, E, F, G" followed by "G, F, E, D, C") at a progressively faster and then slower tempo. When you are ready, repeat your scales, but this time with louder and softer notes, just as in the drum exercise.

☐ STEP 5   HOLDING ONE NOTE FOR A LONGER AND SHORTER INTERVAL

(Whole notes, half notes, quarter notes, eighth notes.) On most electronic keyboards a note will continue to play at full strength while you hold it down. Teach the Apprentice to hold his notes for varying lengths of time along with you. Pre-announce the count you will use in a progression ("Two" for count of two, followed by "Three" for count of three). As the Apprentice improves, you can use increasingly longer counts and then work your way down to gradually shorter counts. You can use visual feedback just as if the Apprentice were reading notes on a score. You can use greater line thickness to represent holding a note longer, or any other symbol system you would like to use, such as numbers ("4" = hold the note and count to four).

☐ STEP 6   RELATIVE CHANGE

As a final step, work with the drums to combine changing degrees of speed with degrees of volume. Try "Slower but stay loud," "Faster but stay soft." When these are mastered, see if you can co-vary both variables at the same time, "Faster and louder," "Slower and softer." The final test is to reverse the combination of variables, "Faster and softer," "Slower and louder." Now do the same thing on the keyboard. Try and add one degree of complexity at a time until you can vary higher/lower, faster/slower and louder/softer in various combinations. This takes some practice but is well worth the effort.

Variations:

Teach the Apprentice to use her senses to determine preferable degrees of change. As you play the drums and keyboard, see if you can agree on the speed that is most fun and the volume that sounds best. In a similar vein, try to agree on the optimum sounds for waking up in the morning, going to sleep at night. See if you can relate volume, speed and intensity of sounds to different emotions such as happiness, or sadness.

Obstacles/Opportunities:

If the Apprentice has trouble playing a scale and skips notes it is quite all right to number, letter or color code the notes and then to announce the changes you are going to make by code.

LEVEL II, STAGE 5, ACTIVITY 22

Walking Together

ACTIVITY HIGHLIGHTS
° Learning to walk side by side with another person
° Keeping pace with your partner's movements

Summary:

One of the most important ways we can teach people to be socially coordinated is to have them practice walking alongside their partner. Someone at this level of development is very rarely aware that he is not keeping pace with you.

Participants:

Apprentice and Coach.

Getting Ready:

Tape a start line, finish line and two parallel "walking" lines on any floor, or outside area.

Coaching Instructions:

This exercise has four steps:

☐ STEP 1   WALKING FASTER AND SLOWER

Count and begin walking together, each on your own parallel line. Make sure the Apprentice remains at your side, but do not vary your own pace. Instruct the Apprentice to slow down and speed up as necessary to keep up with your even pace.

☐ STEP 2   SPEEDING UP

Now instruct the Apprentice that you will be starting off slow and then gradually walking faster on each trial. Begin with one round trip (from start to finish and back to start) at a moderately slow speed. On the next trip gradually increase your speed and so on. Keep working at this until the Apprentice can remain at your side at any reasonable speed. Practice without start and stop lines and in many different settings.

☐ STEP 3   VARYING SPEED

Now you will vary your pace within particular round trips. Tell the Apprentice that you are going to start out slow, then speed up a bit on the "return trip" (coming back to the start line). Continue to increase your pace on each round trip. When the Apprentice has mastered this, tell him that now you are going to increase your speed more frequently. Make sure to carefully announce when you are going faster, as you increase speed every few seconds. When you get to the fastest reasonable step, begin decreasing speed gradually making the appropriate announcements. See how fluidly you can perform this without stopping between round trips.

☐ STEP 4   FIND THE BEST RATE

Try to pick out movement speeds that are best for different types of activities. Find the best speed of walking when you are passing a ball back and forth. Now find the best speed when you are carrying different types of objects. Finally, find an optimal speed for walking together on elevated boards while carrying or passing something back and forth. Make sure you record your findings (on video if possible).

Variations:

If the Apprentice is able and willing to do some simple types of coordinated dancing, you can pick a piece of music that gets gradually faster and faster (such as the theme from the film *Zorba the Greek*) and dance together to it. Another fun variation is to walk together in time to a metronome.

Obstacles/Opportunities:

You can practice walking together any time you are at a shopping mall or just going for a walk. A natural extension is jogging together and then riding bicycles together. In all of these situations, make sure the Apprentice is following your pace. It is all too easy for the Coach to unconsciously fall into step with the Apprentice's pace instead.

LEVEL II, STAGE 5, ACTIVITY 23

Too Far to Whisper, Too Close to Shout

5

ACTIVITY HIGHLIGHTS

° Learning to be aware of body position relative to others

° Using subjective impressions to determine optimal position

Summary:

Apprentices often have a very poor sense of the position of their body in relation to social partners. This activity focuses on learning to be aware of small degrees of change in distance and orientation with social partners. There are many body position variables that can be addressed. In this exercise we have selected one critical variable – physical distance – moving closer and farther apart from one another.

Participants:

Coach and Apprentice

Getting Ready:

"Closer/Farther Apart" is best done in a large area, such as an outdoor patio, or even better, a driveway. Try to pick a flooring surface that is level and on which you can mark off spots that do not have to be erased for a reasonable period.

Coaching Instructions:

We will describe two activities:

■ **ACTIVITY 1   CLOSER/FARTHER APART**

Play a game of "Two-Ball Toss." Choose a center point and mark it with tape. Each partner stands face to face on either side of the centerline. Partners begin backing away from one another, while staying on the line until they are so far apart that in the game of catch they are assured of dropping each other's throws. Partners gradually move closer in small steps while continuing to play. Next, start very close and move progressively far apart, continuing to throw the ball back and forth. As they move, partners try to determine the closest point at which they are still too far away to throw and catch the ball successfully on five successive attempts. Place two taped lines on the ground to indicate the "too far for throwing" point, beyond which a game of "Two-Ball Toss" will not be fun.

Gradually move closer until partners are very close to each other. Then they should move even closer and begin to play "Two-Ball Toss" again. Both then move progressively away in small increments while continuing the throw the balls. They keep moving backwards until both judge that they are no longer too close to have fun. With each step of moving backwards make sure to declare your level of fun and ask the Apprentice to declare his. Find the spots where you begin to have fun again and mark these two spots off as well.

Now start to move backwards again. The goal this time is to try and find the spot where the game is most fun; where there is still some challenge, but also a good chance for success. Mark these lines off as well.

As you become more proficient at the activity, the lines should change. If possible, do not remove the old lines; place the date next to them. If you have a more physically coordinated Apprentice you can compare the "just right" point for "One-Ball Toss" with the optimal distance for "Two-Ball Toss," in order to reinforce one more time the relative nature of physical distance.

■ ACTIVITY 2 WHISPERS AND SHOUTS

Now we will do a similar activity using voices. Stand very close together, touching if possible, and practice whispering short appropriate phrases to one other. Make sure that you can understand one another. Now gradually back away from one other, one step at a time, until you reach a point where one or both of you cannot understand the whispering. When you reach the point of "no whispering" mark it off as a line. Now slowly approach one another and try to determine the point of "best whispering." Repeat the same activity with "shouting" and then with "normal talking voices."

Variations:

Other common physical relationships will need similar practice. Work on "leaning in" and "leaning out." Practice "sitting too close" and "sitting far away." Try to create your own activities that address the variables of "ahead of" and "behind," or facing more towards and more away from your partner. Judging when we are too far ahead or too far behind is a completely subjective event. If we are trying to toss a ball back and forth while running together, falling just a bit behind or ahead can be the cause of immediate failure. The issue of "relativity" is what is so confusing about teaching "appropriate" physical space and distancing. It all depends on your goals. As you move through degrees of movement, changes continue to provide feedback on what you are now too close for, too far apart for etc. A more advanced activity is to reference the degree of comfort as a measure of determining what changes are needed in coordinating movement.

Obstacles/Opportunities:

This exercise is yet another that will have no lasting impact unless it is translated into everyday life. We can all see how we can continue to work on relative body positions outside of any specific practice time. We want Apprentices to be constantly considering the optimal distance in relation to others for every conceivable type of activity.

LEVEL II, STAGE 5, ACTIVITY 24

Ice Cream Happiness

ACTIVITY HIGHLIGHT
° Understanding degrees of emotional expression
° Appreciating your partner's emotional changes

Summary:

In this activity, Apprentices learn to appreciate that emotional expressions are reactions that occur in relative degrees, as opposed to an on/off fashion. We associate degrees of expression change with different events in the Apprentice's life that we believe might trigger that reaction. We are not yet concerned about whether the Apprentice fully understands the meaning of each subtle change in expression. We are more interested in her learning the importance of perceiving that these subtle expression changes provide important information. In this exercise we are equally interested in Apprentices learning the subjective nature of their own degrees of expression and understanding that their partner's expression changes are equally meaningful and potentially evoked by different factors than their own.

Participants:

Coach and Apprentice.

Getting Ready:

Work with the Apprentice (and family members if needed) to choose four events or regular activities that she can easily connect to four different degrees of happiness. If the Apprentice is verbal you can discuss one particular event that makes her, 1. Sort of Happy 2. Happy 3. Very Happy and 4. Really Happy.

Coaching Instructions:

This activity has five steps:

☐ STEP 1

After you have connected one event/activity with each level of happiness, practice different facial expression for each of the four levels of happiness. Have the Apprentice practice four types of happy face in front of a mirror. When you feel that you can clearly distinguish the four different expressions of happiness, take a photo of each one.

☐ STEP 2

The Apprentice views each of the four photos in turn and must correctly associate the photo with the event that would cause that degree of happiness. An example would be seeing a photo of one of your four faces and saying, "That is my chocolate-ice-cream face."

☐ STEP 3

Reverse the game by revealing the event first. Tell the Apprentice one of the events and have her pick out the appropriate facial photograph and then demonstrate the expression.

☐ STEP 4

Discuss your own four different degrees of happiness to specific events or activities in your life. Make sure these are not the events that would trigger the Apprentice's reactions.

☐ STEP 5

The Apprentice learns to associate your four different facial expressions with your personal events/activities. The Apprentice should learn to see one of your faces and tell you which level of happiness you are portraying ("A going- on-vacation smile").

Variations:

After the Apprentice has mastered degrees of happiness, move on to degrees of sadness and fear using the same method. If you think she can be successful, see if she can perceive differences in what her own four degrees of an emotion look like compared to yours.

Obstacles/Opportunities:

Some of our sensory delayed Apprentices have very poor awareness of their own facial expressions. They don't seem to receive the muscle feedback to help them make subtle distinctions. They may require additional feedback and practice to master this activity, but we know it can be done. You may wish to begin with two levels of happiness and gradually build up to four.

LEVEL II, STAGE 5, ACTIVITY 25

What Does Excitement Sound Like?

ACTIVITY HIGHLIGHTS

° Using gradual changes in voice tone to express different degrees of excitement

° Learning voice equivalents of simple emotions

° Becoming sensitive to the importance of attending to your partner's voice changes

Summary:

Prior exercises addressed two essential elements of non-verbal communication, body distance and facial expression. Now we address a third critical element. We will be linking degrees of voice change to a specific emotion, in this case excitement.

Participants:

Coach and Apprentice.

Getting Ready:

You will need a cassette recorder.

Coaching Instructions:

This exercise parallels the last one on facial expressions.

☐ STEP 1

Together with the Apprentice (and family members if needed), choose four events or activities that are clearly related to four different degrees of excitement for him. It helps if you can talk about 1. Sort of Excited, 2. Excited, 3. Very Excited and 4. Really Excited.

☐ STEP 2

After you have associated the events/activities with the four levels, proceed to associate a degree of voice expression with each. Have Apprentices listen to audiotapes of different people conveying the four levels of excitement.

☐ STEP 3

Next, have the Apprentices record each of the four levels using their own voice. Provide lots of audio feedback via cassette recorder and make sure that the Apprentice can distinguish one from another. It may help to can define the four types of voices by degrees of volume, emphasis on key words or any other variable you feel will be helpful. When you and the Apprentice have decided on the best four voices, record them and use them for the next step.

☐ STEP 4

Play a game where you present the Apprentice with one of his own four voices and he has to correctly associate it with the event that would cause that specific degree of excitement. An example would be, "That is going-to-Disneyworld excited voice." Next reverse the game. Tell him the event and have the Apprentice enact the voice that corresponds to the degree of excitement evoked by it.

☐ STEP 5

Relate your own four different degrees of excitement to specific events or activities in your life. Make sure that these are not events that would trigger the Apprentice's reactions. Create a tape of your own "four voices." Now, have the Apprentice associate your degrees of excitement with your personal events/activities. Finally, the Apprentice should learn to hear each one of your excited voices and tell you which level of excitement you are portraying ("A going-to-the-baseball-game excitement").

Variations:

After you have mastered degrees of excitement, practice with other emotions such as degrees of sadness, anger and fear.

Obstacles/Opportunities:

As in the prior exercise, you will come across some Apprentices who have difficulty distinguishing voice qualities and thus enacting four separate excited voices. If this is the case, back up and begin with two levels of excitement and gradually build up to four levels.

LEVEL II, STAGE 5, ACTIVITY 26

Improvement

ACTIVITY HIGHLIGHTS

° Learning to perceive degrees of improvement

° Experiencing the excitement of improving as a team or unit.

Summary:

Learning to understand degrees of improvement is not a social activity *per se*. However, it helps Apprentices to remain motivated to work on any skill that does not provide immediate payoff. As relationship skills get more complex, Apprentices must be provided with temporary "markers" to show they are making progress, even though they may not yet be receiving the benefit of their increasing skill. In this activity we want the Apprentice to see the improvement of our "team" as we become more skilled at a joint activity. The celebrations are because "We did it!" as we cross over one more of the seemingly endless hurdles they face on their developmental path. We love to fabricate "world records" as a motivation for many of our activities.

Participants:

Coach and Apprentice.

Getting Ready:

Choose a specific activity where it is easy to record the Apprentice's progress. Make sure to choose an activity that does not become an obsession for the Apprentice and of course it must be one that requires both of you to work together in order to succeed. Finally, make sure there is no external "payoff" or reward associated with improvement or reaching a certain level of achievement. In other words, your "team" is practicing getting better for the sheer reason of getting better.

Coaching Instructions:

In a prior exercise we demonstrated how to demarcate lines indicating the optimal distance for a game of catch. Now define your joint goal as seeing how far apart your team can stand while completing twenty successful throws, or two-ball tosses without a drop. Begin by standing very close and gradually move farther apart. Use a tape measure to determine your increasing distance apart and record your findings. Photograph, draw and write up brief accounts of your gradual progress. Store your "proof" in an activity journal, which you should briefly review, using a ritualized story form ("First we were only able to do one foot"), starting from the very beginning, each time you practice.

Variations:

Practice degrees of improvement with many different activities so that it will generalize. The sad truth is that life is not always about getting better. Sometimes there are temporary setbacks on the road to success. Along with celebrating our small triumphs, we try to find ways to mutually "mourn" our temporary defeats. There is nothing like keeping a good meaningful record of past successes to provide perspective at the time of a setback. Make sure to keep your activity journal handy and use it as a reference point, each time your "team" encounters a setback.

Obstacles/Opportunities:

Try not to use any criteria based on speed, for example getting faster, as this seems to increase stress and the potential for upset.

STAGE 6: TRANSFORMATION

Goals and Objectives

Until this stage we have focused on only one half of the "Relationship Balance." Apprentices have practiced acting as Co-Regulators, learning to modify their actions to remain coordinated with their partners. Now we begin to address the other half of the balance, learning to enjoy novelty and unpredictability – the creative part of relationships. This will set the stage for Level III, where the Challenger will learn to function as a Co-Creator of novel activities. In the last stage, Apprentices learned to enjoy degrees of change such as moving faster and slower, even when introduced in an unpredictable manner. In this, the Transformation stage, new elements emerge, patterns are altered, and one activity may be transformed into an entirely new one, albeit in a gradual manner. "Follow the Leader" is an activity that epitomizes the Transformation stage. The leader can turn walking into skipping, balancing on a beam etc. at a moment's notice and the "followers" must be prepared to match his change without warning.

Activity Highlights

Activities in this stage revolve around gradual transformations. These occur in an observable step-by-step sequence rather than all at once, so that the Apprentice is not mystified or overwhelmed. Activities are presented in slow motion, like time series photography. We slow down a series of actions that normally occur in a split second, so that they can be studied and mastered. We begin the stage by learning how one activity can gradually be transformed into another one in a surprising, yet enjoyable manner. We go on to explore transformations in functions of objects. In the middle phase we enter "Opposite World," a place where things are always the opposite of the way they were before. Then we move on to exploring the role of unexpected changes in producing the most hilarious humor. We take a side trip into the world of "morphing" emotions, an exercise designed to demonstrate how our emotional world can change dramatically from one moment to the next. Then we return to humor and design wacky role-plays, where characters rapidly change role actions. Moms climb into their cribs for a nap, while babies grab their briefcases and head off to the office. We close with an exploration of the aesthetic world of transformation. Apprentices experience the use of music, to portray transformations in the natural world.

Critical Tips

- Add variations in a slow gradual process so that each change is understood by the Apprentice.

- Make sure to give transformed activities and structures new names, so the Apprentice can remember them as different from the original.

- By the close of this stage, Apprentices should be hungry for novelty and variations as major sources of fun and excitement!

- You should also observe a significant increase in their flexibility and tolerance for change.

- Make sure that humor develops apart from reliance on scripts.

- Remember that the activities we present are only examples. They should whet your "creative juices" so that you can invent many more of your own variations.

LEVEL II, STAGE 6, ACTIVITY 27

Activity Transformations

ACTIVITY HIGHLIGHTS
° Enjoying unexpected novelty and change
° Understanding how one activity can transform into another

Summary:

This exercise introduces Apprentices to a new type of variation, where one activity gradually transforms into another. As before, we present a sample activity that we hope will provide you with ideas for many more.

Participants:

Coach and Apprentice.

Getting Ready:

For the base activity, you will need forty-eight cards, or pieces of paper cut into different shapes. They should be of different colors, evenly distributed between the shapes. Make twelve triangles, twelve squares and twelve circles. You also need twelve cards cut into a shape that consists of rectangles with a "bridge" joining them at the top (in the general shape of a torso with two legs and a small abdominal area).

Coaching Instructions:

☐ STEP 1

Begin by teaching the base activity, which will soon be transformed. Divide the cards into two piles, one for you and one for the Apprentice. Begin a simple matching game, where the Apprentice has to guess which of his cards he should play to match the one that you have turned over. After you turn over a card and place it on the table, the Apprentice turns one over and places it directly below yours. If the Apprentice is incorrect, have him take the card back and try another until he obtains a match.

☐ STEP 2

Lay out three triangles, side by side. The first match should be for shape. Any color triangle is a correct match. Next lay out three yellow shapes. This match is colors. Any yellow shape will be a match. Next, lay out three triangles again. This time only a circle will be a match for a triangle. Now directly below the Apprentice's circle, lay out a square of any color. Next, the only correct match to the square will be a "torso." When you have completed the three rows, if the Apprentice hasn't already noticed, point to the objects and say, "Look what we made! Let's make more!" Lay down three new rows of triangles and see if the Apprentice has caught on. The activity should now have moved from one of correct matching, to building human figures with triangle hats, circle faces, square mid-sections and rectangular torsos. Now take markers and together draw in the facial features and any other decorations you wish to provide for your figures.

Variations:

Build towers out of wooden blocks and then get out a ball and practice knocking them down. Make popcorn together and have one partner hold a basket and the other toss the popcorn into it. We hope that these illustrations give you many ideas of how you can present activity transformations where one activity turns gradually into another one.

Obstacles/Opportunities:

You may have to "tweak" this activity to get it to work, depending upon the age and understanding of the Apprentice. You can use any number of cards, colors and presentations.

LEVEL II, STAGE 6, ACTIVITY 28

Rule Changes

ACTIVITY HIGHLIGHTS
° Flexible adaptation
° Adapting to rapid rule changes
° Enjoying a degree of unpredictability

Summary:

In this activity, we completely alter the rules of familiar games to turn them into something very different. We begin with a simple game such as Monopoly. One by one you will introduce changes in the rules that "morph" the game into a new brand new version.

Participants:

Coach and Apprentice.

Getting Ready:

Choose a game to play. Check the sample transformations below to see what other materials you may need.

Coaching Instructions:

Inform the Apprentice that you are going to practice making lots of rule changes to a familiar game. Prior to any change, you will announce "Rule Change" and check with him to see if he is ready. Between rule changes, keep the excitement and attention focused on the next rule change and make sure the Apprentice does not get too focused on the game itself. Begin playing the game with the standard set of rules. Make your first rule change after you both have taken several turns. Stop, announce

"Rule Change" and say, "Now when we role the dice we have to move backwards instead of forwards." Practice this for several turns prior to the next change and then continue to make regular changes. Record your changes on paper as you are making them. When you are finished, make sure to provide a new name for the game like "Silly Monopoly." Make sure that the Apprentice recognizes that you have created a brand new game that only looks like the old version. Take out the new rules and play your newly created game regularly. Do not forget to celebrate your creation. We provide some sample changes below.

Variations:

We have provided some sample changes but feel free to provide your own. Determine the number of rule changes based upon the Apprentice's reactions. We want excitement, not upset. Remember, you can use any game.

Obstacles/Opportunities:

Remember not to choose any game upon which the Apprentice is particularly focused or obsessed with. With highly competitive Apprentices it might be better to teach them a new game first and, before they get invested in it, begin playing this version.

Sample Changes:

- Move backwards.
- Everyone will trade one property with no regard for value if any player lands on "Income Tax."
- "Ones" now have the same value as "100s."
- When you land on "Chance" you give the card to a friend before you look at it.
- After throwing the dice, you will skip every other block.
- You may try to take properties from anyone who is not looking at you.

LEVEL II, STAGE 6, ACTIVITY 29

Opposite World

ACTIVITY HIGHLIGHTS
° Enjoyment of activities that turn into their opposites
° Appreciation for unexpected transformations

Summary:

Another type of transformation occurs when one thing surprisingly turns into its opposite. We all love these types of surprises and hope that Apprentices come to enjoy them as well. In this exercise, we turn a game of catch into a game of "Drop the Ball," we say "Goodbye" when greeting instead of "Hello" and generally enjoy the silliness of creating opposites. One other important change in this exercise is that now we introduce our transformation at a much more fluid pace and without warning. By this point our Apprentices should be ready for this type of fast-paced change.

Participants:

Coach and Apprentice.

Getting Ready:

By this stage, Apprentices should be comfortable with sudden changes that are aimed at generating mutual laughter. You will need a ball, a whiteboard and markers, a jigsaw puzzle, a board game and some props for a simple domestic role-play.

Coaching Instructions:

You can begin the series of activities by explaining "Opposite World" to the Apprentice. When you enter "Opposite World," whatever you are doing at that time suddenly turns into its opposite. At this stage, only the Coach has the power to turn on "Opposite World." Here are four steps of what can be an unlimited number of "opposite" activities:

☐ STEP 1   SUCCESS OPPOSITES

Begin a game of catch with the Apprentice. See how many times the two of you can catch the ball without dropping it. Now tell the Apprentice that you are entering "Opposite World." The new game is to see how many times you can "just miss" the ball without catching it. Demonstrate how to "just miss" which requires partners to almost catch the ball but not quite. See if you can demonstrate two or three different ways to "just miss" and then start the game.

☐ STEP 2   GOAL OPPOSITES

On the whiteboard begin an activity of taking turns drawing an elaborate figure together. Once you have drawn all over the whiteboard, make an "Opposite World" announcement and tell the Apprentice that the new game is taking turns erasing pieces of the drawing. Do a similar activity with a jigsaw puzzle.

☐ STEP 3   RULE OPPOSITES

Play a game like Monopoly, where you earn money for landing on spaces. At some point in the game make an "Opposite World" announcement and hand out all the remaining money to the players. Now when you land on a space you do the opposite of what it says. Instead of paying rent you get paid. Instead of collecting $50 you have to pay it.

☐ STEP 4   ROLE-PLAY OPPOSITES

Practice a simple role-play where you wake up in the morning, eat breakfast, go to school and/or work, come home, eat dinner and go to bed. You can have parallel roles and pretend to be two brother or sisters, or complementary roles where you are a parent and child. Make an "Opposite World" announcement and teach the Apprentice how to do the role-play backwards. Wake up at night, take off your pajamas, put on your clothes, eat your dinner, go to work, come home, eat breakfast, put on your pajamas and go to bed. Now do the role-play in the original order again. When you announce "Opposite World" this time you will continue to do the play in the right order, but you will use opposite words to describe what you are doing. Lie down and pretend to wake up. Yawn, stretch and say to each other "Good Night, it's time to go to sleep." Get out of bed and go to the "dinner table" and have "dinner." Pretend to be a parent and child. Have the parent go to school and the child go to work. Come home and have "breakfast." Get tired and tell each other it's time to wake up. Go to bed, say "Good Morning" to each other and go to sleep.

Variations:

When he is ready, allow the Apprentice to turn on "Opposite World" but only using the methods you have already introduced. These are just a few examples to get your mind working. Try to come up with many more. You can let the Apprentice help you come up with ideas. As in the prior activity we are sure you can come up with unlimited variations.

Obstacles/Opportunities:

As you might imagine this is excellent training for our Apprentices who have difficulty in flexible thinking and set shifting. After a short time, the most enjoyment should be derived by the unpredictability. The Apprentice never knows when the Coach will shout, "Opposite World" and the fun will begin.

LEVEL II, STAGE 6, ACTIVITY 30

Unexpected Jokes

ACTIVITY HIGHLIGHTS
○ Learning the true function of humor
○ Finding alternative to "scripted" jokes
○ Developing improvised humor

Summary:

Those of you who have read my (Steve's) first book may remember a bittersweet vignette I shared about a child who had worked hard to learn "Knock Knock" jokes only to encounter a younger child who did not know the format and who, though very amused, provided the "wrong" response, which provoked rage from my client. Throughout RDI we work hard to help Apprentices learn that the main function of jokes and humor is shared laughter and rather than performing the joke correctly. In this activity we reinforce the notion by teaching Apprentices to alter jokes so that they deviate way off their scripts in unexpected ways.

Participants:

Coach and Apprentice.

Getting Ready:

Completion of prior humor and absurdity activities is essential for the Apprentice to appreciate the sudden shifts.

Coaching Instructions:

Make sure the Apprentice practices these jokes with family members and familiar people. We will present four formats for transforming jokes, but will expect you and the Apprentice to develop many more. The key is to continue to transform the jokes so that they are always changing. The samples presented below are just starting points. If they do not continue to change, they too will become scripted and stale.

■ *Format 1: Transform one essential element of a joke and make it equally as funny.*

"Normal" Version

    Knock Knock

        Who's there?

    Bee

        Bee who?

    No B2!

        B2 who?

    Knock Knock

        Who's there?

    B2 Bomber

        B2 Bomber who?

B2 Bomber B2 work on time.

"Silly" Version

Knock Knock

Who's there?

Bee

Bee who?

Knock Knock

Who's there?

Bee and H

Bee and H who?

Bless you.

- ■ *Format 2: We "criss-cross" the main subjects of the joke.*

    Why did the insect cross the road?

    To get to the other side.

    Why did the rabbit cross the road?

    To get to the insect.

    What happened when the insect crossed the rabbit?

    It became Bugs Bunny.

- ■ *Format 3: We turn one joke into another joke.*

    Why did the guy throw a glass of water out of the window?

    He wanted to see a waterfall.

    Why did the guy throw a bucket of water out of the window?

    He wanted to make a big splash.

    Why didn't the bucket of water make a big splash?

    He was on a boat.

Variations:

Once you use up our joke examples you need to create your own. Do not worry about whether they are particularly clever. Almost any silly variations will do just fine. Try creating stories that have similar switches and unexpected endings. Now have the Apprentices practice making their own silly endings to these predictable beginning lines. Do not worry whether they have any meaning or not, as long as they make you laugh.

Obstacles/Opportunities:

This activity, like many others we present, sets the stage for framing social encounters as improvisational and creative. This is an invaluable set of skills for our Apprentices to maintain in order to behave in a manner that is inviting to their peers. Remember that you will have to practice this with many joke variations and not just the examples presented above.

LEVEL II, STAGE 6, ACTIVITY 31

Morphing Emotions

ACTIVITY HIGHLIGHTS
° Introduction to rapid changes in emotions
° Exposure to how quickly situations may change

Summary:

Sometimes in life we rapidly go from feeling one emotion to feeling its exact opposite. We may believe that something has happened and find out that, in fact, it was the exact opposite of what we thought had happened. This activity provides an introduction to unexpected emotional transformations. It also exposes Apprentices to the concept that context can change rapidly and that we should not always expect a situation to play out the way we expect.

Participants:

Coach and Apprentice.

Getting Ready:

You may decide to include some props to make the role-plays more exciting and realistic. It is helpful in the first play if the Coach can change hats to indicate his role shift.

Coaching Instructions:

We will present four simple scenes to illustrate this exercise. You and the Apprentice should match your emotional expressions to the characters, pretending to be happy or sad together as the story unfold. You will need to explain each of the role-plays to the Apprentice before enacting them. Make sure to explain that these are supposed to be silly stories and not serious ones. Also, make sure that the Apprentice can assume all the roles.

☐ ONE EMOTION IS QUICKLY TURNED INTO ANOTHER

Scene 1

Teach a simple role-play where the Apprentice is at home and answers the door. The Coach, who is pretending to be the mailman, knocks on the door and the Apprentice opens it. The mailman says "Congratulations, you have just won one million dollars. Here is your check. Have a great day." The Apprentice should be quite happy and excited. Now there is another knock on the door. The Apprentice opens the door and it is the "tax man," who says, "Hello. I am the tax man. I heard that you just received one million dollars. Is that correct? Well, you will have to pay taxes on that." The tax man pretends to add up numbers on a calculator and then says, "Well the total taxes you owe come to…one million dollars. Please pay me now or I will have to take you to jail." The Apprentice hands over the check to the tax man. Now the Apprentice is very sad.

Scene 2

In the second version, the Apprentice plays a student and the Coach is the teacher. The scene begins with the teacher, who is not wearing his or her glasses, handing out test grades. Pretend to hand out different grades and then stop in front of the Apprentice and announce, "Class. I want to tell you how proud I am. This student has received one hundred per cent on the test. This is the highest grade in the class." Stop for the Apprentice to stand up, take a bow and wave to the class. Pretend that the class is applauding. Now have the teacher look puzzled and put his or her glasses on and examine the test paper. Suddenly the teacher says, "Class. I'm sorry to announce that I made an error and read this student's test grades wrong. He received a ten on the test not a hundred. This is the lowest grade I have ever seen!"

□ SOMEONE REACTS WITH TOTALLY UNEXPECTED EMOTIONS

Scene 3

The Apprentice comes to the door and knocks. The Coach answers the door. The Apprentice says, "Congratulations, you just won a million dollars." The Coach begins to cry in sadness. The Apprentice asks, "What's wrong. Didn't you hear me? You just won a million dollars!" The Coach still crying, says, " I heard you. But, I needed two million dollars to pay my bills. How terrible that I only won one million!"

Scene 4

In the final play, the Apprentice pretends to be a robber. He breaks into the Coach's house and steals a TV set. Then he yells, "Ha ha, I just stole your TV" and proceeds to run away with the TV. The Coach hears this and acts very worried and scared. Later there is a knock on the door and a policeman is there. When the policeman sees the Coach he notices that the Coach is laughing and smiling. The policeman says, "Hello, I am a policeman. Don't you know your TV was stolen last night? Why are you so happy?" The Coach continues to smile and says, "I have two TVs. One TV is broken and it was so big I could not lift it to throw it out. The robber stole the broken one. If you catch him, thank him for helping me get rid of it!"

Variations:

You can vary the last role-play by having the robber feel great about getting away with the TV, then going home to turn it on and finding out that it is broken. You can also play a game of role-reversals, where one character suddenly turns into another one. Robbers can be wearing police badges under their "robber uniform." Mommys can go to sleep in their cribs, while babies pick up their briefcases and head off to work. Remember to continue to vary scripts and add new ones so that the transformations themselves do not become scripted.

Obstacles/Opportunities:

You will have to practice these scripts for the Apprentice to become fluent with them. Remember to break them up into parts before combining them. You will also have to adjust the scripts based upon the age and level of understanding of the Apprentice.

LEVEL II, STAGE 6, ACTIVITY 32

The Thunderstorm

ACTIVITY HIGHLIGHTS
° Aesthetic judgment
° Making subjective impressions

Summary:

In this exercise, we make a leap into a new area we call "Aesthetic Transformations." As our activities have progressed we have moved from very concrete structural changes to altered rules, roles and humorous elements. Now we transform our subjective reactions based upon changes in musical rhythm, volume and speed.

Participants:

Coach and Apprentice.

Getting Ready:

You will need a small amount of proficiency on piano or keyboard for this exercise. If you have absolutely no musical skill or knowledge, find someone who can "mark" the keys for you numerically, so you know which ones to play.

Coaching Instructions:

This exercise has four steps:

☐ STEP 1

Begin by teaching the Apprentice to recognize how different types of music can evoke either a peaceful, relaxed feeling or a "stormy", scared or angry feeling. You can play recordings of musical compositions and demonstrate how different passages evoke a certain type of feeling. Only proceed when you are sure that she can easily make the distinction.

☐ STEP 2

Teach the Apprentice to use her two index fingers to play a "G, C" combination one octave below middle C. She should learn to play only when you nod to give so that she plays in time with you. When the Apprentice has learned her part, begin to play a simple note progression in the octave above middle C. The pattern you will play has three notes progressing up the scale "E, G, C" and then down for the final note, "G." The piece you will be playing consists of combining your pattern with the Apprentice's two-note combination in a very soft and peaceful manner. When you feel that you and the Apprentice have mastered your parts together, make a tape recording. End the piece with your "E, G, C, G" followed by a progression down to the lower "C" note to finish the piece. Give this piece a name like "Peaceful Day."

☐ STEP 3

Next you will practice the "stormy" part of your piece. Teach the Apprentice to play a slightly different, "B flat, E" two-note combination. After she has mastered this, you will play a pattern that begins higher and progresses lower, "G, F sharp, E flat and C." When you are both ready, play together, providing emphatic nods for the Apprentice to signal when to play. This time you will begin softer but progressively get louder and louder. When you are playing very loudly, see if you can abandon the progression and play your notes all at once to create a real "storm-like" effect. When you are ready, record this piece as well and name it "Thunderstorm."

☐ STEP 4

The final part of the exercise entails combining the two pieces on the tape recorder. You can also try combining them "live" if you think you are both up to it. When you are successful, play the tape for yourselves and other people with the new title "Peaceful Day turns into Thunderstorm."

Variations:

Try using drums to turn a soft song called "Raindrops" into a loud raucous version of "Thunderstorm." See if you can create a song where a "happy day" turns into a "sad day." You should experiment with an unlimited number of "feelings" songs

Obstacles/Opportunities:

Besides being a great vehicle for working on emotions, visual perception and motor skills, this exercise is an introduction to our next stage, Synchronization.

STAGE 7: SYNCHRONIZATION

Goals and Objectives

Now we move to a stage where Apprentices take more responsibility for regulating their interaction to make sure they remain coordinated. In Stage 7 we engage in more complex coordinated activities. The Apprentice learns more of the elements needed to be a partner in real-life, complex interactions. "Ring around the Rosie" is a good Stage 7 example. This provides participants with a framework, but success requires mutual regulation and coordination. Gathering sand together at the seashore, placing it in a large pail and then carrying it together to your "castle" provides another example of a Stage 7 activity.

Activity Summary

We begin the stage by working on a simple, yet critical part of synchronizing actions – learning to start and stop together. Apprentices learn several ways of referencing their social partner's state of readiness, as well as communicating their own degree of readiness. This leads us to the new skill area of Self Talk. For Apprentices to synchronize their actions in complex activities, they must have a means of rapidly altering their own actions. Self Talk supplies the means for ongoing regulation. Now we are ready for the move into more complex requirements for synchronized movements. For the first time we deliberately practice breakdowns of coordination. Communication and relationships are constantly breaking down. In this stage, we use systematic, predictable breakdowns that are incorporated in the activity. We want Apprentices to get used to the breakdowns and so we practice them over and over again. We make them into games. This also increases the sense of competence and confidence and the flexibility of our Apprentices.

Jokes become even more important. We emphasize that humor is a relative thing, completely dependent upon what we find funny. It does not have to be scripted. It can be absurd and even meaningless. We also practice synchronizing our conversational topics, our first foray into the world of reciprocal conversation. For the first time we teach Apprentices to consider the potential future actions of their social partners. "If we are playing soccer and you have to pass to me and we are both moving, are you going to kick the ball to where I am now or to where you think I am heading?" The idea that you can anticipate what someone is going to do or say, and plan your actions based upon their future actions is a critical breakthrough. Stage 7 contains activities that for the first time include peer partners working together.

Critical Tips

- Remember to modify the speed and complexity of motor activities based upon the motor skills of the Apprentice.

- Reinforce the pride Apprentices will feel for taking greater responsibility in synchronizing their actions.

- Learning Self Talk and Self Instruction takes a great deal of practice. They need to become automatic habits that the Apprentice uses on an everyday basis.

- Practice the "Tricky Partner" exercise sufficiently to prepare Apprentices for the large increase in rapid adaptation they will need to be able to deal with when partnered with peers.

- Remember to "back up" to early activities when first introducing Apprentices to one another.

LEVEL II, STAGE 7, ACTIVITY 33

Talk to Yourself

ACTIVITY HIGHLIGHTS
° Translating instructions into Self Talk
° Using Self Talk review, plan and evaluate actions

Summary:

In a number of prior activities, we asked you to narrate your actions in Self Talk. Self Talk has two critical virtues. First, because you are not directly addressing the Apprentice there is no "demand" element in the information you present. This makes it much easier for him to process information without worrying about providing the right answer. Second, you are modeling Self Talk, a skill that is essential for planning, reviewing and guiding your actions. This activity formally introduces Self Talk. In the first application, the Apprentice learns to "translate" your instructions into his own words. Translating information is a critical step in "owning" communication and moving from being a passive to an active information processor. Later in the exercise, we move onto a second major function of Self Talk, using narration to guide our behavior. Now we expose the Apprentice to various forms of Self Talk used to regulate his actions. We begin by teaching him to narrate an action he has just taken. Then we progress to using Self Talk to anticipate an action he is about to take. Finally, we progress to evaluating Self Talk, in which he learns to provide a simple evaluation label for a just-completed action.

Participants:

Coach and one or two Apprentices.

Getting Ready:

No materials are needed for this exercise.

Coaching Instructions:

There are seven steps in this exercise. In each step, make sure the Apprentice is narrating out loud and using language to indicate that he is not talking to you. Also, make sure to avert your gaze while he is Self Talking, so he is not confused between Self Talk and communicative language.

☐ STEP 1   FROM MY WORDS TO YOUR WORDS

Begin this exercise by having the Apprentice translate very simple instructions into Self Talk. For example, "Walk to the door" can be translated as "I need to walk to the door," or even "I walk to door now." Keep practicing simple translations until the Apprentice demonstrates proficiency. This will take at least several weeks. If he is having difficulty, model out loud how you would translate your words into Self Talk. Do not rush through this step.

☐ STEP 2   MORE COMPLEX INSTRUCTIONS

Now make the instructions more complicated. Work on two-part instructions and directions such as "First walk to the door and then open it." This can be translated into "I walk to door and then open it." You can continue to add complexity for as long as the Apprentice can be successful. Try to use meaningful instructions and directions, so the Apprentice can see some payoff for his translation efforts. Again, do not rush through this step. Remember, we are trying to develop a life-long skill. Try to make a habit of requiring him to translate your instructions into his own words, prior to expecting him to carry out any action.

☐ STEP 3   REVIEW

In this step, the Apprentice learns to use Self Talk to narrate an action he has just taken. Make a request for the Apprentice to complete some relatively simple activity that is within his capability for remembering and narrating. After he has finished the activity, instruct him to tell himself out loud what he has just done, such as, "I put the dishes into the dishwasher and turned it on." Once again, take a photo that represents the activity.

☐ STEP 4   MULTI-STEP REVIEW

In this step, Apprentices are taught to stop at regular intervals to review actions they have just taken. This is a more complex activity and it has several different steps. There should be natural places to stop and review. A sample activity could be following a Lego construction set that has several clearly demarcated steps of construction. After each step, the Apprentice stops and narrates to himself what he has just completed. Have the Apprentice take a photo of the activity at each of the stages of completion and then "tell the story" of the whole project when he has completed it.

☐ STEP 5   PREVIEW

In this phase, the Apprentice uses the stopping interval to "preview" the actions he is about to take. Have the Apprentice review what he has just done. But before proceeding, ask him to "preview" the next step out loud by telling himself what he is about to do. Make sure the Apprentice uses future-oriented language. When he has completed the actions he has just previewed, ask him if his preview was accurate.

☐ STEP 6   EVALUATION

Now, Apprentices learn to stop and make simple evaluations of an activity like, "That was great," "That was fun," "I did a good job." After completing all the steps of the activity, ask the Apprentice to provide a simple evaluative label for the activity. If he is unable to come up with a label on his own, provide visuals for several and have him choose one or two.

☐ STEP 7   RECORDING

The final step entails preserving a review of actions in a simple manner. Take the photos and the Self Talk statements and place them together in an "activity journal." The photos should be placed in order with the narrative under them. The final stage of completion should contain the evaluative label.

Variations:

If the Apprentice is a good reader, have him practice translating what he is reading into his own words. This is a particularly good method for increasing reading comprehension in readers who are already decoding well but not really understanding at a deep enough level. You can do the same activity with a multi-stage drawing of a scene. You can add critical elements stage by stage. Another great idea is to use this method for everyday things such as cleaning up their room, or helping to prepare a meal. It is highly motivating for an Apprentice to see his room in various stages of completion and then finally to feel the satisfaction of getting it right.

Obstacles/Opportunities:

This is a great exercise for Apprentices who believe they are "listening" to instructions while engaged in some other activity such as TV or video games, but are not really stopping to actively process the information. An added element for our more oppositional Apprentices is requiring that they not only put the instructions into their own words but also tell themselves the consequences for not complying with the instructions, for example, "If I don't shut off the computer I lose my privileges for two days."

Apprentices with little or no language will have difficulty verbally reviewing multi-stage activities. This is where the photos come in really handy. These Apprentices can sequence the photos and, with very little language, create an excellent review, preview and evaluation.

LEVEL II, STAGE 7, ACTIVITY 34

Synchronized Rhythms

ACTIVITY HIGHLIGHTS
° Making rapid modifications to remain coordinated
° Adapting to fluid variations

Summary:

In this activity we take advantage of the skills learned by Apprentices in collaboratively using the electric keyboard to create a true duet between Apprentice and Coach. Your duo will fluidly change speed, volume and pattern without stopping. Apprentices get a first taste in making rapid modifications so that they remain coordinated.

Participants:

Coach and Apprentice.

Getting Ready:

Apprentices should have completed prior keyboard and rhythm exercises.

Coaching Instructions:

This exercise has three steps:

☐ STEP 1

Review prior instructions for keyboard activities. Now begin to play a simple pattern, which the Apprentice should match. Play this pattern faster, slower, louder and softer in a fluid manner. Announce and then make the change with only a brief pause. Continue to have the Apprentice use just two fingers. Remember to use an exaggerated motion to indicate which note you are about to play.

☐ STEP 2

Next, play your scales together on the piano or keyboard. First go up the keyboard for five keys ("C, D, E, F, G") and then back down the keyboard together. After this is mastered, teach the Apprentice to go up the keyboard, one key at a time, while you proceed down the keys, always keeping your speed and volume synchronized:

- Apprentice plays "C," while Coach plays "G"
- Apprentice plays "D," while Coach plays "F"
- Apprentice plays "E," while Coach plays "E"
- Apprentice plays "F," while Coach plays "D"
- Apprentice plays "G," while Coach plays "C"

☐ STEP 3

Play a simple duet. Teach the Apprentice to play a steady rhythm of "C,G,C,G" etc. You can use a metronome to help keep the tempo if you think it will help. Have the Apprentice begin to play his rhythm, then you join in with a harmonious repetitive pattern such as "C, C, E, E, G, G, E, E," with each note played at twice the speed of the Apprentice's notes. Make sure the Apprentice maintains the tempo you have taught him. Vary degrees of loudness together, while you are playing.

Variations:

If the keyboard appears too daunting, you can synchronize rhythms on the drums quite effectively. Make sure that the Apprentice begins with a simple drumbeat and then join in by drumming at twice the speed, while he maintains his pace. Try to record your music so the Apprentice can enjoy it later and share it with others.

Obstacles/Opportunities:

You can go on from these humble beginnings to create many different compositions together. Remember to modify your speed and complexity based upon the motor skills of the Apprentice.

LEVEL II, STAGE 7, ACTIVITY 35

Tricky Partner

ACTIVITY HIGHLIGHTS
° Enjoy the challenge of synchronizing actions with an unpredictable partner

Summary:
Now we are ready to focus on a key element of synchronization; carefully observing and rapidly adapting your own actions based upon your partner's sudden changes. In this activity we create a "tricky partner" who may move or act in an unexpected manner. This is a critical exercise in preparing the Apprentice for the realities of interactions with peers, where changes occur on a constant basis and without warning.

Participants:
Coach and Apprentice.

Getting Ready:
No special materials are necessary.

Coaching Instructions:
You will not be announcing in advance what you are going to do. For each trial explain to the Apprentice that you are going to be tricky and she has to remain with you no matter what you do. You will vary whether you are going to count and "go" or count and "stay." Also vary whether you will go to the end line and "stop" or go to the end line and "fall." If this succeeds, switch roles and tell the Apprentice that it is their turn to be the "tricky partner" and that you will have to keep up with them. Suddenly vary your rate of movement in midstream.

Variations:
Remember to practice many different types of "Tricky Partner" variations. Any of the previous activities can and should be used in this manner. An important variation which teaches Apprentices to be highly sensitive to their coordination is "Getting it Wrong." In this activity we practice deliberately introducing small and large degrees of being uncoordinated. For example, we might practice moving and falling together onto beanbags with instructions that the Apprentice should land just before the Coach, not at the same time. Similarly we can practice playing the drums and have the Apprentice be a bit too loud, or a bit too fast to synchronize with the Coach.

Obstacles/Opportunities:
These are critical exercises that should not be bypassed just because they appear simple. In the next stage, when we introduce Apprentices to peer dyads, they will be exposed to a great deal more in the way of unexpected variation and will have a partner who will not take as much responsibility to keep actions coordinated. This

exercise will provide the practice they need to quickly notice and adapt to loss of coordination.

Variations:

Running and Falling onto Beanbag Chairs

- Count to three, pretend to move but stay on the start line.
- Count "One, two," and move your mouth and body as if you are going to say "Three" but remain silent.
- Run alongside the Apprentice but stop abruptly, just short of the "falling" line.

Tricky Drum Partner

- Hold your hand high as though you are going to hit the drum hard, but come down softly.
- Direct stopping and starting. After you announce "Stop" and you both have ceased playing, begin to say "St ..." in a very exaggerated manner but then say "Stop more" instead of "Start."
- While drumming, use a very loud voice to say, "Soft," and a soft voice to say "Loud."

LEVEL II, STAGE 7, ACTIVITY 36

Synchronized Humor

ACTIVITY HIGHLIGHTS
° Working as a team to deliver jokes
° Appreciating the enhanced enjoyment of collaborating in joke telling

Summary:

As in previous humor activities, we again emphasize that the critical element in a joke is the enjoyment of the participants and not the specific "script" of the joke. Jokes are for laughter not for obeying the rules. In this activity we begin developing the skill of being part of a "Joke Team." Apprentices collaborate to enact a joke or simple routine. The key to this activity is to synchronize your timing with your partner, whether your partner is a listener or part of your Joke Team.

Participants:

Coach and two Apprentices.

Getting Ready:

Apprentices should already be familiar with the concept that humor is whatever makes social partners laugh and is not connected to a specific script.

Coaching Instructions:

Apprentices are told that they are going to learn how to be a Joke Team. Go through the following three steps:

☐ STEP 1 "TELLER" AND "STRAIGHT MAN"

Teach Apprentices four or five simple jokes. Apprentice and Coach now practice telling each other jokes, with each fluidly taking turns playing the "teller" and "straight man." Pay special attention to the pair's timing and their ability to share a "belly laugh" at the end of the joke. The "teller" has to wait until the "straight man" communicates that he does not know the answer. The "straight man's" job is to communicate with emphasis that he is puzzled and has no idea what the answer is. Make sure that after delivering the punch line, both "teller" and "straight man" share their laughter and joy. After practicing with jokes that have been learned, make the transition to "made-up" jokes, where the "teller's" punch line, provided by the Coach, is a different response from the original one. It does not matter if the new punch line makes any sense, as long as it makes both Apprentices laugh. We do not want the joke to be scripted in any manner.

☐ STEP 2 JOKE PARTNERS

This step provides the Apprentices with practice in telling jokes as a team. They stand side by side and look towards one another as they deliver their lines. One Apprentice tells the first line of a two-line joke and the other tells the second line. There is no "straight man" in this exercise. After the punch line, both partners share laughter. Make sure to practice the jokes as learned and also as made-up variations. In both Steps 1 and 2, the Coach should provide the new variation if the Apprentice cannot come up with anything.

☐ STEP 3 JOKE ROUTINES

Now partners practice being a "non-stop" Joke Team. Combine as many simple jokes as you can in a "comedy routine" that Apprentices will tell together in a syn-chronized manner. When you feel they have mastered the routine, find people to act as an audience for their performance. After one partner delivers the first line, the second partner must wait for the audience to either guess the answer, or indicate that they do not know, prior to telling the punch line. After they tell each joke they both need to wait for the response of their audience, before proceeding to the next joke in the routine.

We have provided a few simple jokes below. Feel free to use many of your own.

Variations:

We like to prepare our Apprentices for the possibility that some listeners will not appreciate their humor. Role-play a joke routine where the listener clearly demon-strates that he does not find the jokes funny. Apprentices learn to respond by briefly apologizing, and asking if the listener would like to hear a different joke.

Obstacles/Opportunities:

It is crucial to quickly provide variations to the original jokes that the Apprentices have learned. If an Apprentice becomes too invested in getting any joke "right," be sure to eliminate it quickly from the repertoire. You may be surprised that some Apprentices may need to practice "laughing" hilariously. Be sure not to skip this step!

Sample Jokes:

Why was the broom late?

It over swept.

What's red and flies and wobbles all over?

A jelly copter.

How can you double your money?

Look at it in the mirror.

What birds are always unhappy?

Bluebirds.

What cat lives in the ocean?

An octopus.

What did Napoleon become after his thirty-ninth year?

Forty years old.

What did one broom say to the other broom?

"Have you heard the latest dirt?"

What did Tennessee?

He saw what Arkansas.

What did the big watch hand say to the small hand?

"Got a minute?"

What's gray and squirts jam at you?

A mouse eating a doughnut.

Can April March?

No, but August May.

What do you call a blind dinosaur?

I-don't-think-he-saurus.

What do you call two rows of cabbages?

A dual cabbageway.

Why do Teddy Bear biscuits wear long trousers?

Because they've got crummy legs.

Why did the chicken cross the playground?

To get to the other slide.

What goes ho-ho whoosh, ho-ho whoosh?

Santa caught in a revolving door.

What does a dentist call his x-rays?

Tooth-pics.

LEVEL II, STAGE 7, ACTIVITY 37

Conversation Frameworks

7

ACTIVITY HIGHLIGHTS

° Introduction to reciprocal conversation

Summary:

In this exercise, Apprentices learn three simple, structured frameworks for having brief reciprocal conversations. At this early stage, we are primarily interested in Apprentices appreciating that conversations require both partners to remain focused on a topic. We provide three simple frameworks they can use to do so: "Telling and Telling," "Telling and Asking," and "Asking and Telling."

Participants:

Coach and Two Apprentices.

Getting Ready:

Apprentices should have completed prior conversation readiness exercises.

Coaching Instructions:

Apprentices face each other during this exercise. They should be the center of each other's attention.

☐ STEP 1   TELLING AND TELLING

Both partners tell each other something about a common topic area. The Coach provides the topic, for example:

Topic: What you did yesterday.
Apprentice 1: "I went to the zoo yesterday."
Apprentice 2: "I went to the movies."

Topic: Restaurants you like to go to.
Apprentice 1: "I like to eat at Chili's."
Apprentice 2: "I like McDonalds."
Apprentice 1: "I also like McDonalds."
Apprentice 2: "I like Burger King."

☐ STEP 2   TELLING AND ASKING

Now Apprentices practice first making a statement "telling" and then "asking" their partner to respond to the same topic.

Apprentice 1: "I went to the zoo yesterday. What did you do?"
Apprentice 2: "I went to the movies yesterday."

☐ STEP 3   ASKING AND TELLING

Apprentices express curiosity about each other in a reciprocal manner.

Apprentice 2: "What did you do yesterday?"
Apprentice 1: "I went to the zoo?"
Apprentice 1: "What did you do yesterday?"
Apprentice 2: "I went to the movies."

☐ STEP 4   FLUENT COMBINATIONS OF THE THREE VARIANTS

As Apprentices become more skilled in these simple conversation sequences, begin chaining them together. Combine "Asking and Telling" with "Telling and Asking."

☐ STEP 5   TELLING, ALONG WITH TELLING AND ASKING

Eventually try and combine all three in a more natural manner.

Variations:

This is a good time to practice getting off topic, so that Apprentices can recognize the difference. Practice all three frameworks in a manner where Apprentices are deliberately venturing off topic. After a while, you can play a game where Apprentices try and function as a "tricky partner" and deliberately get off topic, to see if their partner will recognize it.

Obstacles/Opportunities:

Some Apprentices may have difficulty generating their own topics or responses. At this stage it is perfectly acceptable for the Coach to provide the material. However, in order to progress to Level III, Apprentices will have to learn to introduce their own variations.

LEVEL II, STAGE 7, ACTIVITY 38

Anticipation

ACTIVITY HIGHLIGHTS
° Learning to anticipate partner's actions
° Basing your actions on anticipated partner actions

Summary:

When I (Steve) was writing this activity I couldn't get the old Carly Simon lyrics, "Anticipation. It's making me wait" out of my head And for some reason I kept picturing bottles of ketchup. Oh well. This exercise is not about making people wait.

On the contrary it is about being able to take a brief look into the future and figure out where your partner is going to be next. Now our Apprentices are learning to coordinate their actions with the future, "not-yet-occurring" actions of their social partners. The best example we could come up with is that of the "Lead Pass." We are most familiar with the concept in sports such as soccer, football and basketball, but it is equally applicable to baseball. When there is a man on base and his team-mate hits a long fly ball, both the fielder and the base runner are playing the game of "Anticipation" and trying to gauge their actions based on their assumptions of what the other is going to do next. Anticipation is a critical skill to empha-size as we leave Stage 7 and move to Stage 8, with the variations and unpredictabil-ity that will be introduced by peer partners.

7

Participants:

Coach and two Apprentices.

Getting Ready:

You need a ball, a music keyboard and some masking tape.

Coaching Instructions:

There are two activities involving movement and music. Make sure that the Appren-tice enacts each role in both activities:

■ **ACTIVITY 1   ANTICIPATING MOVEMENT**

This activity has four steps:

☐ STEP 1

To practice this, we often begin with a simple back and forth catch. Tape a four-foot line on the floor, with two squares at either end of the line. One Apprentice will walk back and forth between the two squares. The other Apprentice stands several feet away and has to throw the ball to the square the first Apprentice is walking towards and deliver it just as he reaches the destination. When partners have mastered this, they practice a more fluent version in which the Apprentice in motion practices moving back and forth between the two squares and receiving the ball at each square. As Apprentices becomes proficient, first remove the line and then remove the boxes. Apprentices have to learn to "lead" their throw so the ball ends up where their partner is going to be.

☐ STEP 2

When simple throwing is mastered, practice with a "lead" soccer kick, basketball pass or any other ball action.

☐ STEP 3

After this is mastered, practice having one Apprentice move directly towards and then away from his partner with the partner's job once again being to deliver a "lead" pass, anticipating where the first Apprentice will be.

☐ STEP 4

A final step entails practicing with both partners in motion at the same time. As they become proficient, increase and decrease their speed fluidly. Eventually see if they can vary direction and speed of movement without any pre-announcements.

■ **ACTIVITY 2   ANTICIPATING MUSIC**

The Coach plays a simple five-note scale twice. The third time, stop after the third note of the five-note scale. One Apprentice has to immediately play the fourth note of the scale and the second Apprentice immediately follows with the fifth and final note, all done without a pause. After this has been mastered with a scale, practice in a more fluid manner. Play a simple pattern and have the Apprentices ready to fill in the missing notes, each time you pause in the midst of the pattern.

Variations:

We can practice an "Anticipation" variation of "Tricky Partner." The Coach has two soft balls. He throws one up in the air and then tosses the next at an Apprentice while his eyes are on the first ball. Teach Apprentices to play this game with one another. A similar variation is playing "Monkey in the Middle" and anticipating where the next throw is going to be.

Obstacles/Opportunities:

It goes without saying that you will modify this activity based upon the motor skills, eye–hand coordination and age of the Apprentices. Use video replays and Self Instruction as you practice and perfect this exercise. In a later stage we will be practicing anticipation in "Two-on-Two Soccer" and other small team activities.

STAGE 8: DUETS

Goals and Objectives

As you might expect from the name, this stage is a typical time for emphasizing peer relationships and for Coaches to move to more peripheral position. When we introduce peers we have to be careful to begin with simpler activities than the Apprentice has already mastered with an adult guide. No matter how you have tried to simulate a peer, you will never present the same degree of challenge and unpredictability. So after introducing peers, we typically return to earlier activities and replicate them.

Activity Summary

In Stage 8 we give Apprentices more of the responsibility for partnership, negotiation initiation, rules, roles, and coordinating movements. They also take responsibility for referencing and evaluating their partner's level of enjoyment. In Stage 6 we systematically introduced predictable breakdowns. Now the breakdowns are unpredictable. By Stage 8 Apprentices should be old hands at managing coordination breakdowns. They should know that relationship encounters are like an old boat that will only stay afloat through the efforts of the crew to keep patching and bailing. Social encounters are continually being disconnected and will inevitably "spring another leak" just when you finish patching the last one. Things not working do not deter peers at this point. They know that usually, with enough effort and joint negotiation, things sort of work out.

The stage begins with two activities, "Zoom Ball" and "Drumming Duets" that provide an opportunity for the new partners to collaborate and become a team. This is followed by an activity that teaches the two Apprentices to use non-verbal signals to aid each other complete their tasks such as obtaining the needed puzzle pieces from their partner. This is followed by an activity that reinforces the value and enjoyment of maintaining connections with their partner. The "Curious Conversations" exercise, teaches peers the importance of maintaining curiosity, in order to have a successful conversation. We end the stage with "Play on Words," which is an exercise that teaches peer partners to function as a Joke Team.

Critical Tips

- When introducing peers to each other remember to return to simpler activities until they are comfortable with one another.

- Spend enough time teaching Apprentices how to observe their joint interaction so that they can regulate and make repairs without your help.

- Remember that you are no longer the center of attention, the Apprentices are!

- Make yourself less conspicuous. At times avert your gaze so that the partners reference each other and not you.

- Do not intervene too quickly when Apprentices are a bit frustrated. Give them a bit of time to work things out.

- If they are available use persons who have completed the higher levels of the program, such as Explorer and Partner, as Assistant Coaches.

Zoom Ball

ACTIVITY HIGHLIGHTS
° Enjoyable cooperative motor activity
° Rapid adjustments to keep the ball in play

Summary:

A Zoom Ball is a football shaped plastic ball that is suspended on two long ropes with handles at each end. As partners move their arms in and out, the ball zooms back and forth between them. Moving your arms wide apart sends the ball away and towards your partner, while bringing your arms close together brings the ball back towards you. Apprentices have to coordinate their arm movements to keep the ball quickly moving back and forth. The excitement of this activity is heightened by an anxiety that the ball will move so quickly that it will come free and propel itself into one or other of the participants. If partners don't work together continuously, the ball simply drops to the floor. It may even become tangled. Thus, using cues to begin, slow down and ultimately stop the zooming are essential.

Participants:

Two Apprentices and Coach.

Getting Ready:

You can purchase a Zoom Ball at a local toy store or on our website. Apprentices should be far enough apart to ensure safety of objects and people. Space between partners must be adequate for ropes to be taut.

Coaching Instructions:

You may have to do extensive modeling and practice to teach the motor skills for "Zoom Ball." Often we temporarily enlist an Assistant Coach to help demonstrate. The Assistant Coach will be a temporary partner while the Coach stands directly behind an Apprentice and guides his hands, until he learns the rhythm of opening and closing the ropes needed to make the ball move smoothly. When the Apprentice is ready, you and the Apprentice practice. Slowly move the ball back and forth along the ropes. When both Apprentices are ready and have practiced with the Coach, they each take one end. The secret for the success of this game is that the players must not mirror each other but move their arms in complementary, opposite directions. Each action is narrated out loud so that it is easily understood, "We are going slower now," "We are going faster now," "Uh oh, I forgot to move my arms, it stopped."

Variations:

You can actually purchase a Zoom Ball that glows in the dark. Get one and see if you can set a "world record" for moving it back and forth in the dark without stopping. Later on, when Apprentices are more proficient, you can play "Two-on-Two Zoom

Ball," with four persons, each of whom grasps one of the handles on each side. The partners now have to coordinate their actions with the person next to them as well as the Apprentices at the other end of the ropes.

Obstacles/Opportunities:

For Apprentices with serious motor problems, "Zoom Ball" can be a difficult task. But, ironically, your fear may be the most serious obstacle. In fact we have found that our most seriously motor impaired Apprentices have been able to accomplish this task.

LEVEL II, STAGE 8, ACTIVITY 40

Drumming Duets

ACTIVITY HIGHLIGHTS
° Collaborative rhythms
° Enhancing the feeling of connection of peer partners

Summary:

Music is a great way to cement a feeling of unity and connection between new peer partners. For a number of weeks we may begin each meeting with a short period of synchronized drumming, having first introduced our partners to one another.

Participants:

A Coach and two Apprentices.

Getting Ready:

Apprentices should have extensive experience on drums and keyboard.

Coaching Instructions:

☐ STEP 1

Begin by playing a simple several-beat rhythm on your drum (e.g. long, long, short, short). Apprentices are asked to match the rhythm. After they are successful, demonstrate a simple variation and ask one Apprentice to carefully add the variation to the pattern (e.g. long, long, short, short, short). All partners match the new rhythm. Now demonstrate a variation and ask the second Apprentice to match you (long, short, short, long, short, short). All three drummers should now match the new rhythm. Practice this until all of you know your distinct rhythm and can play it without any help.

☐ STEP 2

Practice more smooth transitions where each of you takes turn "leading" by playing your specific rhythm and having the other two partners match it. Go from one variation to another without stopping, using only a signal from you to indicate that it is time to change.

☐ STEP 3

Now fade out of the interaction and teach the Apprentices to vary their rhythms without your participation.

Variations:

You can perform endless variations of this exercise using a music keyboard. You can teach simple patterns that are assigned to a specific Apprentice. You can alternate one Apprentice playing an ascending scale and the other playing a descending scale, while they match each other note for note.

Obstacles/Opportunities:

There is a strong temptation to urge or allow Apprentices to improvise their own variations and to make this a true "jam session." Try and hold off on this until the Apprentices are very proficient in the initial exercise and are ready to move into Level III, which does teach improvisation, but in a careful systematic manner.

LEVEL II, STAGE 8, ACTIVITY 41

Mixed-up Puzzles

ACTIVITY HIGHLIGHTS
° Using non-verbal signals for problem solving
° Shifting attention between tasks and social partner
° Collaborating with a partner to reach a mutual desired goal

Summary:

In this exercise, Apprentices coordinate their non-verbal signals to help each other complete their puzzles. This is another good activity for work on de-emphasizing words and increasing the importance of visual referencing. It is also very good practice in shifting attention between communication and task actions.

Participants:

Coach and two Apprentices.

Getting Ready:

Use two puzzles with twenty-four or fewer pieces.

Coaches Instructions:

Take the jigsaw puzzles and mix them up into two piles. Make sure that each pile contains about two thirds of one puzzle and about a third of the other. Place the piles at opposite ends of a table – out of potential "grabbing" distance of partners. Seat one Apprentice by each puzzle. Explain that there are two different puzzles, but they are all mixed up. Each has some pieces from the other person's puzzle. They have to finish their puzzles, but without talking to each other, and they will not be allowed to grab pieces from their partner's pile. They have to find another way to get the other Apprentice to give them the pieces they need. When Apprentices master this initial activity, repeat it, but this time instruct them that not only are they not allowed to speak, they are also not allowed to point to the piece they want.

Variations:

If Apprentices are more proficient, this is a great opportunity to add one or two more participants. Now do the same thing mixing up three or four different puzzles. Another variation is to divide the pieces from each puzzle evenly between the various piles. For example, if there are four Apprentices, each puzzle would be divided into "fourths" with a quarter of each puzzle in each of the Apprentice's piles. Provide the same instructions. However, now Apprentices have first to decide who is going to work on which puzzle. Once again, this must be accomplished without words. There are many work-related projects that can be done in this manner. Try digging a hole together without talking, or planting a garden.

Obstacles/Opportunities:

This is another great activity for our overly verbal Apprentices. This exercise may also motivate you to try many other collaborative projects that can be done without a word.

LEVEL II, STAGE 8, ACTIVITY 42

Curious Conversations

ACTIVITY HIGHLIGHTS
° Learning to have curious conversations
° Remaining on a shared conversational topic

Summary:

The one thing that makes conversations work, is the perception that the other person is genuinely curious about what you are saying. In this exercise, Apprentices learn the meaning of having a curious conversation.

Participants:

Coach and two Apprentices.

Getting Ready:

You will need a container of matchbox cars or similar small objects. Two or three should be of similar color – three different model red cars, three different model blue cars and so on.

Coaching Instructions:

This activity contains five steps:

☐ STEP 1

Remind Apprentices of their previous work on conversations and practice some of the basic formats such as "Telling and Asking." Now explain that we will use the pictures in our minds to have a conversation, where we stay on the same topic.

☐ STEP 2

Practice with one Apprentice at a time. Take a car and keep it hidden from the Apprentice. Make sure he is gazing at you and say, "I like the red Jeep, do you know which car I am talking about?" The red Jeep is then placed on the table, "Is this the car you thought I liked?" Now it is the Apprentice's turn. He removes a car from the container without displaying it and tells you "I like the blue Jeep? Do you know which car I mean?"

☐ STEP 3

Now gradually include both Apprentices. When they seem to be proficient, move yourself out and let them proceed on their own.

☐ STEP 4

As the activity progresses, make sure that from time to time you purposely "misunderstand" each of the Apprentices. When asked, "Is this the car you thought I liked?" you might respond, "No, I thought you said the blue Chevrolet."

☐ STEP 5

The next phase of this activity centers on a similar script but one that lacks important information and concrete details. The Apprentice's job is to be curious about important details. Remove a car from the basket, hold it beneath the table and say, "I like the yellow car." (**Note:** the make and model are not identified.) "Do you know which car I mean?" If the Apprentice guesses correctly, respond with, "Yes, I was thinking about the yellow race car." If the guess is incorrect counter with, "No, I don't like the Oldsmobile, it is too big. The car I like is a really fast car." If the Apprentice guesses the school bus, respond, "No, I don't want all those kids in my car. The car I like is a really fast car." If the Apprentice still guesses incorrectly, produce the car. Prolonged guessing will only be discouraging. Have the Apprentices practice this same framework with each other.

Variations:

After they have mastered the above framework, omit concrete objects and practice curious conversations again.

Obstacles/Opportunities:

Apprentices who become overly focused on the object – the car – neglect their partner present an obvious obstacle. Be sure to substitute less competitive objects if this happens.

LEVEL II, STAGE 8, ACTIVITY 43

Play on Words

ACTIVITY HIGHLIGHTS
° Introduction to improvising humor
° Using language in a playful, creative manner

Summary:

We introduced Joke Teams in the previous stage. Now humor moves to a new stage as Apprentices begin to play with words and use them in a creative manner. Various meanings of words will be humorously explored in a round table fashion.

Participants:

Coach and two or three Apprentices.

Getting Ready:

Make sure that Apprentices have mastered the earlier joke exercises. Also, make sure to choose words that you believe are within the Apprentice's understanding and that have several different well-known meanings. You will need a computer or a whiteboard and markers to visually display the words, definitions and sentences.

Coaching Instructions:

You are going to expose Apprentices to three different types of word play. The first consists of words that sound similar but have different meanings. The second type consists of words that have the same sound but are spelled differently. The third variety of word plays are based on words that sound and are spelled the same, but that have more than one meaning. In this exercise we are only concerned with juxtaposing the context. Provide plenty of illustrations before Apprentices practice with each other. Each Apprentice is only allowed to contribute his part of the play. They can take turns starting and finishing the joke. We have provided examples of ways that you can share humor with each of these word plays.

Variations:

Apprentices can begin to practice jokes at the dinner table. Each evening, every family member will have to bring a new joke to the table. It has to be different each night. This helps the Apprentice realize that they should not expect a laugh if they try an old joke on people who have already heard it.

Opportunities/Obstacles:

This exercise is designed for those Apprentices who already have good verbal proficiency and can recognize and understand the word meanings. Make no mistake, the ability to understand humor is extremely difficult. Puns are the most easily mastered form of verbal humor and for this reason they are introduced at this stage. Concrete thinking and a desire for predictability make mastery difficult. In the beginning, Apprentices may resist and refuse to laugh, but they quickly learn the pleasure in shared laughter. They tend to get hooked on it and usually take on the hard work of double entendre in order to keep the experience fun.

Types of Word Play:

Similar sounding but different meanings

Cape and Kate

I met a girl named Cape. She always wore a kate.

Pass and Past

He threw me the past as I ran for the pass.

Poor and Purr

The cat that liked to poor lived in the purr boy's house.

Kill and Kiln

I put a pot in the kill while I kilned a roach that I spotted.

Missiles and Measles

He shot off the measles because he had the missiles.

Same sound but different spelling

Sorry and Sari

I am Sari that I spilled saki on your sorry.

Cellar and Seller

I asked the cellar to stay in the seller.

Red and Read

I red the little read book.

Gate and Gait

He had an odd gate as he went past the gait.

Same spelling but different meanings

Plant

I potted the plant inside the plant.

Yarn

I told a yarn about some yarn.

Fast

Boy, that fast went by fast!

Drop

It's only a drop so how could you drop?

Spat

In the midst of a spat one boy spat on another.

Play

During a play is not the right time to play.

LEVEL III: CHALLENGER

Introduction

Summary

Challengers relate most successfully within groups of two or three. Like very young children, they still have trouble both in initiating and maintaining their relationship in larger groups. Success in Level III can be thought of as mastering the balance of Co-Regulation and Co-Variation. Relationships are a mixture of comfort and spice: the more there is comfort, the more we can safely add spice. This is the level of learning how to add variation while maintaining coordination with a peer partner. Ritualized activity evolves into spontaneous actions. Common frameworks are established, then new elements are added. Challengers can now change or even violate prior rules, upsetting expectations and using things in ways that they were not originally intended for.

Participants

Now our peer partners are taking more responsibility. The adults are becoming true Coaches and are no longer the center of attention. Both Challengers systematically add variations to enhance each other's enjoyment.

Settings

In Stage 9 we are still primarily working with physical movement and action settings. However, such physical settings become much less important as we progress into the later stages of Level III. We still want to guard against the intrusion of other individuals and so we do not yet conduct these exercises in larger groups. We also still make sure that objects and activities that are obvious temptations do not tempt Challengers into departing from interaction. However, we no longer need to conduct activities in specially designed, minimal stimulation rooms.

Language

In Level III, Challengers use language as a major interaction enhancement. We frequently hear interesting verbal variations, made up words and names and improvised "silly" conversations, songs and sayings. Language is also put to work as a means of regulating encounters. It is used for explicitly introducing variations. It is also used to obtain agreement and check with social partners for their acceptance and appreciation. Because peers are constantly introducing novelty and variation, there is much greater potential for confusion and conflict. Language is employed for on the spot negotiations, checking for understanding, communicating confusion and making compromises. Finally, language is used for Executive Functioning – to aid in reflection, planning and evaluation of actions.

Coaching Points

- Remember to celebrate each of the Challengers' co-creations.

- Record co-creations with journaling and photographs.

- Challengers will still require you to provide structure for negotiations and complex decisions.

- Watch out for the "need to win" at all costs. It will sabotage collaboration!

- Remember, you are still in charge of the pace and progression of activities.

- Certain objects can still distract the Challengers and cause them to stop referencing their partners. Be careful to limit objects that compete for attention.

STAGE 9: COLLABORATION

Goals and Objectives

Stage 9 celebrates peers as interactive partners. While you are still present, you are truly in the role of a Coach and no longer the primary interactive partner. Rather, you assume the functions of a facilitator, referee, boundary keeper and limit setter for the peers. The two Challengers face the "challenge" of adapting their actions, based upon their peer partner's reactions, to maintain the relationship balance of predictability and creation that is the hallmark of relationship encounters.

Activity Summary

The stage begins with activities that teach Challengers to function as a coordinated team. Next, we take a brief detour to practice a slightly more advanced form of Self Talk called Self Instruction. Following this, Apprentices practice reflection and planning. Towards the end of the stage we introduce activities that require more complex negotiation and competition against another team. Challengers have to juggle their desire to win with their desire to function as a good team member and maintain a friendship with team-mates and competitors alike. We end the stage with "Map Reader and Scout," an activity which requires a more sophisticated level of cooperation and teamwork.

Critical Tips

- This stage is a critical time to introduce reflection and planning skills.

- Collaboration takes place both for enhanced enjoyment and learning about "strength in numbers!"

- Continue to stress non-verbal communication, especially for language-dependent Challengers.

- Make sure to continually assess readiness for this level. Be prepared to return to Level II if demands for improvisation are too challenging.

- Be sure to emphasize the importance of encouraging and "cheering" for your partners.

LEVEL III, STAGE 9, ACTIVITY 44

Ball and Net

ACTIVITY HIGHLIGHTS
° Taking collaborative actions towards a common goal
° Coordinating actions so you can work together

Summary:

"Ball and Net" could be considered a metaphor for conversation – keeping the ball in the air and sharing responsibility for doing so. Our Apprentices love it because it's fun. Teamwork is necessary and each person must participate with skill and attention to his partner's actions.

Participants:

Coach and up to three Apprentices.

Getting Ready:

For "Ball and Net" you will need a mesh net approximately four feet by four feet. Each corner should have a handle for holding the net. You will also need three small air-filled balls.

Coaching Instructions:

Coach and Apprentices stand in the center of a room. Lack of clutter is important due to the activity level and possibility of breaking objects. Although the game is intended as one of increased challenges for keeping the ball in the air, Apprentices often enjoy knocking it off the net after a period of keeping it going. This provides a convenient endpoint to the game and has been incorporated into the basic rules. Coach and Apprentices hold a corner of the net in each hand and place one ball in the center of the net. They agree to a reasonable goal such as five bounces without any of the balls falling off. The Coach should keep in mind that success is a great motivator for this game. Together the partners say, "Ready, Set, Go" and begin to bounce the ball in the air with the net. If the ball falls to the floor, they pick it up and begin again. After reaching the agreed upon goal, they fling the ball as high as they can (assuming there is nothing fragile above them) and let it fall where it will.

Variations:

Balloons, different size balls or other objects can also be bounced on the net. Once competent, Challengers can also learn to bounce it lightly, vigorously or gradually harder and harder. Balls can be rolled from side to side. Partners can walk or jump as they bounce the balls.

Obstacles/Opportunities:

"Ball and Net" is a game that becomes more challenging as it is played. Disconnections and lack of attention meet with immediate consequences. Communication is essential for modifying one's own actions as well as a partner's. Information is gathered quickly when the game does not go well and strategies develop quickly during this exciting vigorous game.

LEVEL III, STAGE 9, ACTIVITY 45

Self Instruction

ACTIVITY HIGHLIGHTS
° Using Self Instruction to review, modify and plan your actions
° Increased self-regulation

Summary:

The key to remaining synchronized in complex social environments is to be both a careful observer and a rapid adaptor, as circumstances require. Self Instruction is a special kind of Self Talk, essential in directing ourselves to take adaptive actions. In this exercise we teach Challengers to use Self Instruction in an applied context.

Participants:

Coach and teams of two Challengers.

Getting Ready:

Challengers should be well versed in using Self Talk from prior exercises. Use a number of different simple activities that have already been practiced, such as drums, moving and falling, or any similar activity.

Coaching Instructions:

There are three steps in this exercise:

☐ STEP 1   SELF INSTRUCTION TO PREPARE

This step entails Challengers translating instructions for an upcoming action into their own words. For example, if you say, "This time we are going to run halfway and then walk slowly until the endpoint," Challengers should translate this into "I have to run half the way and then slow down." They should also include, "I have to stay next to [partner's name]."

☐ STEP 2   SELF INSTRUCTION FOR RAPID ADAPTATION

As you change elements of the activity, Challengers learns to use Self Talk to translate the necessary change into their own words – "Now we have to go slower," "Now we wait till we count to 'four.'"

☐ STEP 3   USE SELF INSTRUCTION FOR CORRECTION

Challengers accept feedback from you and translate it into Self Instruction to improve, "I went too fast. I have to slow down." After using Self Instruction for correction, Challengers should review their actions to see if the Self Instruction helped – "Did I slow down?"

Variations:

We like to use Self Instruction for rehearsal, prior to entering any new situation, or any setting where Challengers have previously had difficulty. They rehearse potential difficulties and the alternative behavioral strategies they can employ. Afterwards, they review the success of the rehearsal.

Obstacles/Opportunities:

Self Instruction is a key element in the development of Executive Functioning. It opens the door to useful reflection, self-evaluation, preparation and planning. Once again, make sure that Challengers use Self Instruction in all activity settings including schoolwork. Model your own Self Instruction out loud.

LEVEL III, STAGE 9, ACTIVITY 46

Replays

ACTIVITY HIGHLIGHTS
° Reviewing completed activities for evaluation
° Spotting the need for corrective actions

Summary:

This is the first activity to use video replay for feedback on the success of synchronizing behavior with a partner. In the last activity, Challengers practiced using Self Instruction to translate feedback so they could modify their actions. In this activity, they learn to rely on their own observations and evaluation to provide feedback that they will use in subsequent attempts of the activity.

Participants:

Coach and teams of two Challengers.

Getting Ready:

You will need a video camera and monitor for playback. Remember to set up your camera to capture the critical elements of the activity you are recording.

Coaching Instructions:

To practice this exercise, return to three previously practiced movement activities eg. "Two-Ball Toss," this is the easiest exercise in which to observe, in terms of making corrective actions, becoming more coordinated. After several trials, stop and play back the video. Pause the replay at critical moments, so Challengers can observe themselves acting out of "synch." Practice using "we" language, when it is clear that both partners need to take an action such as slowing down, moving closer, or counting together. Remember to incorporate the lessons learned from the previous Self Instruction activity. The combination of video feedback and Self Instruction becomes a powerful method of developing Executive Functioning skills.

Variations:

Deliberately take actions that place you out of "synch." Replay the tape and see if Challengers can spot the problem and tell you what actions need to be taken to be more coordinated. You can, if you wish, now begin to use regular video feedback as a routine part of working on many activities.

Obstacles/Opportunities:

Challengers who are perfectionists may have trouble watching the video without an emotional reaction. Make sure that you make as many errors as the Challenger. Also, try to keep framing the issue as corrective actions that both of you need to take and not problems that are specific to the Challenger.

LEVEL III, STAGE 9, ACTIVITY 47

Two-on-Two Soccer

ACTIVITY HIGHLIGHTS
° Developing an understanding of teamwork
° Encouraging your team-mate
° Coordinating your actions to reach a shared goal

Summary:

This activity requires Challengers to stay focused on the goal of winning but also on their actions as good team members. In addition, they have to coordinate their actions to out-maneuver members of the opposing team. This rapid shifting of attention is another challenge for people who frequently manage only one thing at a time well. Previous skills such as moving more quickly, more slowly, communicating availability to your partner, and rapidly modifying responses now come into play, but with a higher demand for timing and spontaneity.

Participants:

Up to four Challengers.

Getting Ready:

Challengers need to first learn the rudiments of soccer. This will include making sure not to use your hands, the need to stay in bounds etc. In our version, we emphasize the importance of no physical contact. Of course, Challengers must understand the point of the game – to kick the ball past the goalkeeper into the goal. All participants must first become proficient in making a lead pass (kick). You will need a soccer ball, some type of tape or other boundary markers and two goal areas. Remember to contain the game to an area that is easily manageable for the two teams. We will often initially conduct this activity indoors in a room with few distractions, before moving it outside. We use masking tape to indicate the perimeter of the field.

Coaching Instructions:

This activity has three major steps:

☐ STEP 1

The team-mates learn the basic rules. One person on each team is the "Goalie" and the other is the "Fielder." There are two major rules in our version of the game. Only the Fielder can score a goal, the Goalie cannot. But the goal will only count if it comes right after a good lead pass from the Goalie. So a goal only counts if it combines a good pass from the Goalie with a good kick by the Fielder. Goals made in any other manner do not count. Second, there is a "three second rule." If the Fielder or the Goalie keeps the ball for more than three seconds, their team loses possession of the ball and it goes to the other team. This means that the team-mates must keep passing the ball back and forth in order to keep it.

☐ STEP 2

Teams spend a good deal of time in practice sessions prior to their first competitive match. They become proficient at frequent back and forth passing and at making and receiving lead passes. Make sure that each of the team-mates spends equal time practicing both the Goalie and Fielder roles.

☐ STEP 3

Before you allow any competitive match, team-mates must practice making mistakes and responding in an encouraging manner. Participants must first pass a "buddy" test, where they demonstrate that they are emotionally going to support their team-mate no matter what, before being allowed into the competitive arena. Furthermore, they must pass the sportsmanship test, where they demonstrate that they can be good winners and losers. When the opposing team scores a goal, you must congratulate them and encourage each other that you will score the next goal.

Variations:

If Challengers have difficulty, you can begin with a simpler "practice" version. Set up teams of three Challengers. Teams take turns practicing. One Challenger acts as the Goalie and the other two are Fielders. One Fielder begins by making a lead pass to his team-mate, who then tries to score a goal. We are sure you see the natural extensions of this activity to basketball and volleyball and even relay races.

Obstacles/Opportunities:

Some Challengers hate the idea of losing. Their difficulty in handling loss may have led parents and siblings alike to create artificial "wins" to avoid tantrums and meltdowns. Two avenues of intervention will prove helpful. The first is direct teaching and a direct consequence. You will have to practice losing, "My turn to lose, your turn to lose," in a structured way. With each practice, Self Talk is critical. "I hate to lose, but that's OK. I'll feel better later." A penalty for outbursts should also be imposed.

9

LEVEL III, STAGE 9, ACTIVITY 48

Map Reader and Scout

ACTIVITY HIGHLIGHTS
° Simple collaborative problem solving
° Experiencing the power of team-work
° Practicing joint attention

Summary:

Map reading and "treasure hunting" seem to lend themselves to teamwork. In this exercise, Challengers learn to work together to reach their destination. They follow a map from marker to marker until they arrive at a "treasure." The "Map Reader" holds and "reads" the map, while the "Scout" looks for markers and retrieves them.

Participants:

Teams of two Challengers each.

Getting Ready:

Materials include handmade maps of a designated area based upon the age and map-following abilities of the Challengers. Colored markers are needed to signify when a specific area has been reached, and carefully construct maps that are as simple or complex as the ability of the Challengers to follow them. It is a great idea to have Challengers actually construct the maps.

Coaches Instructions:

There are four steps to this exercise:

☐ STEP 1

Challengers may first need instruction in how to use a map as a representation of an actual area of physical space. This is a crucial organizational skill in its own right.

☐ STEP 2

Once Challengers have sufficient map skills, provide them with a map that has colored points on it. Each point signifies a same-colored marker that is placed along the route. Make sure Challengers understand how to use the map to retrieve all the markers and bring them back.

☐ STEP 3

Designate and teach the two role assignments. One person is given the job of Map Reader. Only he is allowed to read the map. The other is the Scout who accepts the directions of the Map Reader and is the only one allowed to retrieve the markers.

☐ STEP 4

Practice a structured format for managing the journey. Upon reaching a new location and retrieving a marker the Scout must ask, "Where do we go next?" and wait for the Map Reader to indicate the direction using words and gestures. The Map Reader and Scout must make sure they understand one another before the Scout goes off on the next phases of the mission. While the Scout is scouting, the Map Reader remains at the prior location. When the Scout spots the next marker, he calls out "I see it" and the Map Reader then moves to join the Scout.

Variations:

As Challengers become more adept at this activity, allow them to walk together from marker to marker. You can also increase distances between markers. Markers can be "landmarks" such as a specific pieces of furniture that have clues taped to them, making this a true "treasure hunt." Challengers can also learn to go on a walk and make a map together as they walk along. They can then use this map to construct a treasure hunt with markers that other people have to follow.

Obstacles/Opportunities:

The goal of this activity is not winning or reaching the treasure. Like many of our activities, this exercise has the potential for becoming primarily a means to an end, with Challengers focusing more on reading the map correctly than on functioning together as a team, and the coach needs to watch out for this.

STAGE 10: CO-CREATION

Goals and Objectives

In Stage 10, Challengers experience the excitement of acting as partners in a creative process. Together they produce something that can only result from their equal collaboration. Challengers experience an intense pride in what they have accomplished together. They frequently reflect on their accomplishments and record their new creations. The products they create are solely for their own enjoyment, not for an external source. They do not require the appreciation of family members, though they are certainly proud when they receive praise.

Activity Summary

Stage 10 begins with two activities "Creative Rhythms" and "Creative Songs," which gradually familiarize Challengers with the excitement of Co-Creation. Choices are still structured and limited by the Coach. In "Creative Games" Challengers produce a lively new version of a game that may constitute the first time they have had something unique to share with a new peer. Co-Creation progresses to jokes, and poems, as Challengers practice Co-Creation in different media.

Critical Tips

- Make sure to record creations and review them frequently.

- Work in as many different media as you can think of.

- Carefully watch to make sure peers retain a fifty/fifty partnership.

- Do not become personally invested in the product. All that matters is that the peer partners enjoy it.

LEVEL III, STAGE 10, ACTIVITY 49

Creative Rhythms

ACTIVITY HIGHLIGHTS
° Jointly creating unique rhythm patterns
° Increased feelings of unity

Summary:

This activity presents the characteristic elements of all Co-Creation exercises. The activity begins by presenting a basic framework. Challengers each choose their own distinct variation, from limited choices. The choices are integrated with a little help from you (as little as possible) into something new and unique. Challengers name their creation, celebrate it and return periodically to reflect on it.

Participants:

Up to four Challengers.

Getting Ready:

Challengers should provide their own drums if they can.

Coaching Instructions:

There are six steps in this exercise:

☐ STEP 1

Each person chooses his own rhythm on the drums. Make sure that each rhythm selected is different and that none is too complex. Make sure that you record each rhythm.

☐ STEP 2

After they have each chosen their rhythms, Challengers play them in succession as a single piece. They can also try playing the rhythms together.

☐ STEP 3

Now they jointly agree on a final rhythm to be used as an ending for the piece. Once again, record the rhythm so that it can be duplicated.

☐ STEP 4

You will need to add some simple connecting beats to tie the piece together.

☐ STEP 5

The Challengers practice playing their simple piece until they can replicate it. They make a final recording.

☐ STEP 6

As a final step they give their composition a distinct name and the piece is saved for future reference. Following the naming, lead them in a brief celebration of their accomplishment. Remember to play their piece periodically.

Variations:

Once Challengers have the hang of the Co-Creation process, give them opportunities to create other different distinct rhythms to add to their "album." Also, once experienced, allow them to choose longer and longer rhythms to combine. Try to gradually eliminate your role and see if they can "bridge the gaps" in a piece with their own efforts. Remember to let them struggle a little. Make sure you periodically play their "oldies" so they can reminisce. If they are willing, encourage them to create a unique dance to go along with the rhythms they create.

Obstacles/Opportunities:

While we refer to this stage as Co-Creation, we are not yet ready to give Challengers unlimited creative license. The key to this stage is learning to share a creative event with a partner. Make sure that no one's creative desires dominate or become the center of attention. The key is that the participants are not interested in creating a specific thing or the "right" thing. Ideally, they can't wait for the surprise of finding out what their shared efforts will create.

10

LEVEL III, STAGE 10, ACTIVITY 50

Creative Songs

ACTIVITY HIGHLIGHTS
° Creating your own novel songs
° Using familiar lyrics to integrate contributions

Summary:

People have made up their own unique version of popular songs from time immemorial. It is a great way of fostering a feeling of comradeship. In this activity, Challengers take elements from familiar songs and use them to co-create a completely new version.

Participants:

This exercise is best conducted in teams of two.

Getting Ready:

Practice this exercise yourself prior to trying it out on Challengers. Make sure that you have pre-selected several songs that Challengers are familiar with.

Coaching Instructions:

This exercise has six steps:

☐ STEP 1

Present several simple "standard" songs and have each person pick the one they like best. Make sure that the song is a simple one and not a modern hit.

☐ STEP 2

Each partner chooses a line of words from their song. You should help them to each pick a line that will not be too difficult to integrate in the final product.

☐ STEP 3

Challengers make this selection from their chosen song three times, until they each have picked three lines.

☐ STEP 4

Now type the lines on the computer and have partners try to fit each other's lines together to make a song. Allow the Challengers some poetic license to change words, make them sillier and take more "ownership" of them, as long as both partners are happy with the changes and neither dominates. Provide help when absolutely necessary to eliminate or modify a particular word.

☐ STEP 5

Now supply teams with a choice of melodies, none of which is from the two songs that have been chosen. Challengers pick the melody they will use for their new co-created lyrics.

☐ STEP 6

The final job is to shape the lyrics to fit the song. This will typically entail some minor editing efforts by you. Take one line of music and lyric at a time and fit lyrics into the music. When both partners are satisfied with a line, you should record it. When you are done with all six lines, have the partners sing the song and make a final recording.

Example:

This is a mixture of three American classics, "Oh Susannah," "Frosty the Snowman" sung to the tune of "Yankee Doodle:"

Happy jolly souls

Corn cob pipe and button nose

Riding on a pony

Waved goodbye saying don't you cry

My banjo's on my knee

Variations:

The obvious but more difficult variation is to have Challengers each pick out a melody from a song and combine melodies and then using the words of a third song. Give it a try and see what happens.

Obstacles/Opportunities:

Like all of these exercises, you will only see real benefit from multiple trials of co-creating songs. Although you will have to help the partners, do not get hung up on producing a quality song to the point where you become the central figure in the composition. If the partners do not see the piece as their creation you have defeated the purpose of the exercise.

LEVEL III, STAGE 10, ACTIVITY 51

Creative Games

ACTIVITY HIGHLIGHTS
° Jointly create inventive new games
° Gain popularity through creativity
° Develop pride in cooperative effort

Summary:

Good friends have always invented their own unique games. Sometimes they are impossible to explain to others and only provide enjoyment to the friends, but they are a great source of bonding and shared experience. In this exercise, Challengers learn to work together to create a new game. The point of the exercise is for Challengers to feel pride in their joint creation.

Participants:

This exercise is best done in teams of two or three.

Getting Ready:

You will probably have to choose the particular game genre that you wish to start with. Be prepared to pursue this activity with many different types of games.

Coaching Instructions:

This exercise has eight steps:

☐ STEP 1

Team-mates each pick a favorite game within a specific genre. Initially you should pick a single genre such as card games, chess/checkers type games, or simple board games.

☐ STEP 2

Next each Challenger must write down three important rules of the game she has chosen.

☐ STEP 3

Challengers take turns presenting one rule from each of their games until there are a total of six rules, three from each game (nine rules if there are three team-mates).

☐ STEP 4

This step entails integrating the physical structure of the chosen games. If the game is a card game or a checkers/chess equivalent this should provide few problems. However, if you work with board games (as you eventually should), each partner will write down three features of his game and then will take turns adding features from this list, until all six are included.

☐ STEP 5

Now Challengers create the new game that combines the rules and features that have been selected. Your job is mainly to record the results and to modify any elements that would make the game unworkable or too complicated.

☐ STEP 6

Give this game a new name, which typically is a combination of previously used names.

☐ STEP 7

Teams play their game and make any modifications needed to make it more fun.

☐ STEP 8

As a final step, help the teams make a short "documentary" video demonstrating how to play the game.

Variations:

Try the same exercise with movement-oriented activities such as soccer, basketball, baseball, hide and seek, tag, dodge ball etc. How about "Ping Pong Pool?"

Obstacles/Opportunities:

Make sure to choose games that participants are not overly invested in. A great aspect of this activity is that if partners are successful, and you aid them in creating a game that really is fun, they can teach this new hybrid game to other peers and gain some respect as someone who started a new fad!

Creative Role-Plays

ACTIVITY HIGHLIGHTS
° Creating unique role-plays
° Creative collaboration with team-mates

Summary:

Now we are ready to make our Co-Creators into budding playwrights. Challengers modify a script to make it uniquely their own. Then they perform and videotape it for future enjoyment. One key to success is to make the play as wacky as possible.

Participants:

Use teams of two Challengers.

Getting Ready:

Challengers should already be familiar with taking on role-play characters and coordinating their actions to make the play work.

Coaching Instructions:

There are six steps in this exercise:

☐ STEP 1

Practice at least three different simple role-plays. Each role-play should have two distinct characters who do not appear in any other play. This will create six characters from which to choose.

☐ STEP 2

Each team-mate now chooses one character from the prior role-plays that they will portray in the new play. Make sure that the characters are from different role-plays.

☐ STEP 3

Now choose a theme for the play. The theme can be from one of the role-plays in which no characters were chosen.

☐ STEP 4

Write a simple script for the new play. Add absurd, comic elements to liven it up. Make sure that the Challengers give it a title.

☐ STEP 5

Now practice and enact the play, making sure to videotape the final version.

☐ STEP 6

Videotape the play and provide "screenings" for friends and family.

Variations:

See if you can write continuing episodes for the play, as if it were a soap opera. Gradually add other characters from the initial role-plays into the play by adding additional members to the team. If you want to, you can "kill off" some of the older characters as you add new ones. See if the Challengers can add new characters to the play without creating too much confusion or conflict.

Obstacles/Opportunities:

This is another activity where a Challenger's perception of needing to get it "right" can interfere with the enjoyment and thus the purpose of this activity. We care not at all that the play is enacted with any skill or technical prowess, just as long as it leaves team-mates in stitches.

LEVEL III, STAGE 10, ACTIVITY 53

Joke Factory

ACTIVITY HIGHLIGHTS
° Jointly created humor
° Enjoying wacky improvisation

Summary:

In this exercise, we provide a simple "Joke Factory" that Challengers tap into as a team, to create novel pieces of humor. Each partner picks a topic from a short list of choices. Then they combine their topics into a joke that makes absolutely no sense. Once again we emphasize that the point of jokes is laughter and shared silliness and not "getting it right."

Participants:

We recommend no more than three Challengers on a team to begin with.

Getting Ready:

Make sure that Challengers have experienced prior activities where we practiced absurd, meaningless but funny jokes.

Coaching Instructions:

Tell Challengers that you want them to help you develop a Joke Factory. This will be a computer program that can produce endless numbers of jokes. Challengers will try out the factory by testing it with three basic joke formats:

1. Why did the _____?

2. What do you get when you mix a _____ with a _____?

3. How do you make a _____? You _____.

Examples of each of the formats are presented at the end of the exercise. One Challenger works on the first line and the other Challenger does the second line. Then they practice telling the joke together in a coordinated manner. Make sure to laugh uproariously.

Variations:

There are an unlimited number of joke structures that you can set up in this way. See how many different ones you can come up with.

Obstacles/Opportunities:

Challengers can learn to be creative and funny after they practice this exercise. It provides enough structure for the participants to feel safe, so that Challengers can explore their creative sides.

Joke Factory Structures:

1. **Why did the** *(name an animal)* _____
   - Elephant
   - Rhino
   - Ant
   - Skunk
   - Alien
   - Dinosaur

   (name an action) _____
   - Cross the road
   - Pick blueberries
   - Hop on one leg
   - Run around in circles
   - Wear a cabbage on his head
   - Swim in spaghetti
   - Wear a bathrobe
   - Swim the backstroke

2. **Because he** *(add a reason)* _____
   - Just took a bath
   - Was very hungry
   - Wanted to eat
   - It was on sale
   - Wanted to go home
   - Had to blow his nose
   - Had to scratch his toes

3. **What do you get when you mix a** *(animal)* _____ **with a** *(animal)* _____ **?**

10

159

- Elephant
- Rhino
- Ant
- Skunk
- Alien
- Dinosaur

(add your own categories)

You get a _____

- Mixed-up creature
- Whoknowswhatasaurus
- Headache
- Mess

(add your own)

3. How do you make a *(animal)* _____ *(action)* _____

- Do the backstroke
- Cross the road
- Eat a pickle
- Go to sleep

(add an action)

You *(action)* _____

- Put a cabbage on his head
- Count to three and close your eyes
- Twirl him around and hope for the best
- Tell him there's a McDonalds down the street
- Tickle him with a turkey feather

(make up your own action)

LEVEL III, STAGE 10, ACTIVITY 54

Poetry Factory

ACTIVITY HIGHLIGHTS
° Viewing oneself as a creative writer
° Participating as part of a creative poetry team

Summary:

Kenneth Koch has mastered the art of teaching children to love poetry by creating structures that help them make beautiful poems without needing to have sophisticated organizational and literacy skills. We will use Koch's poetic structures again in later stages. This is a simple version that allows a pair of Challengers to experience joint poetry creation without frustration. Using Koch's methods, each partner contributes one line to a poem structure. Note the similarity to the "Joke Factory" exercise.

Participants:

Try this exercise in teams of two.

Getting Ready:

Challengers need have no experience with poetry to do this exercise. It is much easier to do this with a computer.

Coaching Instructions:

Explain that you are creating a "Poetry Factory" computer program. You want the team-mates help in testing out whether it works. You should also talk about how you know that they are good poets and will create wonderful poetry if they work together. We have presented several poetry structures adapted from Koch's work. Samples are provided at the end of the exercise. Have partners take turns contributing each line. When the poem is complete, they should collaborate on a simple title. Make sure to save the finished work in a journal, so that team-mates can show it to others and review their creations from time to time.

Variations:

We highly recommend that you read Koch's works, including *"Rose, where did you get that red?"* for many other ideas for poetry frameworks that you can use. You can also use your poems as lyrics for co-created music.

Obstacles/Opportunities:

This is a wonderful opportunity for Challengers to feel that they can compose and create. For many this is the first time they can enjoy being a writer and the boost in self-esteem and desire to write more is amazing.

Color Poem

Red is like a _____ in the *(season)* _____

Blue is like a _____ in the *(season)* _____

Green is like a _____ in the *(time of day)* _____

Yellow is like a _____ in the *(time of day)* _____ .

Sounds Poem

The dinosaur cried out with a *(sound)* _____

But the little bird cried out with a *(sound)* _____

The volcano exploded with a *(sound)* _____

But the snowfall made a *(sound)* _____ as it fell

The roaring waterfall made a *(sound)* _____

But the peaceful forest stream made a *(sound)* _____ .

Day and Night

In the day I can _____

But at night I can _____

In the morning I can _____

But at night I can _____

In the afternoon I can _____

But at night I can _____ .

Different Days

On Mondays I must _____

But Saturdays are for _____

On Tuesdays I must _____

But Sundays are for _____

On Wednesday I must _____

But holidays are for _____ .

STAGE 11: IMPROVISATION

Goals and Objectives

This stage introduces Challengers to the demands of peer play and conversation, where topics, themes and movements may change at a moment's notice. Challengers have now become the major contributors to these "on-the-fly" changes made without stopping to discuss or negotiate. This requires rapid referencing, regulating and repair skills.

Activity Summary

The stage begins with exercises aimed at preparing Challengers to rapidly introduce their own ideas in a coordinated manner. Challengers learn flexible thinking, rapid adaptation and alternative ways of using familiar materials and actions. Practice in improvisation expands over a number of different areas, including rhythms, music, song and movement. Challengers learn to emphasize the fun of their joint activity over reaching any particular endpoint. The joint creativity of this stage comes to full fruition when partners improvise their own role-plays and jokes.

Critical Tips

- Remember to stay with simple materials.

- You may have to work individually with Challengers who have difficulty coming up with their own contributions.

- Begin each activity by providing a simple framework that serves as a base for later improvisation.

- Once again, remember not to get caught up in the quality or meaning of an improvised product. What is important is the peer partner's enjoyment, not whether they produce something that you think is worthwhile.

LEVEL III, STAGE 11, ACTIVITY 55

Co-Variations

ACTIVITY HIGHLIGHTS
° Accepting and showing appreciation for your partner's contributions
° Effectively communicating the reasoning for your actions
° Remaining coordinated in the face of unexpected variation

Summary:

While on the surface this may seem like a turn-taking activity, in actuality we learn how to add variations while keeping related to social partners. It is also an important exercise in learning to acknowledge and appreciate your partner's contributions.

Participants:

You can do this exercise with a team of up to four Challengers.

Getting Ready:

You will need a large set of "architectural" blocks. You will also need a white board and markers and a marble. Participants sit facing each other. The blocks are in a container next to you.

Coaching Instructions:

There are four steps to this activity:

☐ STEP 1

Tell partners that they are going to build a sculpture out of the blocks. They will take turns choosing a block and adding it wherever they want in the structure – but they have to make sure that their idea is connected to their team-mates'. They have to stay connected. But they also have to add something new to the structure, some sort of variation. Challengers must use one of the following choices for their "Connections" and "Variations." Choices should be provided in writing, so Challengers can reference them.

Connections:

1. I used the same shape block.

2. I used the same size block.

3. I kept going (in the same direction).

4. I put my block next to yours.

Variations:

1. My idea makes it larger.

2. My idea makes it taller.

3. My idea makes it wider.

4. My idea makes it stronger.

☐ STEP 2

After each person takes his turn, he must explain which of the four ways he has chosen to remain connected, and in which way he has chosen to vary the structure. He is asked to explain his contribution by saying, "This is my idea. The way my idea is connected to yours is _____." Next, he explains his variation, "The way my idea changes the sculpture is _____." Do not accept any variation that is not listed in the choices above.

☐ STEP 3

The other partners are encouraged to compliment each contribution by acknowledging that they see how the sculpture has changed in the way that was described and that it is a positive change. Continue to take your own turn the first few times this exercise is practiced, in order to model the process. As you build, you should use opportunities to create ramps without mentioning why you are doing so.

☐ STEP 4

Now remove a small marble from your pocket, place it on one of the sloping surfaces and say, "This is my idea. I'm turning the sculpture into a marble racetrack." Hand the marble to one of the partners to place on the sculpture. Now each member has to maintain the process of acting in a way that is similar and also a variation, this time using the marble. After each person is done, he passes the marble to the next partner.

Variations:

Cardboard sculptural kits with beautiful colors and shapes are available in gift shops and toy stores. These may be used to co-create sculptures.

Obstacles/Opportunities:

Some Challengers simply can't accept that their ideas are being changed as part of the ongoing process. We have had some break down and cry without consolation because an idea was changed. While this exercise is difficult for these Challengers, they clearly most need these skills.

LEVEL III, STAGE 11, ACTIVITY 56

Improvised Activities

ACTIVITY HIGHLIGHTS
° Learning the joy of improvisation
° Flexible thinking
° Divergent thinking

Summary:

With this activity we move full force into the joy of improvisation. Challengers are given basic materials and improvise together to create a new activity. They are successful because by now they have a storehouse of ideas and can recombine the elements of the many activities they have already mastered.

Participants:

You can do this with several teams of two Challengers if you wish.

Getting Ready:

Select materials that you believe will be simple and familiar enough so that they will not become the focus of attention. We like to begin with some of our "veteran" materials such as beanbag chairs, balloons, balls and blocks. Typically, by this stage Challengers can use relatively few materials to create quite an assortment of activities.

Coaching Instructions:

The activity has three steps:

☐ STEP 1

Lay out the materials that the team-mates are going to use. Tell them that you want them to use the materials to make up their own game. They can make up any game they like, as long as they both participate and agree and it is fun for them.

☐ STEP 2

To provide a reference source, visually display the names of many of the activities that they have already mastered. Typically this review is enough to get teams going.

☐ STEP 3

If you see a team getting stuck and running out of ideas, take one of the materials and say, "Let's see. Here are some beanbag chairs. What are some ways that you like to use beanbag chairs? Will any of those uses work now?" If partners are still having trouble, you can make a list of the different ways they can use each material. For example, blocks can be bowling pins, obstacles, houses, forts, or roads.

Variations:

Practice a very different form of improvisation. Tell team-mates that you want them to do a certain activity, but do not provide the usual materials needed. Rather require them to improvise from materials that would not normally be used. For example, tell them to make up a game of tennis, but do not provide rackets or a net. Instead you can provide several cardboard cylinders, a pile of beanbag chairs, some Scotch tape, several plastic plates and some sheets of paper. Do this with as many activities as you can think of and you will be surprised at how quickly the Challengers develop flexible and divergent thinking skills.

Obstacles/Opportunities:

The need to have it "my way" is the biggest obstacle in this activity. Another obstacle can be the lack of imagination. These are both good reasons to keep working at this exercise.

LEVEL III, STAGE 11, ACTIVITY 57

Improvised Structures

ACTIVITY HIGHLIGHTS
° Flexible thinking
° Rapid coordinated improvisation

Summary:

In typical children's play, themes suddenly change without warning. A scenario where two children are spacemen fighting aliens abruptly changes into one where two doctors are operating on a wounded lion, with only a brief suggestion by one of the partners triggering the transformation. In this activity we practice this type of thematic improvisation in a more gradual format. Challengers take turns adding new features to their co-created structures. Periodically they pick a card that allows them to change the entire framework into something else.

Participants:

Several teams of two Challengers can participate.

Getting Ready:

You can use any type of construction materials that you like. We prefer to use simple building blocks, or architectural blocks. Provide a number of pretend "props" that might be associated with different types of structures such as airports, fire stations, schools, garages, shopping malls, etc. You will need to construct a deck of cards that has two types of cards: one that says "Keep the same structure" and the other that says "Change the structure." The deck should contain two "Keep the structure" cards for every "Change the structure" card.

Coaching Instructions:

Explain the two types of cards to team-mates. They will take turns making additions to a basic structure. Each time it is their turn, they will pick a card from the deck. If they pick a "Keep the structure" card, they should make an addition that does not change the structure. For example, if you were building a house, you would add a door, a window, a chimney or some other part of a house. However, if you pick a "Change the structure" card, this means you must turn it into something else. If you are building a house, then you could add some props that will change it into another structure, such as a garage or an airplane terminal. You should choose the initial building theme. It should be something simple like a house. There is one more rule. When you choose a "Change the structure" card and make a change, you must check with your partner to see whether they are enjoying the change. If they do not like it, you must try another change, until you find one your partner enjoys.

Variations:

The corollary to this activity is to turn one prop into another without varying the basic structure of what you are building. For example, if you are building a house and you pick a "Change the structure" card you could take the chimney and transform it into a satellite dish. Make sure to require partners to check with each other for enjoyment, prior to completing their turns.

Obstacles/Opportunities:

Concrete, literal thinking can be an obstacle in this activity, but this also represents a great opportunity to improve cognitive flexibility.

LEVEL III, STAGE 11, ACTIVITY 58

Improvised Rules

ACTIVITY HIGHLIGHTS

- ° Increased flexibility
- ° Ability to adapt rules as needed
- ° Creating variations that increase your partner's enjoyment

Summary:

Some Challengers tend to be very rule-oriented. Rather than viewing rule variations and changes as exciting novelty, they often perceive them as disruptive. This activity brings out the potential excitement we can feel when together we continually change the rules of a game so that we never know what is going to happen next.

Partners play a board game where, on each turn, they have to change one of the rules in order to move their piece.

Participants:

Several teams of two Challengers can participate.

Getting Ready:

Participants should all have mastered several of the earlier flexible thinking activities before attempting this. Use a simple board game that is not too challenging and somewhat age-appropriate.

Coaching Instructions:

Explain to Challengers that they are going to play a familiar game in a brand-new way. They will take turns. Each person rolls the dice and moves her piece just as she always does. But there is one big difference. At each person's turn, before she rolls the dice, she has to change one rule of the game. The change cannot be one that favors her, rather it must be one that makes the game more fun and interesting. At the end of this description, we present a number of possible changes using the example of Monopoly. Prepare a list of possible changes that Challengers can use if they cannot come up with any of their own.

Variations:

Of course you can do this activity with any game or physical activity. Try playing improvised volleyball or tennis.

Obstacles/Opportunities:

This is another opportunity to learn flexible thinking and rapid adaptation. It is a great way to help partners to focus on their fellow players rather than on winning the game.

Possible Monopoly Rule Changes:

- ° You must move backwards.
- ° You must skip every other space.
- ° When you land on "Free Parking" you get a free property.
- ° You can put up motels and shopping malls along with hotels and houses.
- ° Every time you "Pass Go," you have to tell a joke and make the players laugh.
- ° Before you get to move, you have to spin around three times and say your name backwards.

LEVEL III, STAGE 11, ACTIVITY 59

Improvised Rhythms

ACTIVITY HIGHLIGHTS

° Reviewing the evolution of a final product from a series of variations

° Creating activity variations for your social partner's amusement

Summary:

This is an exercise in how to influence and accept influence. In prior musical activities, you have largely been responsible for the introduction of variety and the framework of the composition. In this activity Challengers begin to take responsibility for composition. Excitement is generated from the ability to work as a team and from the increased complexity of the composition.

Participants:

Try this with up to four Challengers.

Getting Ready:

You need one drum per Challenger, a container with additional instruments, carpet squares, a video camera and a cassette recorder.

Coaching Instructions:

This activity has five steps:

☐ STEP 1

Play a simple five beat pattern on a drum. "Hard/slow, Hard/slow, soft/fast, soft/fast, soft/fast." Narrate the pattern as you drum. This pattern is repeated four times. Instruct Challengers not to change the basic five beats of the rhythm. What they are going to do is to vary the rhythm within the five-beat framework.

☐ STEP 2

Provide variation choices to Challengers who are free to choose from among them:

        Soft/slow, soft/slow, hard/fast, hard/fast, hard/fast

        Hard/slow, hard/slow, hard/fast, hard/fast, hard/fast

        Soft/slow, soft/slow, soft/fast, soft/fast, soft/fast

☐ STEP 3

After learning to play the variation choices, Challengers take turns choosing a variation and playing it. The drumming should gradually become more fluid, as they learn the three choices. Continue to take a turn playing the same basic pattern without variation. It should be the Challengers who play all the variations.

☐ STEP 4

When the team-mates master Step 3, allow them to add their own variations, as long as they stay within the framework of the five-beat rhythm.

☐ STEP 5

As a final step, allow Challengers to vary the creation by maintaining the five beats but varying the loud/soft and fast/slow relationships to whatever they would like. Initially require that they stop after introducing their new variation to make sure that all Challengers approve and that it fits the boundaries of the activity. Gradually allow them to drum in a more fluid manner, still maintaining the five-step pattern.

Variations:

As participants become proficient, allow more leeway in introducing rhythms and begin to move from a structured turn-taking format into a more fluid and "natural" one.

Obstacles and Opportunities:

It may be difficult for some Challengers to remember the basic framework and stay within it. This type of sequential organizational problem may require additional practice. Providing visual structure, such as symbols to represent the different pattern combinations, may also help the Challenger with this problem.

LEVEL III, STAGE 11, ACTIVITY 60

Improvised Role-Plays

ACTIVITY HIGHLIGHTS
° Practicing natural fluid role-playing
° Rapid flexible thinking and adaptation

Summary:

Typical children's play is a completely improvised event. Role-plays rarely stay with a theme for very long. Plots interweave. Characters are abruptly added and deleted. Even if characters remain, their roles may change dramatically. In this activity, partners learn to enact fluidly improvised role-plays, choosing from a selected cast of characters, themes and events. People of any age should greatly enjoy this exercise.

Participants:

Teams of two Challengers can participate. If you are working with several teams, have one team at a time be the "Players" with the other teams being "Watchers."

Getting Ready:

Your major job as Coach is to prepare the "raw materials" from which the participants will improvise their role-plays. Select a number of different characters and add brief descriptions for each. Provide different "props" for each character, such as hats, glasses, fake noses, diaper, baby bottle, stethoscope, police badge, mailbag, computer, computer repair tools, jackets and other distinguishing characteristics. Next, make a list of simple plot lines. These should be no more than one or two simple sentences in length. Finally, tape-record a number of sample silly voices using exaggerated high, low-pitched, nasal, and other silly features.

Coaching Instructions:

This exercise has five steps:

☐ STEP 1

Practice to make sure that all "Players" know how to enact each of the basic characters in their "non-improvised" forms. Review each of the characters and their related plot elements so that participants understand each one. Review the different available props. Review different silly voices that participants can use.

☐ STEP 2

Now begin the basic role-play by asking Players to choose roles that fit together easily, such as mother and father or teacher and student.

☐ STEP 3

When Players have had a bit of time to practice their roles, stop the action. Ask each of the players to choose a new character, a new voice, new props and a new plot line. Tell them to make sure that the new characters and plots fit together.

☐ STEP 4

Now, stop the actions more frequently and have Players switch characters and plot lines. This time make sure that, along with matching characters and plot lines, they also choose voices and props that are unexpected and make their characters really silly, like a baby with a deep voice, or a policeman wearing a diaper with a badge pinned onto it. Tell them to surprise each other with the voices and props that they choose. Stop the action frequently and tell them to switch voices and props but continue in character and with the same plot line. Make sure that they continue to identify who they are to each other to avoid confusion.

☐ STEP 5

As a final activity, have Players surprise each other by choosing characters, props and voices without consulting with each other. Then they have to collaborate on a plot line that will be enjoyable for them all.

Variations:

Gradually allow participants to introduce their own characters and plot lines. They are always welcome to introduce new voices and props. If you believe participants will enjoy it, try having the two teams of Challengers combine for a role-play.

Obstacles/Opportunities:

You know you are doing this exercise correctly if Challengers (and you) are frequently falling to the floor with laughter. Videotaping the role-plays really heightens the enjoyment. Keep your eyes on the mutual referencing for shared joy during playbacks of these hilarious videos.

Sample Characters:

- Postman
- Policeman
- Computer repairman
- Talking computer
- Mother
- Father
- Child
- Teacher
- Student
- Robber
- Doctor
- Invisible patient
- Baby
- Pet dog
- Pet cat

Sample Plot Elements:

- I am a postman having to deliver an important message.
- I am a person at home waiting for a message to see if I won the lottery.
- I am trying to catch a robber.
- I am a robber, trying to rob a bank.
- I am a computer repair person trying to fix a computer.
- I am a computer who is refusing to work until I get fed.
- I am a mother telling my child to go to sleep.
- I am a child who doesn't want to go to sleep and is sneaky.
- I am a mother preparing dinner for the father.
- I am a baby crying in my crib.
- I am a doctor who is trying to examine an invisible patient.
- I am an invisible patient who is trying to get the doctor to help me with my tummy ache.
- I am a dog who wants to catch a cat.
- I am a cat who wants to scare the dog, so he will stop bothering me.

LEVEL III, STAGE 11, ACTIVITY 61

Improvised Jokes

ACTIVITY HIGHLIGHTS
° Appreciating improvised humor
° Emphasizing shared creation over scripted joke-telling

Summary:
As you can already see, we love to use humor in our exercises. When our partners develop a good improvised sense of humor, both as a Co-Creator and appreciative audience, they immediately become attractive to their peers, despite any other limitations they may have. We all love someone who genuinely laughs at our jokes and comes up with zany additions to our ideas.

Participants:
A small group of Challengers.

Getting Ready:
Remind team-mates of the simple joke frameworks that they used in the "Joke Factory" exercise in Stage 10. Make sure to review this exercise with participants to refresh their memories. The three basic joke-types that we used were:

- Why did the _____?
- What do you get when you mix a _____?
- How do you make a _____?

Coaching Instructions:
There are three simple steps:

☐ STEP 1

Teach participants to use three additional joke variations:

- What did the _____ say to the _____?
- What is the capital of _____?
- What is the national *(food, bird, animal)* of _____?

Provide plenty of examples of each, so that all participants are proficient in using these frameworks.

☐ STEP 2

Now the real fun begins. Participants use a round-table format, where they rapidly go around with each team-mate having a turn beginning a joke and one of the other participants volunteering a ridiculous ending. Make sure to emphasize that they should not care whether the joke makes sense or not, as long as it makes everyone laugh. You will often initially participate as part of the round table and will typically be the one who models ridiculous endings, so that everyone feels comfortable using this framework and does not worry about getting it "right."

☐ STEP 3

Stay within one framework for a while before signaling a change to another one. After everyone is comfortable, try to initiate a more fluid process where each participant picks another framework and the group quickly rotates through all six. You should gradually withdraw participation and become a highly appreciative audience. Over time, you should also gradually withdraw the need for turn-taking and allow participants to provide their contributions as they think of them.

Variations:

Have each participant bring in one new joke format each time that you meet together. Allow them to provide some examples of the format. Then incorporate them into the improvisational mix.

Obstacles/Opportunities:

As you might expect, the biggest obstacle is a participant's unwillingness to accept the nonsensical nature of jokes as they rapidly change and "morph" into new entities. This is a sure sign that you must backtrack to earlier stages. As we stated in the summary, this type of practice will pay off in immediate benefits in the world of peer relations. The reason for this is that this exercises reinforce the essential truth that the key to humor is not the need to get it right but to have fun and make sure your partners are having fun too. All you have to do is study the totally improvised and oftentimes nonsensical humor in the Marx Brothers films to know that this is so. If you stopped to analyze them, you would have no idea why their jokes were funny, but that does nothing to keep you from rolling on the floor with laughter!

11

STAGE 12: RUNNING MATES

Goals and Objectives

In this, the last stage of Level III, Challengers begin to perceive their relationships in a more self-aware manner. The Challenger has become aware of the need to act in a way that will be attractive to peers. He knows that others will not tolerate a cheater, or a sore loser. Nor will they want to be with someone who does not find ways of compromising and collaborating with them. He also knows that, to keep a friend, he must provide something that is meaningful to them. By this stage he knows that communication will not always be effective. He is actively checking for misunderstandings and seeking to correct them.

Activity Summary

The stage begins by exploring the relationship between emotional expressions and internal feelings. Challengers learn that their feelings emanate from within themselves and not from another person. They learn to be accurate "readers" as well as "senders" of emotional expressions. We practice non-verbal "conversations" where children learn the different components of non-verbal language and manage emotional expressions in a more deliberate manner. Challengers also learn to be more aware of their communication environment. They learn to choose physical space carefully and regularly check for accuracy, understanding and topic connection. In mid-stage we return to formal conversation practice, as Challengers work on maintaining the connection of their topics in ongoing conversations. As the stage progresses, we teach several critical relationship skills: learning to be a graceful loser, managing mistake-making without emotional upset and joining in a peer's activity without interrupting and intruding. At the end of the stage we introduce Challengers to the concept of examining their behavior from another person's point of view and then close the stage with a "Friendship" exercise. Here we teach Challengers that even early friendships require maintenance and effort to sustain them.

Critical Tips

- Remember to have everyone use similar emotion labels to avoid confusion.

- Learning progresses much faster if we all use Self Talk out loud regularly.

- Remember to continue to amplify your emotional expressions.

- Non-Verbal communication must be practiced all day long. Practice should be part of a daily routine.

Emotions

ACTIVITY HIGHLIGHTS
° Learning that emotional expressions emanate from internal feelings
° Identifying the non-verbal expression of basic emotions
° Meaningfully sharing emotions with social partners
° Linking feelings with their causes

Summary:

This is the first activity to work directly on understanding emotions. We begin with four basic feelings: happy, sad, angry and scared. In this exercise emotional expressions are taught as a meaningful communication of something the person is experiencing. Don't be surprised if you spend months on variations of this activity. It is critical for further development and combines many different elements of emotional awareness and communication.

Participants:

Up to four Challengers can participate.

Getting Ready:

In the initial phase, you will use four "emotion cards" with line drawings of faces expressing the basic emotions. You will need a mirror but a video camera and monitor will be quite helpful as well.

Instructions:

There are eight steps to this activity:

☐ STEP 1

Explain that we have expressions because something happens to cause us to have a feeling. When we have a feeling, the feeling turns into an expression. Move in front of a mirror and make the appropriate expression while speaking as follows:

> "I have this sad expression because I feel sad inside."
>
> "I have this happy expression because I feel happy inside."
>
> "I have this worried expression because I feel worried inside."
>
> "I have this angry expression because I feel angry inside."

☐ STEP 2

Now have each participant practice making each of the expressions and relating it to a feeling, just as you did.

☐ STEP 3

Practice "passing" the emotion to one another. Sit in a small circle and take turns making an expression and sharing the feeling. After making her expression, each Challenger reaches out and gently places her hands on the cheeks of the partner to her left. This signals that she is "passing" her same emotion to the partner. The

12

person who has received the emotion makes the appropriate expression and states that she is having the feeling. The Coach indicates when it's time to change expressions and begin passing a new expression.

☐ STEP 4

Once Challengers master passing basic expressions, we work on linking feelings with simple causes for these feelings. Explain that we have feelings because something happens to cause these feelings. "We are going to practice having feelings and saying what makes those feelings." Demonstrate as much as needed. For example, you may say, "I am happy because I get to see my friends today." Each participant practices a happy emotion and its cause. Continue for all four emotions.

☐ STEP 5

The activity becomes more fluid and Challengers get to choose their emotions and explain why they have it.

☐ STEP 6

Challengers practice guessing the emotions of other group members based upon their facial expressions. After this much practice they should be able to do this very quickly.

☐ STEP 7

After guessing the emotion, they practice responding in a caring manner. Insert some simple conversation as follows:

- Person notices sad expression: "Are you sad?" *(affirmative reply)* "Why are you sad?" *(wait for reply)* "Is there something I can do to cheer you up?" *(wait for reply)*

- Person notices a happy expression: "You look happy!" *(wait for reply)* "I am glad you are happy. I'm happy too."

- Person notices worried expression: "You look worried." *(wait for reply)* "What are you worried about?" *(wait for response)* "I get worried too sometimes."

☐ STEP 8

Continue to regularly add emotions to this activity, until you have a large repertoire.

Variations:

Play a variation of the "Pass the Emotion" game. One partner picks an emotion and explains why she has it and then passes it onto the next one. The next partner must explain why he has the emotion, using a different but valid reason and so on, until you indicate a need to change emotions.

Obstacles/Opportunities:

This is a great opportunity for everyone involved with Challengers to use emotion labels in the same manner as they are practicing. It helps if those involved make an extra effort to narrate their own emotions and the simple reasons for their feelings out loud. It is also crucial to encourage Challengers to use their new skills to ask those close to them about their emotional expressions. Be careful not to minimize your facial expressions by saying things like "I'm fine. It's no big deal." You may think you are protecting the Challenger, but in reality you will be confusing him.

LEVEL III, STAGE 12, ACTIVITY 63

Talk without Words

ACTIVITY HIGHLIGHTS

° Practicing the different components of non-verbal communication
° Learning to have non-verbal "conversations"

Summary:

Now we return to the world of non-verbal communication. In this exercise we break down the various elements of "speaking without words" into two main areas: "Body Language" and "Sound Language." We practice each separately and then integrate them into more complex non-verbal "conversations"

Participants:

Try this exercise in groups of up to four Challengers.

Getting Ready:

You will need a video camera and monitor for this exercise. Prior to starting you should choose a range of non-verbal expressions you wish participants to practice. Make sure to clearly distinguish the different "body" and "sound" expressions that characterize each one. Make a videotape to illustrate each expression. Do not add any words for your sound portion of the tape, just the non-verbal accompaniments. You will also need to make a videotape of two people having each of the non-verbal "conversations." Examples of these conversations are presented at the end of the exercise. (If you wish, you can purchase this videotape for a modest fee on our website.)

Coaching Instructions:

The activity has eight steps:

☐ STEP 1

Learn to read your partner's body language. First turn on the video without the sound and have participants watch the body language in the different segments. If you have the ability, play the segment in slow motion and pause at critical points so you can capture important components. Carefully observe one segment at a time. Test each person's ability to read body language by playing different segments out of order and seeing if they can recognize the communication. Now ask each partici-

12

pant to enact a "body" conversation. Stay with one at a time. After participants have accurately modeled all of the basic forms, quiz them by seeing if they can recognize each other's "body talk." Work with one pair of Challengers at a time, with the others acting as "watchers." Finally, have each participant practice reading body talk accurately without benefit of video playback.

☐ STEP 2

Learn to read your own body language. Now repeat the procedure, but have each participant view their own video segments and learn to correctly identify their own body talk.

☐ STEP 3

Make sure that not only can they visually identify their body language but that they can also do so kinesthetically (feeling the different muscle groups that they use for the expression). Return to each segment and have participants identify the changes they can feel in their face, their arms and their trunk, when they enact the different responses.

☐ STEP 4

Learn to read your partner's "sound" language. Repeat the procedure for Step 1, but turn off the video and just work with the audio portion of the tape. Make sure not to use any words in the sound recording.

☐ STEP 5

Learn to read your own "sound" language. Repeat Step 2 and similarly just use the audio portion.

☐ STEP 6

Use only body language to have a conversation: Now you are going to work with reciprocal expressions. These come in both "symmetrical" and "complementary" forms. Have participants watch the video and then practice their own simple "body" conversations. When they are ready, videotape each conversation and have them analyze it. When they have enacted all of the conversations, make sure that they can recognize each one without any hints.

☐ STEP 7

Use only "sound" language to have conversations.

☐ STEP 8

Use both "body" and "sound" language to have conversations.

Variations:

The possibilities for non-verbal conversations are endless. Watch your favorite movies with the sound off. Stop the action regularly and have participants guess the conversations that are going on.

Obstacles/Opportunities:

This is another opportunity for highly verbal Challengers to learn to rely less on their words. Practice non-verbal conversations at regular times in the day. Make it a part of the daily routine!

Sample Non-Verbal Conversations:

Symmetrical

- ° We are both members of a team that just won the championship.
- ° I am angry with you and you are angry with me.
- ° We are brothers and our pet dog just got run over.

Complementary

- ° I am sad and you are wondering what's wrong.
- ° I am angry with you and you are confused about why.
- ° I am feeling very scared and you are trying to comfort me.

LEVEL III, STAGE 12, ACTIVITY 64

Can You Hear Me Now?

12

ACTIVITY HIGHLIGHTS
- ° Heightened awareness of personal space
- ° Learning the impact of physical position on communication effectiveness

Summary:

Challengers may still be rather unaware of the impact of their physical position on others. This activity provides practice to increase awareness of the effect of our position in space on the person we are interacting with. In this activity, social partners practice the dimensions of "too far away," "too close," "too soft," and "too loud."

Participants:

You can work in pairs or with three Challengers, with participants rotating and one serving as a "watcher."

Getting Ready:

No materials are needed for this activity.

Coaching Instructions:

There are three steps to the activity:

☐ STEP   TOO FAR AND TOO CLOSE

Tell participants that this will be a lesson about being too far from and too close to each other. When you are talking to someone, you can be too far away from them, so they can't hear you, or too close to them, so they feel uncomfortable. Start by practicing being too far away. Ask each pair or threesome to stand far apart and try to conduct a conversation about what they see, while using a normal speaking voice. Tell them to keep moving back to determine when they can no longer accurately hear each other.

☐ STEP 2   WALKING AWAY WHILE TALKING

Now tell partners that they will practice how walking away while talking may leave the other person unable to hear you. Ask partners to slowly walk away from each other while talking, again using a normal speaking voice. Have one partner slowly walk out the door and continue talking while the other remains inside.

☐ STEP 3   TOO LOUD AND TOO SOFT

Practice speaking too loud and too soft. Have partners practice talking very softly so that they cannot hear each other. Finally have them practice getting within normal speaking distance and then talk too loudly.

Variations:

An excellent real-life exercise is to walk down a fairly noisy street together, and walk far ahead or behind your partner while talking about something that he absolutely needs to talk with you about. Hopefully he will be amazed at the number of communication breakdowns and misunderstandings. Contrast this with how much easier it is to communicate when you remain side by side while you walk.

Obstacles/Opportunities:

As the previous variation illustrates, this activity is an excellent introduction to the concept of "Communication Breakdowns" and the need for continual monitoring of accuracy. We will be continuing this theme in the next activity and in later stages. But this activity certainly can be a strong example.

LEVEL III, STAGE 12, ACTIVITY 65

Connected Conversations

ACTIVITY HIGHLIGHTS
° Practicing remaining on topic
° Practicing conversation "repair" skills

Summary:

In Level I we introduced the concept of connected and disconnected topics to Novices. A good deal of work has already been undertaken to help participants maintain connections with their peers; without which this particular exercise would have little value. Now we enact a much more sophisticated version of the earlier activity. This time, participants make up their own statements and questions and use them in the proper manner

Participants:

Up to four Challengers.

Getting Ready:

Each participant needs one blue, yellow and red card with his name on each card. "Good Idea" is written on the blue card alongside the name. "Connected" is written on each yellow card. "Disconnected" is written on each red card. A Post-It note is attached to the blue and yellow cards.

Coaching Instructions:

This exercise is taught in three steps:

☐ STEP 1

Maintain control of all cards and explain the meaning of each through demonstration. Place your blue card in the center of the table and say, "I have a good idea." Choose a fairly broad but definable category so that participants will clearly understand the activity. "I want to talk about birthdays." Now write "Birthdays" on the Post-It note attached to your blue card. Also, place a Post-It on each participant's "Connected" yellow card. This is a visual reminder of the subject. We often begin with a simple topic such as birthdays because everyone has something to say about it.

Connections:

As each participant responds to the birthday idea in a connected manner, place his connection card on the table. Every time a participant says something that connects with the topic, a line is made on his connection Post-It.

Disconnections:

Disconnections will be treated as follows: "For my birthday we went to McDonalds. I had pizza with pepperoni last night for dinner." In an exaggerated manner produce the participant's red card and explain that he has "disconnected" and must say, "Uh oh, sorry" followed by a connected statement about the topic. Once the person makes a connection, the red card is removed and a connected mark is placed on his yellow card.

☐ STEP 2

It is now time for the participants to have "good ideas." In the beginning any idea is acceptable.

☐ STEP 3

Once the exercise is understood, a final component is added. An idea presented by a participant must be agreed on before the connection/disconnection activity occurs. For example, a partner might say that his good idea is train whistles and ask "Do you want to talk about train whistles?" If there is disagreement, he will need to find another topic. By this juncture, the Coach is simply in charge of the cards.

Variations:

The cards should be used only in the initial, explanatory stages of this work. Participants should quickly be taught to produce and read facial expressions that signal a disconnection has occurred.

Obstacles/Opportunities:

You may be surprised by the topics that lead to long series of connections. A young man who said he wanted to talk about "train whistles" suggested one of our favorite examples. We assumed that the connected comments would last for about two go-rounds. In fact, we thought this would be an opportunity to do a small lesson on selecting topics that might also be of interest to others. We finally brought his idea to a halt because there was no stopping the flow of information that this group of individuals with Asperger Syndrome brought up about train whistles.

LEVEL III, STAGE 12, ACTIVITY 66

Learning How to Lose

ACTIVITY HIGHLIGHTS
° Learning how to lose gracefully
° Prioritizing your relationship over winning a game

Summary:

People hate a sore loser – someone who always has to win to feel good. Having friends means learning how to lose without ruining the enjoyment for your partners.

Participants:

Up to four Challengers.

Getting Ready:

You can choose any simple game like checkers that has winners and losers and can be conducted very rapidly.

Coaching Instructions:

There are four steps to this exercise:

☐ STEP 1

Tell participants, "Every time you play a game with a friend you are really playing two games. One game is the game in front of you. The other game is the Friendship Game. Which game is more important? Of course, the Friendship Game! When you play with a friend, winning the game is not important. Winning the Friendship is much more important than winning the game. Let's see if you can learn how to win the Friendship and lose the game that's not important."

☐ STEP 2

Team-mates play a game and purposely try to lose, "I want to see how fast you can lose without cheating. The faster you lose the more points you get." This is a simple and enjoyable way to get Challengers who have trouble with losing to learn to relax.

☐ STEP 3

Challengers are told that they will play a simple game but this time they will add a new element. Tell them, "Now you are going to play two games at the same time. There is the "Checkers" game (or whatever you are playing) and the Friendship Game. I want to see if you can win the Friendship Game. You get Friendship points for each thing you do that makes you a good friend." There are five things you can do:

1. Encourage your partner, "You can do it!"

2. Complement your partner, "That was a good move."

3. Share good feelings, "This is fun!"

4. Talk to yourself about losing, "Friends are more important than winning a game. I can win the Friendship Game!"

5. There is a final thing you can do. If your friend wins you can congratulate him.

☐ STEP 4

Spend time practicing and role-playing all five of these skills. Once Challengers are proficient, it is time to incorporate the skills into the game. Tell participants that this time when they play, they can earn Friendship "points" for encouraging, complimenting, sharing good feelings, and bonus points for talking to yourself and congratulating your partner if he wins, "Let's see how many Friendship points you can each get."

Variations:

Just as people hate a sore loser, they dislike someone who always wants to do what he wants to do and doesn't seem to care about his partner's interests or desires. In this variation, Challengers practice doing things that are not particularly interesting to them, just because it makes their friend happy.

Obstacles/Opportunities:

This activity will take some practice for Challengers with serious emotion regulation problems. If any of the partners shows any signs of distress, stop the action and request that he remember what his true goal is.

187

LEVEL III, STAGE 12, ACTIVITY 67

Mistake Practice

ACTIVITY HIGHLIGHTS
° Staying calm after making mistakes
° Using Self Talk to overcome perfectionism
° Learning to tolerate others mistakes

Summary:

A large obstacle for some Challengers is their fear of, or over-reaction to, making mistakes. Relationships, even for those of us born with innate talent, inevitably require making many mistakes in order to become proficient. And even when we become experts in relationships we will still make mistakes every day. In this activity, Challengers learn to see mistakes as a common experience, necessary for learning and development.

Participants:

This exercise is suitable for a group or small class.

Getting Ready:

No special materials are needed. You can, if you wish, make up "mistake" index cards to signal when it is time for someone to make a mistake.

Coaching Instructions:

There are five steps in this activity:

☐ STEP 1

Tell Challengers that you are all going to have "mistake practice." In "mistake practice" you get a point for making the right type of mistake.

☐ STEP 2

Demonstrate different types of "small" mistakes, such as misspelling, over-drawing a circle, leaving out a step in a problem and making the wrong decision in a game. Practice making different kinds of small mistakes and then telling about them.

☐ STEP 3

Now have each Challenger decide on one type of mistake to make. She is not to tell anyone what she has chosen. See if her team-mates can guess what the mistake was and when it was made.

☐ STEP 4

Now insert Self Talk into mistake-making. Practice simple self-statements that Challengers can make after a mistake. Examples of statements are provided at the end of the exercise.

☐ STEP 5

The final step concerns mistakes that other people make. Tell Challengers that soon they will do some activity together. But first they will choose in advance a mistake that one partner will make that will affect the other. Choices include things like accidentally spilling a cup of candy belonging to your partner, taking your partner's turn, coloring together on a single sheet of paper and accidentally coloring over your partner's area. Before partners begin, they are to choose from a short list of responses to their partner's mistake. A sample list is provided at the end of the exercise description.

Variations:

Challengers can keep a simple "mistake diary" which chronicles the mistakes they and others made and the way that they managed the mistake.

Obstacles/Opportunities:

For some Challengers, mistakes are unfortunately associated with extreme negative self-perceptions. We will return to mistakes at a later stage to learn more sophisticated means of dealing with them.

Sample self-statements after a mistake:

- "It's no big deal."
- "Everyone makes mistakes."
- "I can fix that."
- "Well, at least it's not a big mistake."
- "I'm only human."

Sample communication after partner makes a mistake:

- "Hey, it's no big deal."
- "It was only an accident."
- "You're only human. We all make mistakes."
- "I'm sure you didn't mean to do it."

12

LEVEL III, STAGE 12, ACTIVITY 68

Joining In 1.

ACTIVITY HIGHLIGHTS
° Learning effective strategies to successfully join in activities
° Learning to be a good observer of others

Summary:

In this exercise, Challengers practice simple strategies for joining in an activity. They are taught methods for trying to join in and also for inviting another person to join in their activity. The key elements practiced here are observing, narrating what the peer is doing, approaching, and trying to join in. In a later stage we will work on the more complex aspects of joining in.

Participants:

You can try this with up to three Challengers, with each taking turns playing the role of a "Joiner," a "Watcher" and an "Actor."

Getting Ready:

The only materials needed are those the Actor will use, such as some simple blocks.

Coaching Instructions:

To begin with one Challenger is given the role of Actor another is the Joiner and the third is the Watcher. They should switch roles often. The Actor is given some blocks, or similar simple materials to play with. We will work on dealing with rejection in a later stage, so in this activity the Actor's role is simple. The Joiner has to practice four steps: Getting Ready, Narrating, Approaching and Joining In.

Getting Ready:

☐ STEP 1

During the initial phase, the Actor waits for the Joiner to make the first move. The Joiner first practices moving to "observing" distance – close enough to see what his peer is doing, but not close enough to bother him. Joiners will require practice in determining the correct distance for observing. The Actor is to act interested in his building task and not to notice the Joiner unless he comes too near, at which point he should communicate annoyance in a simple manner.

☐ STEP 2   NARRATING

Once he has figured out a good spot for observing, the Joiner stops and briefly "narrates" what his partner is doing. He should already possess this skill from prior activities.

☐ STEP 3   APPROACHING

After "narration," the next step is to approach to "joining" distance. Practice how to physically approach to get near enough to indicate interest, but not to interrupt the Actor.

☐ STEP 4   JOINING IN

The actual "joining" act entails four simple steps:

1.   First, the Joiner compliments the Actor with a phrase like, "Hey that's a great thing you are building."

2.   The compliment is immediately followed by a simple, curious question such as, "What is it?" The Actor is instructed to answer accurately with a neutral manner, not inviting the Joiner to join him.

3.   Then the Joiner enacts the third step and asks to join in saying, "Can I help?" In this initial simple version, the Actor accepts the request and allows the Joiner to join in.

4.   After this is successful, we insert the fourth step. Prior to asking to help, the Joiner asks "Mind if I watch?" After this is agreed to, the Joiner sits down near the Actor but not so near as to interfere with his actions and remains there for several minutes. He should practice making non-verbal comments to indicate his interest and admiration for the Actor's efforts. Only after this should he ask "Can I help?"

Variations:

A second version of the exercise involves the Actor behaving in a more inviting manner. The activity begins the same way. However, when the Joiner moves into joining distance, the Actor briefly narrates his current activity and then invites the Joiner to play with a phrase such as, "Hey, I'm building a _____. Would you like to do it with me?"

Obstacles/Opportunities:

The inevitable question to be asked here is "What about rejection?" This is an important concern, as we know that in typical children's play, for example, about half of all attempts to join in with peers are rejected. While having a simple strategy like the one in this exercise should reduce rejections, it certainly will not eliminate them. We will address rejection in a later exercise.

191

LEVEL III, STAGE 12, ACTIVITY 69

What's More Important?

ACTIVITY HIGHLIGHTS

° Examining your behavior from a friend's point of view

° Finding ways to make visiting friends feel important

° Taking responsibility for determining which objects distract from attention to friends

° Using methods that increase the feeling of control over success of social encounters

Summary:

Parents often tell me how they work so hard to arrange a "play date" only to have the desired child come over and be ignored, because their son or daughter became too focused on a video, computer game or similar activity. In this activity, Challengers practice keeping their primary focus on a friend, while being tempted by some object or activity that is very compelling to them.

Participants:

Four Challengers can participate in this activity.

Getting Ready:

Carefully select the objects and activities that will be used as "temptations" to pull partners away from their friends. Make sure to have several options, in case one is too powerful and you need more practice to work up to it.

Coaching Instructions:

This exercise has five steps:

☐ STEP 1

Tell Challengers that they are going to practice how to make a friend feel important. Explain about how people feel when they are ignored. This is a good way to tiptoe into the emotion of loneliness.

☐ STEP 2

Use Self Talk to demonstrate how you might feel when you come to your friend's house and she ignores you for something, or someone else.

☐ STEP 3

Have all partners role-play coming to a friend's house and being ignored. Make sure that everyone gets to experience both roles.

☐ STEP 4

Sometimes you do not ignore your friend completely, but you may still make her feel as if she is not very important. Perform role-plays where the person is not being totally ignored, but she is made to feel less important than some activity. An example of this is watching a video together and being told to be quiet when you make some comment about the movie. Then role-play how she might be made to feel more important.

☐ STEP 5

Have partners each pick activities that make it easier and harder to put their friend first and then try them out. Challengers should experiment with different activities and gradually compile a list of activities that are "friend-friendly" and "not friend-friendly."

Variations:

The natural extension of this exercise is for Challengers to take more responsibility in pre-planning activity choices when they have a friend coming over. If a friend insists on an activity that is on the "not friend-friendly" list, make sure that the Challenger has a good excuse for declining to do the activity.

Obstacles/Opportunities:

We want Challengers to learn to be aware of those aspects of the environment that are difficult for them and to take actions, whenever possible, to minimize environmental obstacles. Carefully considering which activities will distract too much attention away from a friend is one critical step in this process of "ownership."

LEVEL III, STAGE 12, ACTIVITY 70

Friendship

ACTIVITY HIGHLIGHTS
° Learning basic definitions of friendship
° Learning how to make good friendship choices

Summary:

Many Challengers initially have little understanding of the definition of friendship. For some, anyone whose name they know is a friend. For others, someone who will play or work at their side qualifies. This activity introduces Challengers to the concept of friendship at a very basic level. We are not yet working on a more mature definition. Rather, we focus on what constitutes what we can think of as a good "beginning level" friendship.

Participants:

This activity is suitable for a group of four.

Getting Ready:

Make up a set of eight cards with the different attributes of a good friend. Each card has one good attribute on one side. Sample attributes are provided at the end of the activity description.

Coaching Instructions:

There are seven steps in this exercise:

☐ STEP 1

Tell Challengers that they are going to learn about the attributes that make a good friend. Ask them if they can tell you who their friends are and why they believe that the person is a friend. Often, at this stage participants cannot tell us very much about why someone has received that designation.

☐ STEP 2

Take out a set of "Friends" cards for each participant. Place the cards in a stack. Go through each of the eight cards. After you read the card, provide a brief role-play demonstration of what the description on the card means.

☐ STEP 3

Now Challengers participate in simple, structured role-plays that illustrate the positive sides of each of the eight attributes. Clearly identify which attribute you are working on. Continue role-plays until you are sure everyone can perform all eight elements without any prompting.

☐ STEP 4

Now tell participants you are going to practice how "Not to get chosen as a Friend." See if the group can generate eight "Un-Friend" cards that correspond to the initial "Friend" cards. Place each "Un-Friend" attribute on the flip side of the corresponding positive attribute. Now have participants role-play each of the "Un-Friend" attributes. Continue until you are certain that they fully understand each one.

☐ STEP 5

Mix up positive and negative attributes when taking on the role of either "Friend" or "Un-Friend." One participant serves as your Friend for the exercise. The others have to observe carefully and "Stop the Action" when they see you doing one of the attributes. After stopping the action, the Challenger holds up the card he believes corresponds to your behavior and/or says out loud first whether you are being a good Friend or an Un-Friend, and second, which of the attributes he believes corresponds to your behavior.

☐ STEP 6

After each person has been successful in recognizing the attributes, gradually substitute participants and have them enact the different attributes without telling in advance which they are doing. Rotate participants through this role.

☐ STEP 7

About four weeks after you have finished working on this exercise, ask again about their friends. Determine if they have generalized the concepts enough. If not it is time for a "refresher" course.

Variations:

We like Challengers to learn some structured ways of remembering how each of these attributes works for them in real life. We often ask them to add a short journal entry of what they did to be a good friend, following every extended peer encounter. We also encourage repeated rehearsal of these attributes prior to a play date with a peer.

Obstacles/Opportunities:

Some of our Challengers may at this stage require some additional "tutoring" in observing what makes others laugh and what does not, even though the "initiator" may think what he says or does is funny. They key is referencing your partner's reactions and then recording what worked.

Good Friends:

° Show that they are happy to see each other.

° Know how to make each other smile and laugh.

° Want to play the same things.

° Do not act bossy or controlling.

° Play fair and do not cheat.

° Do not walk away in the middle of an activity.

° Act like people are more important than things.

° Care more about a friend than winning or getting their way.

(Can you think of some more?)

12

LEVEL IV: VOYAGER

Introduction

Summary

As we progressed through Levels I, II and III, the topic of relationships remained constant. We concentrated on behaviors such as facial expressions, sounds, gestures and movements that can be directly referenced, compared and coordinated. Level IV marks the beginning of a permanent, dramatic change in the primary reference point for relationships. Rather than continuing to concentrate on overt "public" behavior, Voyagers now learn to understand and value inner, "private" experience. It will take enormous energy to learn to coordinate their unique perceptions, ideas, and feelings with those of their social partners. Until now, the focus of communication has been our actions, our bodies, voices and words. Now the focus changes to sharing our perceptions and reactions to what we see, hear and feel in the world around us. By the end of this level, Voyagers will have learned to understand and share their inner perceptions as they tackle the problem of emotional regulation.

Participants

By Level IV, Voyagers can successfully coordinate their actions while in small groups and teams. Coaches become less critical and more frequently act as initial instructors and then fade out, only to appear as facilitators and occasionally conflict mediators. Level IV marks the period in typical development when peers begin choosing peers over adults as interaction partners. They choose those peers who are fun and who provide a greater challenge to them. But they are also attracted to those peers who carry their own weight and don't make them work too hard.

Settings

By mastering Joint Attention, Voyagers make a crucial breakthrough, one that makes it much easier to initiate and sustain interactions with more people and in varied settings. Just about every parent of a child in the Autism Spectrum can recite stories about times they have arranged for a peer to come over to play, only to watch as their child ignored his "pal" and focused completely on his Nintendo or a favorite video. By the close of Level IV, we finally reach a point where the lure of interesting objects and toys is no longer as much of an impediment to friendship. When pals come over, they can receive undivided attention. Voyagers learn to be more deliberate about the objects they use and activities they engage in when their friends are over. By the close of this level, they know that no matter how exciting a Nintendo game or TV show might be, it does not produce the joy and excitement that people can provide.

Language

A common activity in this stage is looking out at the world together to share what we see. This is also a good method for beginning conversations. In this level Voyagers learn to structure conversations around the reference point. Language becomes even more creative and is used to add imaginative additions for partners' mutual enjoyment.

Regulation and Repair

In Level IV our referencing goes beyond actions. We try and read our partners emotions to understand if feelings are hurt. We attempt to understand and reconcile different perspectives and ways of seeing the world.

Coaching Points

- Be careful to distinguish pointing as a means to an end from the same action done for "Experience Sharing."

- Make sure that you teach Voyagers that their faces are the main reference points, rather than some external stimuli.

- Self Talk and Self Narration are critical skills during Level IV. Be sure to make them regular habits.

STAGE 13: PERSPECTIVE

Goals and Objectives

Perspective taking introduces Voyagers to the world of the relative versus the absolute. This is an enormous cognitive breakthrough. Perspective is inherently subjective. Our perceptions are influenced by our unique reactions to our world. The emotional aspect of perspective means that we can have vastly different reactions to the same stimulus. The music that is so pleasing to you can drive me crazy. We learn that the world is a place where there may be multiple ways of doing things. It is a place where a solution may be good relative to the context. Any given perception may be more valuable depending upon what you are trying to do.

Activity Summary

We begin this stage with activities geared towards sharing personal experience. Voyagers learn that their perceptions are subjective events, valued for their personal meaning. They learn to share personally meaningful photos and to deliberately capture events they wish to bring back and share with partners. As the stage continues they practice juggling their attention between the object world and the relationship needs of partners. Perspective taking quickly becomes more demanding, as we practice observing and reflecting on others' interactions and comparing them to our own, and sharing perspectives with partners who are not physically present. As the stage draws to a close, Voyagers are introduced to the concepts of strategy and the use of perspective taking to develop different and equally valid ways of solving problems.

Critical Tips

- Don't forget to spend time on the technical aspects of photographing, videotaping and journal writing. The goal is not to make Voyagers experts, but to provide them with sufficient skills so that they can be independent.

- Self Talk does not require full, grammatically correct sentences. Simple phrases are sufficient.

- Be sure to spend sufficient time teaching Voyagers to be good "watchers."

- Practice in strategy development and flexible thinking should become an important part of each Voyager's day.

LEVEL IV, STAGE 13, ACTIVITY 71

Returning from a Journey

ACTIVITY HIGHLIGHTS
° Advance planning
° Recording your perceptions for future sharing
° Selecting experiences to share with a friend

Summary:

This activity introduces Voyagers to sharing perceptual events that are uniquely their own. We are also making a second major leap by introducing the idea that you can begin an activity for the sole purpose of later sharing it with someone else. Partners initially use Polaroid or digital cameras to record their observations, while on a short walk. When they return, they practice "asking and telling" about the discoveries they have made.

Participants:

A small group of Voyagers.

Getting Ready:

You will need two Polaroid or digital cameras. Plan a walking route prior to beginning the exercise.

Coaching Instructions:

This activity has five steps:

☐ STEP 1

Begin by teaching each partner how to take pictures using a Polaroid or digital camera. In this part of the exercise we emphasize the technical features of operating the camera and the need to be careful in the number and quality of photos that you take.

☐ STEP 2

Partners practice making decisions about what is important and unimportant to share with others. It is a good idea to practice taking pictures in a room, prior to going on a walk. Make sure that participants understand that they are going to photograph only something that might be interesting to share.

☐ STEP 3

Now partners are told, "We are going on a walk. Take your camera with you. When we are walking, you can stop and take pictures of things you like, or things you want to share. Remember to only take pictures of things that are important to share when you get back from the walk."

☐ STEP 4

Begin the walk. Initially, have Voyagers ask permission prior to taking a photo. They must justify why the intended photo is important. But since this can dampen the fun of the activity, move quickly to allowing them to shoot their pictures without your interference. If you are using Polaroids, each time a partner takes a picture, stop and remove the photo and hold it "To look at when we get back." If using digital cameras, simply tell the partners that they will be able to view each other's photos when they get back and the photos have been developed and printed out.

☐ STEP 5

When Voyagers return, have them attach each of their photos to a page in their respective photo album, putting the photos in the order they were taken. They will then share what they saw on their journey.

Variations:

Share a photo essay of a typical day, or a family trip or vacation.

Obstacles/Opportunities:

Photos can become a critical means of aiding communication, especially for participants who have limited language and those who tend to be verbal but are not able to choose topics of mutual interest. Be careful not to allow hyper-verbal partners to over-talk! Also make sure that you notice whether a participant is shooting photos of things that only he is interested in, with no regard for what his partner might enjoy. This is a sign that he may not be ready for this activity, or may need more rehearsal in deciding what it is important to photograph.

LEVEL IV, STAGE 13, ACTIVITY 72

Play-by-Play

ACTIVITY HIGHLIGHTS

° Using Self Talk to monitor behavior
° Developing Social Memories

Summary:

Perception sharing now takes a large leap, as the "perception" we are teaching Voyagers to focus on is not an external object, but rather themselves. When we move into the area of narration, we introduce a new type of language, called Self Talk that we use to talk to ourselves and not to communicate with someone else. Self Talk does not develop just because language is in place. It has its own separate track of development. Many people with Autism, AS and ADHD seem to lack productive Self Talk, or engage in it in only a rudimentary way. Yet it is the crucial step in behavioral self-control. Learning to be a narrator of our own actions is a critical part of developing Executive Functioning. It is literally the beginning of self-consciousness. When we narrate our actions, for the first time we are attempting to observe ourselves as if from the outside. Learning to use Self Talk to narrate a social partner's actions is helpful in teaching how to observe where your partner is headed, so that you can make decisions about how best to coordinate with them. Self Talk can also be used for communication purposes. By narrating our current and future actions out loud, we communicate information to partners that makes it easier for them to coordinate their actions with ours, if they so wish.

Participants:

Try this with a small group.

Getting Ready:

You can be fairly flexible in your choice of materials. However, make sure materials are not of a sort to make rapid attention shifting more difficult.

Coaching Instructions:

There are eight steps in this exercise:

☐ STEP 1

Begin by demonstrating simple Self Talk while acting. Self Talk begins with simple motor actions such as "I am walking over to the door. I am picking up a pencil." Make sure that all participants are proficient before proceeding.

☐ STEP 2

Narrate more complex acts such as "I am drawing a face," " I am building a tower with blocks." Stop to spend time working on mastery of this skill.

☐ STEP 3

Now demonstrate Self Talk immediately following completion of actions, "I drew a face," "I walked to the door." Voyagers practice Self Talk following an action, until they can perform it without any coaching.

☐ STEP 4

Move to using Self Talk just prior to taking an action. We call this "Planning." Demonstrate simple Planning and make sure that all partners are proficient in it.

☐ STEP 5

Before we move to sharing our Self Talk with another person, we want each Voyager to feel comfortable in fluidly narrating her own actions at three different periods: 1. just prior to doing them – *Planning*, 2. while she is engaged in them – *Self Instruction* and 3. just following their completion – *Reflection*. This will entail speaking in past, present and future tense: "I walked to the door," "I am walking to the door," "I will walk to the door."

☐ STEP 6

Coaches and other significant people in the Voyager's life should model Self Talk extensively, both during practice time and many other times during the day.

☐ STEP 7

We move to the next phase of the exercise, in which Voyagers learn to narrate their partner's actions. Each participant takes a turn watching the other take simple actions and then narrating the action in the form of a "play-by-play" announcer at a sporting event, "Now Jenny is walking to the door. She is opening the door. She is picking up a block." Voyagers should practice switching to the reflective mode, where their narration is about just-completed activities, "Jenny drew a circle," and then to the planning mode where they try to guess what their partner is going to do next. You can ask the "actor" to freeze and stop in mid-action, to give the Narrator a few seconds to predict what his partner is about to do.

☐ STEP 8

The final phase of this activity entails learning how to use your observations to modify your behavior, in order to be more coordinated with your partner. Voyagers practice narrating what the person they observe is doing and where it appears he is heading. We stop the action long enough for the Narrator to plan what she needs to do to coordinate her actions with her partner's. For example, "Jimmy is hopping. He is going to the door." Now Stop the Action. "I need to stand next to Jimmy and get ready to hop with him to the door."

Variations:

Self Talk should go on throughout the day, until we are sure that it is occurring automatically. Challengers should practice narrating several different actions that they took in a reflective manner. "First I _____, then I _____."

Obstacles/Opportunities:

Remember, this may be the very first time that some Voyagers have used Self Talk to better coordinate with a social partner. There is no way we can over-emphasize how important this skill is. It is literally a foundation for all future work and it is fine to spend several months devoted to its development. The amount of time needed to master each activity is of course dependent on the individual and relates to the time it takes him or her to master the *objectives* of the activity.

You may be concerned that delayed language could be an obstacle here, but we have rarely found it to be so. Narration does not have to be in full sentences, and meaningful fragments such as "Walk to door" are just fine.

LEVEL IV, STAGE 13, ACTIVITY 73

Video Narration

ACTIVITY HIGHLIGHTS
° Actively reviewing prior activities
° Narrating collaborative activities

Summary:
In this exercise, Self Talk evolves further and becomes a way of describing the actions of a social unit of two people. Voyagers learn to use the language of a "We-go" – two or more people who, for the moment, identify themselves primarily as a single unit. They practice telling each other what they perceive they are doing together.

Participants:
This is an activity for teams of two or three Voyagers.

Getting Ready:
You will need a video camera, videotape and a monitor that is easily swiveled back and forth so the screen can be temporarily out of either's view. Team-mates sit in front of the monitor with chairs that are at a 45° angle towards each other so that the monitor can be swiveled so that only one of them can see it and then swiveled back, so both can view it. You should prepare a simple, structured script ready for the "silly" video that participants will enact.

Coaching Instructions:
There are three steps to this activity:

☐ STEP 1

Teams are taught how to act in a "silly" video where they are asked to make funny faces and noises together. They can wear silly costumes and props appropriate to their age and take other actions that they would find funny.

☐ STEP 2

Demonstrate how participants will take turns being the "Narrator" and the "Audience." The narrator views a short piece of the video that the pair has just made, tells a bit about what the unit is doing in the segment and then turns the monitor to show it to the Audience.

☐ STEP 3

Team members take turns narrating short segments of the tape to one another. Stop the video every time there is a new event to be described. The following is a brief sample vignette of how the activity progresses:

- The Coach plays a new segment that only the narrator can see.
- The Audience asks, "What are we doing?"
- The Narrator responds with "Now we are _____," or an equivalent "we" description of what he has just viewed.

- The Narrator asks, "Do you want to see it?"
- The Audience affirms that it does.
- The Narrator swivels the monitor so both can see and makes sure that the Audience has a good view. Then the segment is played.
- The video is stopped and team-mates share their emotional reactions to the segment.

Variations:

Each person can make his own video and have another person narrate it. Each person can narrate his own video to his partner.

Obstacles/Opportunities:

This is another opportunity to practice using "efficient" language in communication and omit unnecessary details. Make sure that the climax of the activity is face-to-face emotion sharing. Do not neglect this step!

LEVEL IV, STAGE 13, ACTIVITY 74

Video Documentary

ACTIVITY HIGHLIGHTS
° Exciting team collaboration
° Cooperative planning

Summary:

In this exercise, Voyagers work together to make a simple video documentary detailing how to perform a specific activity. Voyagers take turns being either the "Cameraman" or the "Actor." Voyagers have to coordinate their attention in many different ways: keeping the camera on the Actor, knowing when to start and stop the camera and knowing when to zoom in and zoom out, to name just a few.

Participants:

A small group of Voyagers.

Getting Ready:

You will need a video camera, videotape and tripod, monitor and whatever simple props are needed to make the "documentary" movie.

Coaching Instructions:

There are four steps to this activity:

☐ STEP 1

Team-mates are told that they will be making their own movie. There will be two roles: Cameraman and Actor. Voyagers should first practice the technical side of using the video camera, which should be mounted on a tripod at eye level. They should be familiar with how to start and stop recording, moving the camera gently from side to side, carefully zooming in and out and keeping your subject in the picture at all times.

☐ STEP 2

Voyagers should next practice taping and reviewing very small segments so that they can learn how to communicate while taping. For example when the Actor points to the object that he is demonstrating, this is a signal to zoom in. When the Actor moves from one location to another the camera should follow him.

☐ STEP 3

Now Voyagers rehearse the simple script of the documentary. Choose a subject such as, "How to use a calculator," or, "How to make a peanut butter and jelly sandwich."

☐ STEP 4

When everyone has mastered his or her role, it is time to make the video. Partners will want to review their work when it is done.

Variations:

After Voyagers complete their documentary we like to test out its usefulness. We can choose a younger child as a "viewer" and see if the documentary serves its purpose. Remember to bring out the video periodically to "re-celebrate" its production.

Obstacles/Opportunities:

Using the video camera can be a real temptation to become caught up in the technical "equipment" issues and neglect the relationship issues. Be on the lookout for Voyagers who are totally captured by equipment. On the other hand, learning to master simple video camera work allows Voyagers to begin routinely capturing important events in their lives so that they can replay them and ensure the development of clear Social Memories. It also provides the person with a social "prop" to be used strategically in certain family and group situations that might otherwise be overwhelming.

LEVEL IV, STAGE 13, ACTIVITY 75

Comparing

ACTIVITY HIGHLIGHTS
° Flexible attention shifting
° Learning to find common areas with peer actions
° Communicating appreciation for social partners' efforts

Summary:

One of the critical factors in social success is making other people feel like you appreciate their efforts, even if they are different from your own. A similar valued relationship skill is the ability to find common areas and themes. In this activity, Voyagers work in parallel on the same general task. They shift focus from their own efforts to admiring and contrasting their work with their partner's.

Participants:

Up to four Voyagers.

Getting Ready:

Use whatever materials are needed for the task that you choose to work on. Make sure that the materials are suitable for each group member and that one is not significantly more competent than the other. Seat Voyagers about five feet from each other. Provide each with the same set of materials.

Coaching Instructions:

There are two steps in this exercise:

☐ STEP1

The first step is for teams to learn how to stop their work, glance toward another's efforts and narrate what he or she is doing before returning to their own task. Practice this until each person is proficient.

☐ STEP 2

Now we work on periodically stopping to find commonalities. You should initially stop Voyagers about every two minutes and say, "Let's see what you are doing that is the same." Begin by focusing on simple attributes of their work. For example, if they are drawing, the comparisons could be related to colors, shapes, size and similar attributes. Gradually move to more complex commonalities.

Variations:

Voyagers can videotape their efforts. They can practice being an excited curious "Audience" and "Shower" in them as they watch each tape together and learn how and why a group member did the task in his unique manner. "Contrasting" is another important variation. They can practice stopping to find contrasts without imposing value judgments. They begin by contrasting simple dimensions. Contrasting is performed in an excited and positive manner, communicating that the "difference" enhances the fun, with no indication of evaluating or competing. In the final step we combine all of these elements. Participants should pause their work periodically to complement, compare and contrast.

Obstacles/Opportunities:

Voyagers who are used to seeing everything as competition may have a hard time adjusting to this positive approach to evaluation. They are the ones who will benefit the most from this exercise.

LEVEL IV, STAGE 13, ACTIVITY 76

Watching

ACTIVITY HIGHLIGHTS
° Learning to observe and narrate social interactions
° Increasing confidence in ability to observe social interactions

Summary:

"Watching" is a type of Self Talk activity. However, instead of observing one person, Voyagers observe two other people interacting. The focus of observation is not the product, but the process – what the two people interacting are doing together as a team or unit. This is an invaluable skill. It enables Voyagers to learn relationship skills by themselves through observation, without always needing a Coach standing by to guide their attention. Success also motivates them to spend much more time observing social interactions.

Participants:

You can do this activity with three Voyagers, or with several teams of two. If you work with several teams, have them alternate between being "Watchers" and "Players."

Getting Ready:

Materials are whatever you decide is needed for the tasks you choose. Prepare the Level II and III activities you wish to use.

Coaching Instructions:

There are three steps in this activity:

☐ STEP 1

Explain to participants that they will be rotating through two different roles. There will be Players and Watcher(s).

13

☐ STEP 2

Provide the activities you want the Players to do and teach them their roles. Players will stop after every activity to narrate what they are going to do next. They will not improvise during this step. They can begin a pre-arranged series of structured Level II activities or any similar activity that is suitable for them.

☐ STEP 3

Now teach the Watcher's job, which is to describe the activity that the pair is doing in a simple format such as, "They're hammering nails." "They're carrying the box." Initially, the Coach may demonstrate being a Watcher with one Voyager at his side. Voyagers gradually assume full responsibility for the role. Make sure to rotate all of the jobs so that each person gets a chance to be a Player and a Watcher.

Variations:

An interesting variation combining the prior few activities is to have the Watchers make a video documentary of the Players doing their activity. The documentary should include a brief introduction and an ongoing narration of the pairs' efforts and achievements. It can also include praise for the Players.

Obstacles/Opportunities:

This can be a frustrating activity for someone used to "doing" and not watching. Adding the element of video documentary maker should help ease the tension of just being an observer. However, we do not think it a good idea to omit the pure observation stage and go right to video film making, which has the potential to be too distracting. Rather, making a documentary can be a context to explain to the Watcher why he must first spend some time watching and narrating the activity as a rehearsal, prior to videotaping it.

LEVEL IV, STAGE 13, ACTIVITY 77

Shared Journey

ACTIVITY HIGHLIGHTS

° Sharing memories of a recent experience
° Learning how to accurately and meaningfully describe a scene to a social partner

Summary:

Now Voyagers begin to work on communicating their memories of events in the recent past. This is a major step in perspective taking, as we now must share our perceptions with another person across a time dimension. Voyagers practice relating information about a "journey" that they took to a place their partner has not yet visited. They describe their journey and make a map of how to go, where to stop and what to see so that their partner can re-create the journey.

Participants:

Several teams of two.

Getting Ready:

Prepare a map of the journey area. Place several very interesting, eye-catching objects strategically at each of the designated stopping points. Choose a journey area that fits the age and abilities of the Voyagers. The area can be indoors, such as part of a house, or it can be a forest trail.

Coaching Instructions:

There are six steps in this activity:

☐ STEP 1

Voyagers rotate roles of "Journeyer" and "Future Journeyer." The Voyager going on the journey first is given a general plan of the area he is to visit, such as a plan of a house, attached to a clipboard. During the first trials a Coach accompanies him and demonstrates how to stop and what to do. The Journeyer uses a pencil to trace the route he is taking.

☐ STEP 2

When the Journeyer reaches a place indicated on the map as a stopping point, he places a number at the point to indicate which stop it was.

☐ STEP 3

At each stopping point, the Journeyer looks around for something interesting to record. He can choose a landmark, a view out a window, a sound coming from a radio, or any similar stimulus. When he determines what he will remember and relate to his partner, he either writes it down or dictates to the coach. This information is placed next to the number on the map. He can also take a digital or Polaroid photo of the object or area if desired.

☐ STEP 4

When the Journeyer returns from his journey, Voyagers sit side by side with the map between them. Using an "Asking and Telling" format, they re-trace each step of the route. The Journeyer relates the sights to be seen at each stopping point on the journey.

☐ STEP 5

Now the Future Journeyer becomes the Journeyer and attempts to re-trace the route and visit the same stopping points as his partner, while the "ex-Journeyer" waits behind. When he returns they repeat the process of reflecting on the journey.

☐ STEP 6

Now the roles are reversed and the person who was the Future Journeyer gets to create his own new journey and the other Voyager gets to follow it as the Future Journeyer.

13

Variations:

The variations are unlimited. This is a great activity to do at a zoo, especially if you can get there at a time when there are no crowds.

Obstacles/Opportunities:

Voyagers with severe visual organizational problems might require assistance. You might also get some resistance from participants who insist they do not need to write anything down and can keep it all in their heads. Do not give in to this.

LEVEL IV, STAGE 13, ACTIVITY 78

Strategies

ACTIVITY HIGHLIGHTS
° Introduction to strategic thinking
° Practice generating alternative problem solving solutions
° "There's more than one way to skin a cat!"

Summary:

A critical breakthrough during this stage occurs when Voyagers learn that there is more than one right way to do almost anything. In this exercise Voyagers play a game where they each proceed in a different manner. Then they have to determine their partner's strategy and attempt to replicate it.

Participants:

Voyagers work in teams of two.

Getting Ready:

Your materials depend upon the activity you choose.

Coaching Instructions:

There are five steps in this activity:

☐ STEP 1

Teams are taught a simple definition of the word "strategy." For purposes of this activity a strategy is defined as a specific way that you go about solving a problem, building something or completing a puzzle. For example, one simple strategy for building a house out of blocks would be to first lay blocks down as the floor, then build the walls and finally build the roof. A second, different strategy might be to first build the walls, then a flat ceiling and finally a peaked roof. Similarly, in drawing a person, you can start with the face and facial features and then draw different body parts, or start by drawing the body and then proceed to the face.

☐ STEP 2

Choose a single simple activity for which there can be several strategies. Each partner is taught to use one of the strategies and begins work, using the chosen strategy.

☐ STEP 3

Following a short period of working on the activity, stop the action and have partners ask and tell each other about the strategy that they used.

☐ STEP 4

Now each team collaboratively chooses one of the strategies. When finished, each team shares the strategy they used with the other teams.

☐ STEP 5

As a final step, teams switch strategies, as each team tries out another's strategy.

Variations:

We want Voyagers to start accumulating "Strategy Cards." These are index cards with simple strategies on them that can be used in specific situations. Voyagers make up cards each time they find a useful strategy. They keep them in card boxes, referenced by specific topics like, "Checkers," "Puzzles" and "Joining in play." At The Monarch School we have had success with students using their Strategy Boxes to become much more reflective and better at planning their approach to tasks.

Obstacles/Opportunities:

Some of our Voyagers need more intensive coaching to accept that there are "many ways to skin a cat." Do not despair if they have not completely mastered this type of flexible thinking by the close of this exercise. Rest assured that this activity is only one in a series we have designed to teach this invaluable skill.

13

LEVEL IV, STAGE 13, ACTIVITY 79

Different Versions

ACTIVITY HIGHLIGHTS
° Practice flexible thinking
° Learning to accept that there is more than one right answer
° Accepting the validity of alternate sets of equally valid rules

Summary:

This activity is similar in concept to "Strategies." In this exercise, Voyagers learn that there are different ways to construct "rules" for the same game and that no one set of rules is the "right" or "wrong" one.

Participants:

You can try this with teams of up to four Voyagers.

Getting Ready:

Once again, materials depend upon the activity that you choose. Do not choose a game that is a particular obsession for any participant. Find an activity, such as a card game, that each partner plays a bit differently. If you cannot easily determine such a game, teach each partner to play a bit differently and then play each version, one at a time. For example, you can play a card game with jokers wild, or with aces high or low.

Coaching Instructions:

Instructions are very simple. Make sure that each partner has learned to use a different "version" of the same game. Have the partners list the similarities and differences in the rules they have learned. Write these on a whiteboard that everyone can use as a reference. Have Voyagers play each of the different versions, making sure that they provide "appreciations" for the way that the rules differ from their version. Make sure they get used to playing all versions, with neither being considered the "right" one. In later meetings the team-mates can decide which version of the game they will play, without your guidance.

Variations:

We can and should generalize this activity to almost anything. Different ways of tying your shoes, cooking eggs, different conduct rules in different classes or schools, different rules for behaving in church.

Obstacles/Opportunities:

Most readers are already familiar with the devastating effects of either being, or living with a person who can only see one way of doing things. Activities such as these really do help to increase flexibility, but they do not create miracles. They require lots of time spent in practicing them and their many variations. The great thing about this curriculum is that by the time our Voyagers have reached Stage 13, they are no longer averse to change. Rather, they look forward to it as enjoyable novelty.

STAGE 14: IMAGINATION

Goals and Objectives

What makes sharing our perceptions so much fun is the way that we can add our own unique imaginative contributions to the perceptual mix. Together we can gaze at clouds and see knights and castles. Gazing at a forested area at night, we can share the spooky feeling of seeing something moving out there. Adding our internal contributions to our perceptions of the external world opens a door into the mind that will play an increasingly major role in relationship growth. No longer will we be satisfied with sharing what we do and see. From this point on, the main "stuff" of relationship is the personal internal twists we place upon our worlds. That is what is most thrilling to share.

Activity Summary

The stage begins with two exercises designed to reinforce the idea that our perceptions are always flavored by our personal experience and that subjective reactions to the same stimulus may be vastly different, while not being wrong or right. Voyagers learn that, without careful consideration, their imaginations can become obstacles to relationships, rather than enhancements. We continue with two "silly" activities, designed to increase Voyagers' desire to integrate their imaginations for mutual enjoyment and hilarity and to give them a greater repertoire of activities they can use to increase their attractiveness with any peers. The remaining activities expose Voyagers to different ways that their shared imaginations can lead to new ideas, resolve confusing, ambiguous situations and provide solutions to difficult problems.

Critical Tips

- Watch carefully for Voyagers who may have difficulty distinguishing reality from fantasy.

- Be careful to value imaginative ideas if their goal is to contribute to the enjoyment of the group.

- Do not reinforce random and meaningless "free association" even if it initially makes team-mates laugh. It will quickly turn into an obstacle to relationship development.

- Continue to emphasize that different perceptions and reactions can both be right.

- Stay away from over-emphasis on "bathroom" remarks.

- The "Silly Soundtracks" exercise may provide a way for Voyagers to invite peers over to their homes to watch TV together and still remain connected to them.

LEVEL IV, STAGE 14, ACTIVITY 80

You Think It's Funny But I Don't

ACTIVITY HIGHLIGHTS
° Appreciating different tastes
° Learning to be sensitive to your social partners

Summary:

Before we move into sharing our unique imaginations, Voyagers must recognize that what they find humorous may not seem so to others. In this simple exercise, we find ideas and jokes that one partner might find hilarious but that others do not. From here, we go on to compare many areas where we might have different reactions to the same thing.

Participants:

One Coach and teams of up to four Voyagers.

Getting Ready:

You will need a whiteboard and markers.

Coaching Instructions:

This is a straightforward activity which has three steps:

☐ STEP 1

Construct a table or spreadsheet in which you can list each of the humorous ideas in the first column. Place each Voyager's name across the top row of the table. Now one by one, go through a number of humorous items including jokes, cartoons, and pictures. Each person privately rates the item and decides whether it is funny or not funny. You can provide each with a list containing a "thumbs up" and "thumbs down" symbol next to each item and ask that they circle one or the other. Make sure to emphasize that they should not rate everything as funny just to be nice.

☐ STEP 2

When the ratings are done, focus on the items that were not endorsed as funny by everyone. Place these items on the whiteboard and alongside place the names of Voyagers that thought they were and were not funny.

☐ STEP 3

Go through the simple exercise of having a Voyager, who thought the item was not funny, address a peer that thought it was funny and explain that everyone finds different things funny. Have him ask the other Voyager to help him see what is funny. If he still cannot appreciate the humor, have him reference the board and point out something he finds funny that his mate did not as an example. Continue in this manner until everyone has had a chance to discuss positively their different sense of humor with all of the other members.

14

Variations:

An important variation is an activity called, "Too Fast for You but not for Me." Voyagers practice all the ways in which a pace of activity is suitable for one but uncomfortable for his partners. For example, someone skilled at throwing a ball might be comfortable with a much faster speed than someone with motor difficulties. Compare all of the differences in speed, position, rate and other factors that distinguish partners' level of comfort and competence. This is also a great time to introduce differences in our aesthetic dimensions. Repeat this activity with famous paintings, sharing differences in what members think are beautiful. Now move onto songs and music as well.

Obstacles/Opportunities:

By now Voyagers should not have difficulty appreciating that there are differences in their partner's tastes and should be interested in comparing and contrasting their perceptions with others. This exercise reinforces the idea that differences are not bad or threatening but an exciting part of a relationship.

LEVEL IV, STAGE 14, ACTIVITY 81

Enhancing or Changing

ACTIVITY HIGHLIGHTS
° Learning to enhance the ideas of your social partners
° Effectively using feedback from social partners' reactions to your behavior

Summary:

This activity is designed to teach Voyagers the difference between actions that "enhance" and those that "change" or interrupt an activity. Friends love it when peers find ways to enhance what they are doing. It is a form of affirmation. However, they have the opposite reaction to someone who butts in and disrupts what they are doing or saying. There is sometimes just a subtle but critical difference between adding more enjoyment to an activity and irritating everyone by butting in and being completely off the mark.

Participants:

A small group of Voyagers can do this activity.

Getting Ready:

The materials you need are a whiteboard, several different color markers, some blank, unlined index cards and some building materials such as wooden blocks.

Coaching Instructions:

There are six steps in this exercise:

☐ STEP 1

Begin by talking about the difference between Enhancing and Changing. You are enhancing when you add something that continues to build upon what your partner is already doing or saying. But when you try and add something that is different from what your partner is trying to do, or attempt to change your partner's strategy, or her topic, then you are changing. Friends love enhancing. But they really dislike too much changing, especially if they are not ready for it. Don't be surprised if participants need extensive demonstration and practice in making this distinction. Provide many examples to illustrate the difference. Explain that even if they ask permission to speak and wait until their partner is finished speaking, if they suddenly change what their partner is doing or saying and try to make it into something else, they are still interrupting.

☐ STEP 2

Conduct structured conversations where partners take turns picking a topic and then make contributions to the topic. Make a three-column chart on a whiteboard. Put "Name" in the first column, "Topic" in the second column and "E or C?" (standing for Enhancement or Change) in the third column. One person provides a topic and then the others take turns providing contributions about that topic. List the name of the contributor, a brief summary of the contribution and then, initially, explain whether and why it is an E or a C – an enhancement of the topic or a change of the topic.

☐ STEP 3

After a while, ask Voyagers to begin deciding whether it is an E or a C without your help.

☐ STEP 4

Move to a less structured conversational format. Voyagers still take turns contributing, but now they act as a team to evaluate whether the contribution is an E or a C. No criticism or negative reaction should be offered whether the response is an E or a C. At this point we are just providing information.

☐ STEP 5

The next phase of this activity involves heightening awareness of when you are making an enhancement or interruption. Give each participant ten E cards and two C cards. This provides a 5:1 ratio of enhancements to changes and is a way of considering the frequency with which each type of communication should be used in typical interaction. The group is jointly provided with some blocks, or imaginative construction materials and told to build something together. You should provide the overall theme such as "You will build a house." Voyagers take turns adding a piece to the structure. They have to first play an E or a C card. Then they explain what they are intending to do, which gives the other partners and the Coach time to decide if they agree that it is an E or a C. Finally, they make their contribution.

14

☐ STEP 6

This game should gradually become more fluid, with your role becoming less involved as the group members become more proficient.

Variations:

Voyagers can vary this activity by jointly working on a puzzle, or any similar type of activity. One partner can elaborate his strategy and then others can take turns putting pieces onto the puzzle, either choosing to continue (enhance) the strategy or change to a new way of working. Another important variation recognizes the subjective nature of enhancements or changes. It also clearly communicates the value of enhancements. Group members divide into two-person teams, play a construction game and also return to the conversation game. This time the person making the contribution tries to only make enhancements. However, only her partner can decide whether to accept her contribution as an enhancement or a change.

Obstacles/Opportunities:

Some Voyagers may get laughs from their compatriots by being completely random in their responses. Be sure to distinguish between the time for "silly" talking, and the right time for enhancing contributions. Similarly put-downs and insults, while unfortunately garnering laughs, should be sharply discouraged!

LEVEL IV, STAGE 14, ACTIVITY 82

Silly Captions

ACTIVITY HIGHLIGHTS
- Understanding that subjective reactions are naturally connected to perceptions
- Learning that sharing imagination enhances our enjoyment of perceptions
- Learning to merge ideas for mutual enjoyment

Summary:

One of the most exciting developments in our program occurs when Voyagers are able to blend their internal worlds of imagination with their external perceptions. This activity is the first and one of the most enjoyable exercises in learning how to share what you see out in the world along with the inner world of imagination and humor.

Participants:

Try to do this activity initially in teams of two.

Getting Ready:

Work with participants to cut out interesting and odd pictures together from magazines such as *National Geographic.* You can also download some very funny and interesting photos from the Internet. Put about twenty pictures in a photo album. We have displayed some samples on our website that you are free to download. Initially have team-mates sit on either side of you to practice. You will quickly be able to fade out of the interaction.

Coaching Instructions:

There are five steps in this activity:

☐ STEP 1

Point to the album and say, "We have put some really interesting pictures in here. Let's look at them and make up some silly things to say about each picture. We can think of funny or scary things we want to say when we look at each picture."

☐ STEP 2

Open the album to the first picture and model a silly phrase.

☐ STEP 3

Now go through several photos in this manner. After you make the initial enhancement to the picture, ask each participant to add something of his or her own. It can be a noise, a word, or a phrase. It cannot be a descriptive statement or fact. Accept it as long as it enhances everyone's enjoyment.

☐ STEP 4

Gradually fade out your participation and allow Voyagers to take turns pointing to photos, sharing what they see and then making ridiculous noises and phrases specifically tied to the perception.

☐ STEP 5

After Voyagers have mastered this basic step, they can move on to integrating their contributions. Practice choosing one silly "caption" for each photo that they can both agree is really funny. Write the caption they have agreed upon under the photo to be reviewed and enjoyed again at a later time.

Variations:

It is always important to practice coordination breakdowns and repairs. After Voyagers become more proficient, from time to time provide feedback that you don't really enjoy their response and request that they try something else. An excellent activity variation is looking at the picture and requesting that the partners pretend together to see something that is not really there. A similar variation entails deciding together to pretend to change what they actually see into its opposite.

Obstacles/Opportunities:

You will be able to use this silly picture album over and over again. You can keep adding photos and new captions. Voyagers who have trouble distinguishing imagination from reality may need more extensive preparation for this activity. Also,

14

Voyagers who do not appear to have much, if any imagination will need some introductory work in how we pretend something is real when it is not really there.

*Note: We use the word "silly" in front of an activity to alert Voyagers that this is just a playful way to do something as opposed to the real "serious" way you would do it in a non-playful setting. Our partners have never been confused.

LEVEL IV, STAGE 14, ACTIVITY 83

Silly Soundtracks

ACTIVITY HIGHLIGHTS
° Learning to watch TV as a meaningful social activity
° Sharing imaginative narrations to movies

Summary:

This is the perfect activity for anyone who has ever seen "Mystery Science Theatre" on TV. Voyagers watch videos, without sound, and make up silly things to populate the "soundtrack" of the movie. They tape-record their voice-over and play it back as the movie is playing.

Participants:

You can try this with teams of up to four Voyagers.

Getting Ready:

You will need a VCR, monitor, audiocassette recorder, videotape and a cassette for each team. Team-mates are seated in front of the monitor. The video they watch should not be particularly interesting to any of them. Make sure that they have not seen the video before. It can be a boring documentary, or lesson video or something equally mundane. Seat them in front of the monitor with the tape already loaded and ready to play. Place a cassette recorder between them so it can easily pick up their comments.

Coaching Instructions:

There are five steps to this activity:

☐ STEP 1

Turn off the sound on the TV. Do not turn on the audiocassette recorder yet. Play a short segment of the video and then pause it. Tell team-mates that they are going to create the sound part of the video they just saw. They can make it as silly as they want, as long as it is funny to all of them.

☐ STEP 2

Now re-play the segment and demonstrate several different ways that they can narrate it. Demonstrate how to make silly sounds and simple, humorous voice-overs. Each time you add something, pause the video and look at the partners for their reactions. If they are smiling or laughing, smile and laugh along with them and tell them, "That one works because it made you smile/laugh. That is how we know which ones we keep. We only keep the ideas that make us smile and laugh."

☐ STEP 3

Allow team-mates to take turns doing short voice-overs. Remember to play a short segment first, to provide a preview, prior to starting the cassette recorder. Make sure that everyone uses the correct procedure. They must turn from the video, make their enhancement and observe their partners' reactions to see if it made them laugh and/or smile, before deciding whether it will be accepted for the "final version" of the soundtrack.

☐ STEP 4

If the comment "works" then rewind to the beginning of the segment, press pause, get the cassette recorder ready to record, then start the VCR while recording on the cassette recorder. Do this until you have recorded about five minutes of soundtrack.

☐ STEP 5

When they have sufficient mastery, Voyagers take turns adding their comments, sound effects, voice-overs and whatever ridiculous additions they wish to contribute in a less structured, more improvised manner. Accept almost anything that the partners decide to add, with the exception of violent imagery, dialogue from other videos, obsessed comments, or hurtful statements. None of the contributions have to make particular sense as long as they are funny to other team-mates.

Variations:

Voyagers can make their own short documentary movies and then "silly" them up with new soundtracks.

Obstacles/Opportunities:

This activity may be quite helpful for those Voyagers who may invite a friend over, turn on the TV and then ignore the friend. Using this activity, watching movies together can actually become a relationship-building activity if the partner is willing to practice their "Silly Soundtracks" with a friend. A major obstacle may be participants' particular obsessions, or tendencies to use actual sound effects and dialogue from other videos. Be careful not to allow this as part of the "soundtrack."

LEVEL IV, STAGE 14, ACTIVITY 84

Imaginative Role-Plays

ACTIVITY HIGHLIGHTS
° Integrating your creative ideas with a social partner
° Adding imagination to pretend play in a coordinated manner

Summary:

Now Voyagers get to use their newly sharpened imagination skills in the arena of imaginative role-plays. Imagination is the element that makes role-plays so exciting. But it has to be added in a coordinated and mutually enjoyable manner to serve as an enhancement for everyone.

Participants:

Try this with teams of up to three Voyagers.

Getting Ready:

You will need simple props for the role-plays you choose. Make sure that all participants are proficient in more structured role-plays.

Coaching Instructions:

This exercise has four steps:

☐ STEP 1

Pick a simple pretend role-play scenario. Make sure the scenario is appropriate to the team-mates ages. Choose a role for each team-mate to begin with. Have the team-mates re-enact it without any embellishment.

☐ STEP 2

When they are successful doing it "straight," Voyagers can take turns adding something funny to their scripts. Stop the action at regular intervals and allow each of the members to make an enhancement to their own actions in the script. Once again either you, or one member of the team should be recording the revisions.

☐ STEP 3

Re-play the scenario with the new scripts.

☐ STEP 4

After the team has managed this more structured format, allow them to do another role-play, this time allowing them to select their enhancements in a more fluid manner.

Variations:

Now is a good time to practice the loss and repair of coordination. Tell team-mates you want them to see what happens if each of them has very different ideas for how the new script should go. Ask one member to make additions to their character so that he is very sad. Ask the other to make additions to his character so that he is very happy. See what happens. Then ask them if they can "fix" the script so that it makes more sense.

Obstacles/Opportunities:

A team member may be sorely tempted to try and influence the other group members to change their characters to fit in with the direction he wants his character, or the play to go. He may become frustrated that the play is being "ruined" because the various contributions are not as perfectly logical as if he wrote the script himself. If this happens, immediately stop the action and remind the team member that in this activity, enjoying your teamwork is more important than how the script turns out. We have to keep emphasizing whenever possible that in most of our relationship actions in life the "means" are more important than the "ends."

LEVEL IV, STAGE 14, ACTIVITY 85

What Could This Be?

ACTIVITY HIGHLIGHTS

° Using imagination to share reactions to ambiguous stimuli
° Integrating ideas where there is no correct perception
° Reaching consensus with a social partner

14

Summary:

This is a lesson in working together in response to an ambiguous perception. Many of our perceptions are not always clear cut and are subject to our subjective impressions. For example, inkblots have no objective form and they can be whatever we wish them to be. In this exercise, Voyagers look at inkblots together, form their own subjective impressions, share them and later try and form a consensus impression.

Participants:

Two Voyagers or several teams of two.

Getting Ready:

For each team you will need five pieces of fairly heavy, pre-folded paper and a tube of safe, washable paint. Team members sit side by side at a table.

Coaching Instructions:

There are four steps to this activity:

☐ STEP 1

Point to the paper and paint and say the following, "You are going to make some inkblots. Have you ever done that? It's fun. Let's start." One team member places a small amount of paint onto the paper, the other is instructed to fold the paper in half and mush the paint together.

☐ STEP 2

Have team members unfold the paper and say, "Wow! Look what you made! The two of you can see lots of things when you look at this. But, there is no right thing. You can use our imagination and see different things. I want the two of you to make up what this could be. Use your imaginations and see what you think it is."

☐ STEP 3

Ask both partners to take turns sharing their perceptions.

☐ STEP 4

After you feel that both partners understand the activity, allow them to take turns interpreting the inkblots. Focus on three types of sharing:

1. Sharing the things that one partner sees and the other cannot. Help your partner to see what you see.

2. Finding out which common things you both see.

3. Choosing one consensus response that you both agree is the best, or funniest.

Variations:

From time to time pretend to have more difficulty perceiving perceptions and ask for help ("Can you help me to see what you see?"). Another good variation is – can you guess it? – playing "Silly Inkblots."

Obstacles/Opportunities:

Since the inkblots that are made create a "projective" stimulus in some ways like the Rorschach inkblots, it is possible for a partner with more disordered thinking to generate some bizarre or frightening stimuli. If this happens, stop the activity and move on.

STAGE 15: GROUP FOUNDATIONS

Goals and Objectives

While Voyagers have typically been in various groups for a while and have even worked with groups in prior activities, they may not be conscious of the value of belonging to a group as a unique entity. This stage provides Voyagers with an understanding of the power of group effort. By the close of the stage we hope that Voyagers have learned to value their group memberships and have sufficient reasons to work hard to support the group. Voyagers in this stage become powerfully aware of the idea of a "We-go," a joint Ego that evolves in well functioning groups. The "We-go" provides each group member with the sense that the group can provide things for him that individual effort could never hope to obtain.

Activity Summary

The stage begins with activities designed to increase the perceptions of group cohesiveness and enjoyment. Voyagers learn to integrate their individual ideas and efforts into collaborative structures that convey an excitement not possible from solo endeavors. This new-found ability that arises from the blending of perceptions becomes part of the emotional basis to support the emergence of friendships. Bonds are strengthened through the creation of activities and games that are unique to the specific group setting within which they were created. Voyagers learn not only to document their accomplishments but to engage in planning social events that include back-up strategies to handle disappointment should the weather turn bad or a member become ill. From this vantage, Voyagers are now ready to begin the hard work and to face the rejection inherent in learning how to join the ongoing activities of more unfamiliar peers. The stage concludes with activities that support an understanding of consensus that includes the interests of both self and others. As members share this journey of hard work they are not only strengthened as individuals but also experience the power that comes from the history of the myths and projects they have created together.

Critical Tips

- Remember to structure activities so that all group members see the advantages of joining forces to work together as a team.

- Consider starting a Group Journal where you highlight the important experiences of the group for continual reference and reflection. The Group Journal is a good way to quickly involve new members in the essence of the group.

- Continue to provide enough structure to the group. Be careful to walk the tightrope between your being seen as the group's leader and allowing the group to degenerate into chaos.

- This is an excellent time to introduce actions, communications and games that are known only by group members. These "secrets" serve as a harmless way to reinforce loyalty and uniqueness in the group.

LEVEL IV, STAGE 15, ACTIVITY 86

Integrating Ideas

ACTIVITY HIGHLIGHTS

- ° Integrating individual efforts into a larger group theme
- ° Enjoying contributions as part of a larger team effort

Summary:

In this exercise, Voyagers learn to integrate their individual efforts and collaborate to create an integrated team product. Teams first individually construct two different structures. After their individual efforts are complete, they are challenged to integrate them into a single unit.

Participants:

Voyagers can participate in teams of three people each.

Getting Ready:

Provide building blocks or similar construction materials for each person. Make sure the teams are working near each other.

Coaching Instructions:

The activity has three steps:

☐ STEP 1

Each team member must first individually build a structure adjacent to one another's. They are asked to keep their relationship connection by narrating their actions. In the initial stage, help team members choose structures that will be easily integrated, such as a house and a garage. After they have some practice in integration, remove this framework and allow team members to choose their own structures. Before they begin to build, tell team members that when they are finished, the team will have to combine their structures into a single one. Team members are asked to briefly discuss what each will be building. This gives them an opportunity to pre-plan how their structures might be integrated later.

☐ STEP 2

When they are finished building their own structures, tell team-mates to create a "play" that combines what each of the team members has built. They can use small plastic people, animals, trees and cars to help them. They must make sure that all three structures are important in the play.

☐ STEP 3

Now tell the teams that you want them to work together and combine their already integrated structures into one group structure that combines all of the structures. Units could be a village, town, airport or anything else that makes sense.

15

Variations:

Once Voyagers have gained proficiency in this task, add challenge by not revealing that they have to combine their efforts until after they finish their own work.

Obstacles / Opportunities:

This exercise provides a good introduction to team collaboration. It is important to structure the activity so that team members see the advantage to integrating their structures into a larger unit, rather than doing so reluctantly. We want to convey the excitement of combining ideas and enhancement that we feel when we join forces with other creative individuals.

LEVEL IV, STAGE 15, ACTIVITY 87

Group Structures

ACTIVITY HIGHLIGHTS
° Engaging in collaborative effort to create new structures
° Participating in a group creative process

Summary:

One of the greatest thrills of early friendships arises from blending perceptions together to create something entirely new. In a variation of the last activity, we now ask Voyagers to work together and create a brand-new structure that reflects their joint contributions.

Participants:

Voyagers can participate in two-person teams.

Getting Ready:

All you need are sufficient building materials.

Coaches Instructions:

This exercise has three steps:

☐ STEP 1

Provide each team with one set of building materials. Tell them that they are going to work together as a team. This time each team is going to work together to build one thing. They have to begin by choosing what they are going to build. Initially limit choices to a house, a school, or a police station. When they become more proficient, allow them to choose their own structure.

☐ STEP 2

Allow teams several minutes to decide. After they have made their choice, ask them to choose a strategy for how they are going to work together. They can take turns adding, or they can each work on a different part, or they can be the builder, architect and parts department. Make sure that partners understand the roles they have chosen and have a clear method of communication.

☐ STEP 3

As in the last exercise, ask the teams to "merge" their structures into a single structure. This will take some re-building and movement, but it is an exciting activity both in terms of reinforcing flexible thinking and in strengthening Voyagers' perceptions of their ability to work as part of a cohesive, successful team.

Variations:

You can try similar exercises with songs and poems.

Obstacles / Opportunities:

Up until now we have seen Journals as individual efforts. Now is a good time to consider Group Journals.

LEVEL IV, STAGE 15, ACTIVITY 88

Group Games

15

ACTIVITY HIGHLIGHTS

° Developing alternative games rules
° Creative team problem solving
° Collaborating to develop new rules for games
° Finding new alternative solutions to problems

Summary:

One of the really neat things that friends do is to make up their own unique versions of games that only they know how to play. It provides a special bond to have created a version of an activity that is ours alone. In this activity, group members make up alternate sets of rules to play a game that they all like.

Participants:

Try this with teams of up to four.

Getting Ready:

Any simple board game or activity that group members enjoy without becoming overly focused.

Coaches Instructions:

Start with any game that group members know really well. Tell them that they get to make up a set of new rules that only they will know. Make sure that the rules that are agreed upon make sense. One member should act as "Secretary" and record the rules. Group members have to make sure that they are all equal contributors to the revisions. Once they have completed their new rules, they should name the game and acknowledge that it is a "secret" only to be revealed to members of the group that invented it.

Variations:

Bring a new person into each team and ask team-mates to carefully teach him how to play the game, using the new set of rules.

Obstacles/Opportunities:

Make sure that all group members know that they cannot teach or use these special rules with anyone but their group without discussing it first with you and their team-mates. With proper coaching, Voyagers can introduce new variations into activities with different peers and be perceived as creative and interesting, rather than weird and crazy. But we have to be careful, as this is another tightrope to be walked.

LEVEL IV, STAGE 15, ACTIVITY 89

Joining In 2.

ACTIVITY HIGHLIGHTS
° Learning sophisticated strategies to join in with peers
° Practicing effective strategic social planning
° Developing alternative strategies as back-up plans
° Learning to re-group after a setback

Summary:

Joining the ongoing activities of a small group is a highly complex, strategic activity. And, no matter how proficient, one has to be able to face rejection and bounce back in order to keep trying. In this activity, partners practice strategies for joining in. They also learn to re-group and try alternative strategies. Finally they learn to determine when it is time to move on and try to join in another time, or join in with another group.

Participants:

Each team should have four group members.

Getting Ready:

You will need cards with the seven parts of joining in written on them. You will also need four "strategy" cards.

Coaching Instructions:

This version of joining in is divided into seven separate phases. Each phase must be extensively practiced on its own, then two or three phases practiced together, prior to integrating all seven into role-plays. The seven phases are:

1. Observing, to figure out the activity that the group is engaged in.

2. Looking for a good moment to join in. Looking for a pause in the action.

3. Compliments.

4. Choose one of four additional strategies for joining in:

    (a) Quietly move next to.

    (b) Show interest and enthusiasm.

    (c) Show a desire to help or enhance.

    (d) Humor.

5. Persist when ignored, up to a point.

6. Try another strategy if the first one does not work.

7. Know when it's time to move on and try again some other time.

Variations:

As you know, we believe that practice in deliberately doing skills wrong creates great learning opportunities, as long as Voyagers are aware of what they are doing. After they are proficient in the seven skills listed above, have them role-play doing all seven the wrong way. It is lots of fun and takes the "edge" off of these exercises appearing too much like "work" or a "class."

Obstacles/Opportunities:

Even with more sophisticated strategies, participants will only be partially successful in joining in. They have to be able to bounce back from rejection and move on. There are unlimited opportunities for social interaction and if they are doing the right things they will obtain the desired results.

15

LEVEL IV, STAGE 15, ACTIVITY 90

Our World

ACTIVITY HIGHLIGHTS
° Building group cohesiveness
° Negotiating with group members to reach consensus

Summary:

As group identity evolves, we provide an experience of group invention, where the group members can transport themselves to a new world of their own creation. Many individuals with whom we work are familiar with the idea because they have computer games that simulate the creation of cities, cultures and environments. This is different, however, because it requires that each individual think not only of his own interests but those of his friends as well.

Participants:

A small group of Voyagers.

Getting Ready:

You will need a whiteboard, magic markers, Post-Its and pencils.

Coaching Instructions:

This activity has four steps:

☐ STEP 1

The group begins by choosing a name for the world they wish to create. A group called "The Drivers" might use a name like "Freeway World." We have had groups choose completely made-up names with no meanings and names that had clear significance to them.

☐ STEP 2

The group decides what their world will look like. They can be provided with several different scenarios including a desert world, a concrete world, a water world, a snow world and a forest world. They have to choose one of these, or come up with an alternative that they all agree to.

☐ STEP 3

Now the group continues to make decisions about a number of characteristics of the world. These include what people do all day, the animal life, the enemies and dangers and the history of this world.

☐ STEP 4

The group creates an adventure that takes place in the world.

Variations:

You must be vigilant for self-absorbed, restricted ranges of interest. This will be easily identified by bossiness and controlling behavior. Be creative in blending in many themes when you create worlds. You can incorporate science lessons, history and government and any other subject. You can even experiment with a bit of science fiction by creating futuristic worlds.

Obstacles/Opportunities:

The value to this exercise is multi-faceted. On a practical level it provides an important experience related to cooperative learning. On a symbolic level it increases group members' sense of cohesiveness and shared creativity.

LEVEL IV, STAGE 15, ACTIVITY 91

Group Journeys

ACTIVITY HIGHLIGHTS

° Developing powerful group myths and stories
° Heightening the experience of group strength

Summary:

Nothing creates group cohesiveness more than a shared journey through life. It can involve something small but special, or something that takes months and a great deal of effort. In this exercise we describe some examples of journeys we have taken with different groups at The Monarch School.

Participants:

A group of Voyagers.

Getting Ready:

Remember, the key to any successful group journey is that it originates in the minds of the group members and does not emanate from the Coach. Group members must feel pride in their planning and execution of the journey and perceive that its success was due to their joint efforts.

Coaching Instructions:

We present the following examples in hopes of stimulating your creative group ideas. In all cases group members developed the initial idea and did the bulk of the work of planning and preparing for the journey:

° During the first year of operation of The Monarch School, young teenagers decided they wanted to take a field trip to "Dave and Busters," a large entertainment arcade about ten miles away. Group members spent about two months planning the event, developing rules of conduct and even agreeing upon a dress code. Now, four years later, it is still brought up as a triumph.

15

- ° Another journey was a trip to McDonalds that was not officially allowed by the school. One day, in the midst of a group activity, I snuck group members into my [Steve's] car and sped away to the local McDonalds, located about a half mile away. The event had all the "danger" and thrills of a POW breakout. The students still speak of that day in reverent tones and the ones who were left out still ask when they will get to go.

- ° A final illustration is of a group journey that consisted of visiting a schoolmate who was terminally ill. The group spent several months constructing a special wagon that he could be transported in, decorated with all of his favorite images. When the wagon was finished, they journeyed to a park near his home to present him and his family with the wagon. The family was clearly impacted in a way that will live forever in the memories of group members.

STAGE 16: EMOTIONAL REGULATION

Goals/Objectives

Relationships with others are dependent not only on awareness of the emotional reactions of our partners but also the ability to read our own emotional reactions. Stage 16 focuses on teaching Voyagers to become more aware of their inner emotional worlds and to recognize that they can take steps to regulate their emotional reactions to be more productive.

Activity Summary

Now the number of skills multiplies. Voyagers begin the stage by learning to recognize and manage different degrees of stress. Then they move onto learning and practicing simple skills for conflict resolution. The stage moves on to three exercises whose focus is developing a more sophisticated understanding and use of emotions. We are preparing Voyagers to enter a new level of friendship where caring about and sharing inner feelings is highly valued. We close the stage by focusing on two more critical relationship skills. The first of these prepares Voyagers for the inevitable rejections they must face. They learn that, like mistakes, rejection is a normal part of life that can be understood and coped with effectively. The final exercise teaches Voyagers how to take responsibility for inviting a friend over to their house.

Critical Tips

- To have value, the skills taught in this stage must become part of a Voyager's daily life.

- Remember to emphasize that conflicts are not bad. They are a normal part of any relationship.

- Once again, it is critical for all those involved with Voyagers to learn the feelings vocabulary definitions, so that they use the emotion labels in similar ways and avoid confusion.

- Try to determine each Voyager's favorite medium for representing their emotions.

- Remember to freely admit your own mistakes and past rejections if you wish to serve as a role model.

LEVEL IV, STAGE 16, ACTIVITY 92

Stress 1.

ACTIVITY HIGHLIGHTS
- ° Distinguishing between levels of stress
- ° Becoming aware of internal cues signaling different levels of stress
- ° Developing simple coping responses to decrease frustration

Summary:

Voyagers have reached a point where they can reference others with regularity and accuracy. However, some Voyagers now face the problem of a deficiency in "Self-Referencing." They may have regular "meltdowns" and highly stressful experiences because they are unable to reference the internal cues that should warn them that they are becoming highly stressed and need to take a break and/or ask for help. This exercise sensitizes Voyagers to several different stress levels. We also help members develop increased sensitivity to both the types of events that might trigger stress and the physical signals that provide the internal reference points. Finally, Voyagers practice taking stress breaks and only returning to the activity they were involved in when their bodies have calmed down. This is a preliminary exercise on emotion regulation. We will follow up with the "advanced" course when we reach Stage 21.

Participants:

While this exercise is mainly focused on those Voyagers with problems in emotion regulation, it is certainly helpful to any group or class members.

Getting Ready:

It is quite helpful if Voyagers who have emotion regulation difficulties are aware of this and motivated to find ways of reducing their meltdowns. By this stage Voyagers have taken sufficient responsibility and ownership of their actions so that this is rarely a problem.

Coaching Instructions:

We cover six beginning steps in learning to manage stress:

☐ STEP 1

First discuss that stress is a natural occurrence for everyone. We all face things that are hard for us to do or do not turn out the way we wanted them to. There is no way we can eliminate stress. However, we should want to recognize it and learn to manage our stress before it "blows up" and results in a meltdown.

Now introduce the "Four Color" system for identifying stress. The colors are "Green," "Yellow," "Orange" and "Red," which correspond with traffic lights. Explain that "green" represents times when we feel calm and peaceful. Everything is going great. We do not feel any demands on us. Provide many examples and make sure that each group member provides his or her own examples in discussion. Then have each member write a list of activities and places where they experience "Green."

☐ STEP 2

"Yellow" represents mild stress. This is the good kind of stress as it means we are being challenged. When we are experiencing "Yellow" we are not sure how we are going to solve a problem. There is a degree of uncertainty. But we still feel we are going to accomplish our goal. We do our best learning in these "Yellow" states. Provide examples of times when you were in a "Yellow" state right before solving a problem or finishing a project. Again, go around the group and have each member recount experiences when they experienced a "Yellow" state. Have each member compile a "Yellow" list of activities and memories.

☐ STEP 3

Now we move on to the most critical type of stress. "Orange" is crucial because it is no longer a productive level like "Yellow," but there is still time to do something about our feelings before it is too late. When we are in an "Orange" state we are uncomfortable and quickly becoming discouraged. There are usually some changes going on in our bodies, though we may not be aware of them. "Orange" is a signal to stop and take a break and then take some action to help reduce our stress. If we do not listen to that signal we will move into "Red."

☐ STEP 4

"Red" is the last level of stress. It signals a meltdown and it means it is too late to take any productive action. If we let our stress get to the "Red" state we will probably be very upset and it will take a longer time to calm down. We may say or do hurtful things without meaning to.

☐ STEP 5   LEVEL PRACTICE

Now members think about times when they have moved from one level to another. Each member tries to think about the information in his or her body that would have provided a signal that it was time to stop and take a Stress Break. For some Voyagers determining these signals is very hard. It is useful to work with Voyagers to plan stress simulations in which they will be presented with tasks that become increasingly difficult and then impossible to complete or solve correctly. Reducing time and increasing demands for perfection also increases stress. The Voyager is always part of the team planning the activity and is aware that it is a simulation. However, despite this, it usually has the effect of providing an excellent practice laboratory to sensitize him or her to the cues signaling movement from one level of stress to the next. The Voyager is given four flags representing each of the colors. It is his job to regularly stop, initially when cued by the Coach, monitor his stress level and place the correct flag.

☐ STEP 6   STRESS BREAKS

Once Voyagers have gained some awareness of their "Orange" level of frustration it is important to provide them the opportunity to take Stress Breaks. At The Monarch School our community members have access to the "Beanbag Room," a workout

16

area, a walking track and a soothing relaxation area with soft music, depending upon what is most beneficial to help them recover from stress.

Variations:

This is a great time for a class to begin maintaining a Stress Journal. Twice each day, students can stop and briefly record their estimates of their levels of stress during different activities. From these journals they can begin to learn about the events that serve as "Stress Triggers" for them.

Obstacles/Opportunities:

Voyagers who are able to monitor their own stress levels and take breaks without being cued feel an immediate surge in pride and self-esteem. No one enjoys having a meltdown (we are not referring to manipulative tantrums). Afterwards we all feel ashamed and remorseful, but often we feel helpless to prevent the next meltdown from occurring. It is great to feel that you can take some control over your body's reactions.

LEVEL IV, STAGE 16, ACTIVITY 93

Agreements and Conflicts

ACTIVITY HIGHLIGHTS
° Perceiving conflicts from a "blameless" position
° Resolving simple peer conflicts effectively

Summary:

Conflicts between peers are a normal part of life. For Voyagers to develop lasting friendships, they must become proficient at quickly and easily resolving normal day-to-day peer conflicts. In this activity we deal with some of the simplest and most common types of conflicts: situations where both partners want to go first, play with the same object, want the other to change to a different activity, want the same materials etc. As you read the instructions, note that we try and remove all of the negative stigma from the word "conflict" and convey that conflicts are a natural part of life and are not at all harmful if we learn to deal with them well.

Participants:

You can conduct this exercise in a group, divided into teams of three. One member serves as "Conflict Spotter" for the pair. Make sure to rotate the roles.

Getting Ready:

A video camera and monitor are quite helpful.

Coaching Instructions:

There are five steps to this exercise:

☐ STEP 1

Tell partners they are going to learn what to do when there is a conflict. First, explain what a conflict is. We are going to work on two types of conflicts:

1. Situations where both want something different.

2. Situations where we both want the same thing.

Provide many examples of each type and teach partners to recognize them.

☐ STEP 2

Next, set up some unstructured activity situations, where two partners have to share a limited supply of materials. Now wait until an inevitable conflict starts. Do not wait until it escalates! Stop the action immediately and in a cheerful, excited voice say "Great! I see a conflict! Now we can practice. What kind of conflict do you think it is? Is it 'We both want something different?' is it 'We both want the same thing?'"

☐ STEP 3

Now ask the group to plan an activity segment that will deliberately cause a conflict. Ask them to choose the type of conflict they are going to have and when they will have it. Videotape the scene and ask partners to review it.

☐ STEP 4

Now ask members to do some activity together without pre-planning their conflict. However, as soon as a conflict is observed, they are to immediately announce "We are having a conflict."

☐ STEP 5

Once Voyagers learn to spot conflicts, the next step is to figure out what to do about them. "When you see a conflict, you will make a decision together about what strategy you will use to solve the conflict." Teach the team to use three simple strategies: Taking Turns, Sharing and Compromising. They should learn to use each strategy and then each time a conflict is spotted, stop the action and decide which strategy to take.

16

Variations:

You can prepare some "Conflict" cards which illustrate a variety of normal conflicts on one side of the card. Teams can practice role-playing them and then reach a consensus on the best strategy for dealing with each conflict, which gets recorded on the back of the card. Next, ask members to start reporting the conflicts that they encounter on a day-to-day basis. They can use these conflicts to write their own "Conflict" cards. On the reverse side of the card have them write the strategy that was most effective in managing the conflict. These can be included in Strategy Card boxes, indexed under the term "Conflicts."

Obstacles/Opportunities:

One great thing about this activity is that it typically takes the emotional "edge" off of conflicts. By labeling conflicts as learning opportunities and normal events we replace anger and distress with curiosity and a feeling of competence. We realize that these simplistic strategies will not work in some conflict situations, but surprisingly they are all that is needed for a great majority of them. In a later section we will be practicing more sophisticated conflict resolution methods.

LEVEL IV, STAGE 16, ACTIVITY 94

Faces and Voices

ACTIVITY HIGHLIGHTS
° Expressing emotions with proper voice tones and inflection
° Learning to integrate non-verbal and verbal emotional expressions

Summary:

In this activity, we expand the definition of emotional expression to include not only faces but voice features as well. We provide Voyagers the chance to practice the auditory dimensions of emotional expression with words removed. Then we gradually put all of the dimensions of emotional expression, including language back together.

Participants:

Divide your class or groups into teams of three to do this activity. Each team will need a tape recorder. One member should serve as the observer on a rotating basis.

Getting Ready:

Make tape recordings of the basic emotion expressions, using intonation and inflection, but make the recordings without using any audible words. (You can purchase recordings for this exercise on our website.)

Coaching Instructions:

There are six steps to this activity:

☐ STEP 1

Make sure that partners are proficient at making facial expressions of the basic emotions. After practicing basic facial expressions for a while, tell the partners, "You can show emotional expressions with your voice as well as your face. You don't even need any words to hear the emotion."

☐ STEP 2

Practice different types of intonation:

- Raise your tone at the close of a sentence.
- Lower your tone after the start of a sentence.
- Begin with a low tone, raise it and then lower it again at the end.
- Maintain a raised tone throughout the sentence.
- Maintain a lowered tone throughout the sentence.

☐ STEP 3

Practice humming basic emotions, using the above intonations, without saying any words. Determine if you wish to add any intonations to the five listed above. Play the taped segment of each emotion for the partners. Have members practice imitating the expression of the voice on the tape recorder, without using any words.

☐ STEP 4

Next, tape each member's vocal expressions of the emotions and ask their team to listen to them on a tape recorder. Do this for all four expressions. See if all group members can learn to correctly identify each member's emotion by listening to the recording.

☐ STEP 5

When members have mastered voice tones, move to combining voice tone with facial expression, still using only humming with no words.

☐ STEP 6

Finally, add words to the mix and practice putting faces, voices and words together.

Variations:

Team members can make and watch videos of their expressing different emotions. They can also mix up the voice tone of one emotion with the facial expression of another and see if other team members can guess what they did. One effective variation is for Voyagers to tape themselves saying the same word repeatedly but use a different tone of voice each time. Then the tape is played back and other Voyagers try to guess what the feeling is.

Obstacles/Opportunities:

Eliminating words from emotions provides a wonderful opportunity for Voyagers to learn to pay more attention to the non-verbal qualities of emotional expression.

16

LEVEL IV, STAGE 16, ACTIVITY 95

Expanding the Feelings Vocabulary

ACTIVITY HIGHLIGHTS

° Understanding many different emotions

° Expressing more complex emotional states

Summary:

Now we are ready to expand our vocabulary of emotions past the basic ones. In this activity we add ten new feelings to the repertoire.

Participants:

Up to six Voyagers can work on this activity together in a group.

Getting Ready:

A video camera and monitor are always useful for emotion activities.

Coaching Instructions:

☐ STEP 1

Explain that we are going to add some new emotions to our feelings vocabulary. The ten new emotions are Joyful, Caring, Enthusiastic, Proud, Optimistic, Annoyed, Anxious, Confused, Disappointed and Pessimistic. Begin with the positive emotions. Group members practice each expression with face and voice, while making sure they know why they have each emotion. They practice all of the emotion sharing games from prior activities. Use the emotion descriptions we provide at the end of this exercise. Feel free to elaborate and enhance them.

☐ STEP 2

Next, members practice using these new emotions by talking with each other about situations they remember in which they felt each emotion. If they cannot remember any specific situations, provide them with simple hypothetical situations where they might have the feeling. Make sure to incorporate all of these ten emotions in addition to the four we have already worked on in everyday life.

Variations:

We encourage Voyagers to learn to make predictions as a routine part of their lives. Predictions enable people to experience a healthy sense of control over their lives, something that is often lacking in a world they perceive as confusing and chaotic. The new expanded emotions vocabulary allows Voyagers to think about upcoming events in their lives and try to predict how they might feel. It also gives them ways to prepare strategies for coping with potential negative feelings. Try to conduct regular "Prediction" sessions, where each group member discusses some future event or activity and tries to predict how they might feel. Remember to follow up after the activity to assess the accuracy of the prediction and wonder why it did or did not turn out the way it was predicted.

Obstacles/Opportunities:

It is critical that important people in our group members' lives become familiar with the way we are defining and using these emotions and try to use them as much as possible in describing their own feelings. Expanding emotional understanding is not an exercise that can be done in several weeks. It is an ongoing event. Voyagers should be using their Emotions Journals and regularly recording and discussing episodes that evoke these new emotions.

Sample Emotions List:

- *Joyful:* "My pal and I have so much fun together, I smile and laugh all the time with him/her!"
- *Caring:* "Something is wrong and I want to know about it so I can help you."
- *Enthusiastic:* "I am really excited about something that I am going to get to do. I can't wait to do something!"
- *Proud:* "I feel like I really did a good job."
- *Optimistic:* "I feel that good things are going to happen soon."
- *Annoyed:* "Something or someone is starting to bother me. I'm not angry yet, but if it keeps up I will be."
- *Anxious:* "I am thinking about something bad that might happen to me and I don't know what to do about it."
- *Confused:* "I have to solve a problem and figure something out, but I'm not sure what to do." Or, "I don't understand what you are trying to say. It doesn't make sense to me."
- *Disappointed:* "I was hoping for something really good to happen and it never happened!"
- *Pessimistic:* "I feel that bad things are going to be happening to me soon."

16

LEVEL IV, STAGE 16, ACTIVITY 96

Representing Emotions

ACTIVITY HIGHLIGHTS

- Using several different media to represent feelings
- Sharing important memories with social partners
- Using poetry as a means for emotional expression

Summary:

Emotions can be represented using any medium. This activity begins by using the visual medium of photographs to represent different emotions and then moves on to poetry.

Participants:

This is an individual exercise. It can be done with a single Voyager or with an entire class or group.

Getting Ready:

The initial job is to scour magazines as well as personal photos. This time we are not looking for pictures that are silly, but ones that evoke different emotions. Ask Voyagers to bring in photos of people and places that are special to them in a positive and negative way and that represent the basic emotions we have worked on.

Coaching Instructions:

☐ EMOTION PHOTOS

Once photos are obtained, group members share their feelings with each other in the following manner:

- When I look at this picture I feel _____.
- Why do you feel _____?
- Because _____.
- What picture makes you feel _____ *(the same emotion)*?

The activity continues as follows, depending upon the photo:

- This is a picture of a place that makes me feel _____.
- This is a picture of an object that makes me feel _____.
- This is a picture of a person that makes me feel _____.

☐ EMOTION POEMS

Tell group members that they are going to be making Emotion Poems. Explain that their job is to fill in the blanks of the structure for the poem. You will provide part of the poem and they will finish it with whatever feels right to them. Make sure that you provide them with a pre-written visual format, regardless of whether you are working on a computer, or with paper and pencil. If you are working one-on-one, make sure that you do the typing or writing and leave your partner free to do the creating. They can use one of the emotions they have rehearsed in prior activities, or another emotion if they demonstrate that they understand it. Do not allow them to use emotions without understanding their meanings.

We have provided four examples of poem frameworks at the end of this exercise. Feel free to create your own frameworks using a similar format. Initially, you may have to provide examples of how to fill in the blanks, but be sure that members do not just copy or imitate your responses.

When they are done, save the poems in an easily retrievable place. Since we will be returning to poetry and stories many times, this is a good time to begin an electronic or paper Journal, where Voyagers can record and organize their contributions. This will make it easier to share their poems and stories. Don't be surprised if they want to return to re-read them many times.

Variations:

Make papier mâché masks to represent feelings. Choose music that represents different emotions. Take Voyagers on a photo expedition to shoot pictures of different emotions. If you feel that they are ready, a natural extension is to attempt collaborative emotion poems, where partners take turns enhancing each other's work on a line-by-line basis.

Obstacles/Opportunities:

When we move into the arena of personal emotions, we have to be careful that everyone is ready to respect their peers in the group. To do activities such as this one, all participants have to trust that no one will belittle them no matter what they express. You must be diligent in establishing a safe environment for emotion sharing.

This is an excellent opportunity for Voyagers who have had writing and expressive language difficulties to feel like competent communicators and writers perhaps for the first time. We take their poetry very seriously, bind it into books and submit it for publication. We are amazed at the pride that these poems engender. Try this activity and you will be equally impressed.

Emotion Poems Sample Frameworks:

Partners repeat the basic framework five times to complete the poem

1. I feel _____ *(emotion)* when _____ *(something happens, a certain time of day, I receive etc.)*.

2. _____ *(name of family member)* is _____ *(emotion)* when _____.

3. A _____ *(animal)* is _____ *(emotion)* when _____.

4. A _____ *(object)* is _____ *(emotion)* when _____ *(more imaginative)*.

5. _____ *(a specific place)* is an _____ *(emotion)* place because/when _____.

16

LEVEL IV, STAGE 16, ACTIVITY 97

Rejection

ACTIVITY HIGHLIGHTS

° Learning to anticipate potential rejection

° Learning to bounce back from rejection

° Tools for coping with rejection

Summary:

Much as we hate to admit it, rejection is a fact of life. One of the realities of social life for children is that about half of children's requests to play are greeted with rejection by peers. While, by this stage, our Voyagers are feeling much more successful and accepted, they, like the rest of us, still have to face moments when a peer says or does something that leaves them feeling unwanted or left out. This exercise practices various common rejection scenarios in the hope of inoculating Voyagers so that the real thing is not as disastrous. We also hope to provide some tools for coping with rejection.

Participants:

You can do this exercise in teams of three or four Voyagers.

Getting Ready:

Before starting this exercise, make sure that all team members are using Self Talk successfully for coping and adaptation. If not, go back and work on some of the earlier Self Talk exercises until they are more proficient. Since our goal is to increase Voyagers' feelings of competence, rehearsal of rejections must be combined with affirming Self Talk.

Coaching Instructions:

This is a four step activity:

☐ STEP 1

We are going to work on dealing with rejection. Rejection is a fact of life for all of us. It is helpful to begin by recounting some true experiences of feeling rejected in your own life. See if this will stimulate group members to discuss their experiences with rejection.

☐ STEP 2

Now explain that there are two types of rejection. One type is accidental. The person who you feel is rejecting you is not even aware that he is doing it. He may not hear you. He may be somewhat insensitive and not aware of your feelings. The second type is intentional. The person is trying to hurt and embarrass you. It is not always easy to tell one from another (in a later stage we will present an exercise that focuses on just this issue). When you feel rejected, you first have to stop and figure out whether you should try again. If you think it was accidental you may want to use a different approach strategy from one you feel was intentional. Discuss and role-play "Rejection Scenarios" 1, 3, 5 and 7 and compare them to 2, 4, 6 and 8 to illustrate this distinction.

☐ STEP 3

Explain that the most important thing in dealing with rejection is learning how we talk to ourselves both before and after being rejected. Work on different ways we can use Self Talk to make the situation worse. Examples are provided at the end of this exercise.

☐ STEP 4

Discuss ways we use Self Talk to make the situation better. Again, rehearse Self Talk strategies. Now practice role-plays of the different "Rejection Scenarios." First, we will practice making the situation worse, both before and after the rejection. Then we practice coping using Self Talk to make it better.

Variations:

This is an important exercise to sensitize Voyagers to times when they have been cruel to peers whether purposely or inadvertently. See if on the heels of this activity you can get your group members to develop an "Anti-Cruelty" pact, where they commit to avoiding hurtful actions with their peers.

Some people keep on setting themselves up for rejection by continually approaching peers who are bound to reject them. Learning to use Self Talk to cope with rejection will not be helpful to them. Rather, you will need to focus on helping them make better relationship choices. It is helpful to practice role-plays based upon "How to spot someone who is going to reject you." The focus should be on observing peers to learn to spot those who are cruel and use public humiliation as a means of increasing their own power and popularity.

Obstacles/Opportunities:

While this exercise may appear simple, we expect you to work on it for at least several weeks and possibly longer. Make sure that group members playing the "Rejecters" do not get carried away in their roles. They have to be realistic but not cruel!

Rejection Scenarios:

° Rejection 1: You invite a pal over and he says that he cannot come this time as his family has other plans.

° Rejection 2: You invite a pal over and he says "No" in a rude manner.

° Rejection 3: You invite two friends and they spend time with each other and ignore you.

° Rejection 4: You invite two friends to your house and they purposely ignore you and show you they do not want you near them.

° Rejection 5: You want to tell a pal a funny thing that happened. You approach him and he acts like you are not there.

° Rejection 6: You want to tell a pal a new joke you learned. You approach him and he tells you to go away and stop bothering him.

16

- Rejection 7: At school your pal is playing with another guy and you cannot get his attention.
- Rejection 8: At school your pal is playing with another guy. You approach them and he tells you to go away.

Negative Self Talk before and after Rejection:

Before

- They will probably reject me.
- Nobody really wants to play/talk with me.
- I always get rejected. What is the use of trying?

After

- I am going to get revenge on him/them.
- Every time I try, I get rejected.
- I must be stupid, bad, *(fill in the negative word).*
- Nobody wants to be my friend.

Coping using Self Talk before and after Rejection:

Before

- I could get rejected but I probably will not.
- If I don't try I will never succeed.

After

- Everyone gets rejected sometimes.
- Maybe he is not really my friend after all.
- Other people do not treat me like that.

LEVEL IV, STAGE 16, ACTIVITY 98

Inviting a Friend

ACTIVITY HIGHLIGHTS
- Learning skills for successfully inviting friends
- Using a calendar for planning
- Taking responsibility for scheduling and preparing for social events

Summary:

This exercise is designed to work out the mechanics of having a friend over to your house. We assume that by this stage Voyagers have enough reasons for wanting a friend to come over. It is time for them to take the responsibility for independently inviting friends over and acting as a good host.

Participants:

This can be done in a group or class.

Getting Ready:

Make sure to purchase calendars or schedule books that are useful for the people that you are working with.

Coaching Instructions:

Start by making sure that Voyagers have good reasons for wanting to have a friend come over to their house. Now explain that you are going to learn all the steps of successfully inviting a friend over. We are going to cover seven steps. Make sure that each person role-plays each of the steps. The seven steps to inviting a friend are:

☐ STEP 1   PICKING THE RIGHT PERSON TO INVITE

- ° Some people have a tendency to invite someone who is the most popular. This is an obvious road to rejection. We want to invite someone who you think really wants to become your friend.

- ° Do not choose someone who acts cruelly to other people and has a need to put them down. You are likely to become the next "victim."

- ° Be careful that you do not choose someone who wants to come over to play a new game or see a new piece of equipment you have. This is the wrong reason to invite someone.

- ° The invitee should be someone who has already been friendly to you. They should be someone with whom you have already had success interacting in another setting, like school or scouts.

- ° You should invite someone with whom you have common interests. Otherwise the visit may become quite uncomfortable for both of you.

- ° Finally, the invitee should be someone who respects the rules of any setting she is in and who is likely to come without any distracting games or paraphernalia of her own. Have each partner try and list some potential candidates for inviting over and help them review their choices.

☐ STEP 2   COORDINATE WITH PARENTS

Talk with your parents about your desire to have someone over, obtain potential dates and time and record them in your date book. You should also determine if there is anyone who is absolutely not to be invited.

☐ STEP 3   MAKING THE INVITATION

Inviting should be direct and to the point. It can be as simple as "I'd like you to come over to my house. Can you come over?" Remember not to wait until the last minute to ask. If the invitation is accepted, move on to picking the date and time.

☐ STEP 4   CHOOSING THE RIGHT DATE AND TIME

We don't want Voyagers to act like executives, so we ask that they memorize two possible dates and times prior to inviting. If those times don't work, they can check and get back to their friend at another time.

16

☐ STEP 5   FINALIZING WITH PARENTS AND FRIEND

Younger invitees cannot make their own decisions about accepting an invitation and have to check with parents. Practice the step of how to follow up to see if the invitee checked and received permission. This is a good time to work on basic telephone skills, if they are not in place.

☐ STEP 6   PUTTING IT ON THE CALENDAR

Once a time and date are agreed to, Voyagers learn to put the date on a calendar, so they can keep track of it and plan for it.

☐ STEP 7   PREPARING FOR THE VISIT

Start with general principles of being a good host. Prepare some activity choices that you know your friend is interested in. Practice being a good host and allowing your friend to make all of the choices. However, limit the choices to activities that will not be too distracting and will allow you to be a good friend. Make a list of "Friend" activities and "Alone" activities. "Alone" activities are those that distract your attention from friends and accidentally lead you to act rudely. Put away all "Alone" materials. You can blame the restriction to certain activities as your parents' prohibitions, "My parents won't let me do _____ when I have a friend over."

Variations:

One obvious variation is to help plan for getting invited over to a friend's house. See if you can construct a similar organized plan to help members be successful when they are at an "away game."

Obstacles/Opportunities:

This exercise addresses only the "how to" part. It does not mean that the Voyager will be motivated to invite a friend. Despite all of this methodical planning, "Murphy's Law" will apply and things will go wrong. Please make sure that everyone is ready for this and has alternative plans and Self Talk methods available for when things do go awry.

LEVEL V: EXPLORER

Introduction

Summary

Friendships at Level V have progressed to a level similar to that of the typically developing late elementary pre-adolescent relationships. External props fade in importance. We work on conversational elements in all stages but here is where they bear fruit. Friends do not need props to converse, but they still may need a common meeting place/setting where they see each other regularly, such as the neighborhood, school, club etc. In Level V, Explorers learn to coordinate unique perceptions, emotional reactions and imaginative embellishments into their shared experiences. Accompanying the move to Level V is an emerging interest in ideas and internal emotional states. The Explorer can now differentiate between what is really felt as opposed to what may be overtly expressed. She becomes interested in deciphering people's intentions as well as observing their actions. The enduring preferences and opinions of those around her become important. At this level we observe a great interest in more sophisticated role-playing and pretense. Peers become highly valued as collaborators in the world of ideas and imagination.

Before the close of Level V, friendships undergo yet another transition. We explore the concept of a friend as an "Ally," someone who will consistently support and stand up for us when we need them. We also expect our friends to be skilled in the highly complex process of empathy. However, before we can become very good at empathy, knowing how others feel, we must develop and perfect our ability to know how we ourselves are feeling. We are congruent if we can honestly interpret our own feelings so that what we do and say matches what we feel.

Participants

Exercises are increasingly geared for larger groups and classrooms. On the other hand, exercises require increased trust and self-disclosure and so also require that group members demonstrate compassion and acceptance for one another.

Settings

From this point on, settings become largely irrelevant. Activities can be conducted without concern for physical space or distracting objects.

Language

Language is now a critical element of all exercises. Explorers with continuing significant language impairments will need special modifications. We typically work first with computers so that they have sufficient time to process language prior to having to respond to it. This can create an immediate sense of comfort with language creativity for an Explorer who heretofore has shied away from language as a medium of playfulness and creation.

Regulation/Repair

By this level, we expect Explorers to be highly skilled at monitoring and repairing communication and coordination breakdowns. By the close of Level V, Explorers recognize that their concern must extend past external reactions to potentially hidden internal feelings and thoughts of their social partners. They become concerned with finding out how their friends "really" feel and not accepting superficial expressions without verification.

Coaching Points

- Learning to be a good listener is the most important part of conversation skills.

- The poetry and story-writing structures provide an excellent opportunity for less verbal Explorers to perceive themselves as competent with language expression.

- Be careful to observe yourself and make sure you are not keeping conversations connected.

- The important people in the Explorer's life must require that she "carries her own weight" by making conversations interesting and coherent.

STAGE 17: IDEAS

Goals and Objectives

The first stage of Level V concerns itself with providing an experience of the different ways we can share our internal worlds with others. Stage 17 is like a survey course in sharing minds. Explorers learn to understand their own interests, preferences opinions and emotional reactions and then compare and contrast them with their partners. The pleasure of integrating different ideas and co-creating new ideas becomes evident, as does the potential of sharing real and hypothetical pasts and futures.

Activity Summary

Stage 17 begins by making sure that Explorers understand that they have their own unique internal ideas that can be expressed in a variety of ways. We quickly move to activities that center on integrating ideas to come up with something new. Following this are activities that explore different modalities of idea sharing including absurdity, shared story-writing and creating new role-plays. We return briefly for two activities that highlight a higher form of perspective taking, where the Explorer has to put himself in his partner's "shoes" and consider how the partner's mind may be different from his own. Stage 17 then transitions to several activities that explore our minds as incredibly flexible "whiteboards" upon which we can explore alternatives, address hypothetical problems and even play with improbable and impossible scenarios that have no real value but are fun to speculate about. The second half of this large stage explores various forms of mental structures including ideas, interests, preferences, opinions and "shades" of emotional reactions. The stage concludes with an exercise "It Can't Be Wrong. It's Mine!" which addresses the distinction between objective facts and subjective beliefs and feelings, and illustrates why the former can be right or wrong but not the latter.

Critical Tips

- Be careful not to overlook problems with either too few or too many ideas (e.g. talking non-stop and freely associating out loud anything that comes to mind). Both can become obstacles if not addressed.

- Remember that the objective when integrating ideas is for partners to enjoy the creations resulting from the blending of different minds, not forcing people to compromise.

- When working with the Explorer on a one-on-one basis be careful to note how much of the work you are doing to maintain the coherence of the work product. What looks like a shared creation could wind up being mostly the result of your efforts if you are not careful.

- Once again, we require participation of the important people in the Explorer's life.

- Remember, journaling becomes a crucial step during this stage.

LEVEL V, STAGE 17, ACTIVITY 99

Idea Poems

ACTIVITY HIGHLIGHTS
° Developing the capacity to generate unique ideas
° Using poetry as a medium of expression for personal ideas

Summary:

Some Explorers have an over-abundance of ideas. Others have difficulty generating any of their own ideas. Poetry provides a perfect medium to explore our internal world of imagination and ideas. As we have discussed, Kenneth Koch developed a series of structures that makes it easier to get right to ideas and feelings, without worrying about all of the other poetic elements. In this activity we include several formats for "Idea Poems."

Participants:

Initially you may have to work one-on-one with an Explorer. After they get the hang of it, these poems are easy to create in a group or classroom setting. Remember that the goal of this exercise is not collaboration but helping the person develop her own sense of competence and enjoyment in creating ideas.

Getting Ready:

Initially you may prefer to do this activity in front of a computer, with the Coach doing all of the typing.

Coaching Instructions:

Have the poetry frameworks already set up on the computer before you start the activity. Explain that, "We are going to write some poems together. I am going to write part of the poem and then you are going to write the other part." If your partner is unable to fill in the blanks you have left, feel free to model with some other formats. When ready, team up Explorers in groups of two for their creation. Begin with a simple structure like the "Color Poem" below. We have included three sample formats at the end of this activity.

Variations:

The poetic variations are limitless. We leave them up to you.

Obstacles/Opportunities:

This simple poetic structure offers a wonderful opportunity for people with expressive language problems to view themselves as writers and to express their voices with an eloquence that may startle those around them.

17

Sample Poetry Frameworks:

Color Poem

Red is like _____ *(an object)* in the _____ *(time of day, season)*.

Yellow is like _____ *(an object)* that _____ *(does some action)* in the _____ *(time, season)*.

Blue is like _____ *(object)* in the _____ *(time, season)*.

Green is like _____ *(object)* in the _____ *(time of day, season)*.

In My Movie

In my movie _____ *(something happens)*

And _____.

In my movie _____

And _____.

(etc.)

In My Adventure

In my _____ *(emotion)* adventure, I _____ *(something happens)*

And _____ *(some consequence)*.

Always and Never

I always want to _____

But _____.

I never _____

But _____.

(I think you have the picture.)

Integrating Ideas

ACTIVITY HIGHLIGHTS
- ° Integrating ideas with social partners
- ° Synthetic thinking skills

Summary:

This activity practices blending our ideas together to come up with something entirely new. Explorers work together to create a new animal that has characteristics of the two they chose. They have the pictures of the animals to be an external focus, but they are really just the background. The real action occurs in the minds of the participants.

Participants:

You can do this activity with several teams of two.

Getting Ready:

Prepare twelve cards with pictures of animals on them. Team members sit side by side with the stack of animal cards between them.

Coaching Instructions:

Begin by saying, "Here are some animal cards. You pick one card and you pick another one." Provide the following instructions in written or oral form:

"Put the two animal pieces together and see if you can make an imaginary animal with parts of each one. You can create a brand-new animal. You must agree on all of the following parts of the animal:

1. The name of the animal.

2. What it looks like. What features you will take from each one.

3. What it likes to eat.

4. Where it lives. *(If they have difficulty say the following,)* 'Does it live in the ocean, or the mountains or the jungle or some other place?'

5. What it likes to do for fun.

6. What is it scared of? What does it fear and why?"

Each partner is allowed to contribute only half of the ideas. Record, or have them record, who contributed which idea to the final answer, so you can check. Next to each idea can be one of their names or the word "both" to signify that it was a collaborative answer.

17

Variations:

You can play this "blending" game with almost anything. For example, try to blend two vacation spots like Hawaii and a ski trip into a single fantasy resort. After they become proficient, have your teams combine and see if they can create mythical animals, places or anything else, that are a blend of two teams, or even three.

Obstacles/Opportunities:

Make sure to keep the definition of "success" focused on the team-mates' ability to work together to create something new that neither would have come up with alone. The key to this activity is the thrill of co-creating as a unit. Forcing someone to give up his idea in order to compromise will not lead to increased motivation to collaborate and unite with others.

LEVEL V, STAGE 17, ACTIVITY 101

Silly Questions

ACTIVITY HIGHLIGHTS
° Sharing imaginative ideas
° Creating humor as a product of collaborative thinking

Summary:

This is a great introduction to sharing imaginative ideas without any external props or objects to link us together. It is a wonderful form of humor that bonds our partners together as nothing else does. We use very simple formats to provide a way for humorous creations.

Participants:

Two or three Explorers can participate in any unit. You can have several units working at the same time if you wish.

Getting Ready:

Provide each team with a whiteboard and markers.

Coaching Instructions:

Tell the teams that they are going to play some games with mixing ideas together. Depending upon their level of imagination, you may have to give a demonstration. You may also have to provide the initial structure, as with the prior poems. Make sure that the different teams get the opportunity to share their creations. Some samples are provided at the end of the exercise.

Variations:

As with poems, there is an unlimited number of formats you can use. Have fun!

Obstacles/Opportunities:

By this stage, our team members do not have to be reminded that there are no right or wrong answers. If a participant is still perceiving the exercise as "getting it right" then we know it is time to back up and evaluate whether we should be working at an earlier stage of the program.

Sample Silly Questions Formats:

Silly Mix-ups

- What do you get when you mix an elephant with a blueberry?
- What do you get when you mix a cow with a rubber band?

Silly Inventors

- Who invented the balloon?
- Who invented the elevator?
- Who invented the first tree?
- Who invented the first mirror?

Mixed-up Vacations

- I want to go on vacation to _____. But I also want to go on vacation to _____.
- I guess that I will go to _____.

LEVEL V, STAGE 17, ACTIVITY 102

Shared Stories

ACTIVITY HIGHLIGHTS

- Learning to understand and appreciate each other's ideas
- Introducing ideas to remain related to your partner's contributions
- Learning to modify or withdraw an idea when your partner does not appreciate it
- Collaborating as a team to produce coherent stories

Summary:

Once Explorers learn the excitement of integrating their unique ideas in a simpler medium, we progress to working on this skill in a more complex story format. Unlike poems or riddles, prose is less forgiving when it comes to coherence – sentences need to relate to one another. When we read stories we expect the meaning of one sentence to flow in a highly coordinated manner into the next one, much like conversations. When we work on co-created stories, we want to be careful to emphasize the coordination of emotions. To enjoy co-writing stories, you have to care about your partner's ideas, as much as you do about your own. Successful shared stories become an important "Social Memory" that binds friends together. They will frequently re-read them with pride and compare their various themes and characters.

Participants:

This activity may begin with you and the Explorers working together in a small group until they get the hang of the basic format. After that, you can form as many story writing teams as you wish. Try and keep the teams together for a while to publish an "anthology."

Getting Ready:

All you need is a computer for each team. It may take anywhere from a few weeks to several months for participants to attain enough proficiency in remaining coherent to progress to peer story-writing.

Coaching Instructions:

There are four steps to this activity:

☐ STEP 1

"We are going to write a story together. First, one of you will write a sentence and then the other one will add one. All the sentences have to fit together so you can have a good story. Do you know what fitting together means?"

☐ STEP 2

"Let's practice first. Here is the first line, 'Jack was sitting in class one day in his school.' Now here is the second line, 'I like elephants.' Do these two fit? Now try this one. 'Jack was sitting in class one day in school. Jane was sitting next to him.' Do these two lines fit?" Continue to practice until you are sure the partner understands "fitting together."

☐ STEP 3

"You can begin with a story about _____ who decided to leave home and travel around the world. I will start the story and then the team will take over. 'Once upon a time there were two _____, whose names were _____ and _____ *(use real first names)*. They decided they wanted to leave home and go all around the world. (Type the sentence so that partners can read it.)* OK, now you can keep going from there." Make sure each partner contributes only one sentence at a time.

☐ STEP 4

Your role from this point on is to be a typist if needed and to point out when there is a loss of coherence. Each time a sentence clearly doesn't fit, say the following, "Does that fit with the sentence that came before? How does it fit? I don't think it fits!" If the partner does not appear to understand how to make sentences connect with one another, it is best to stop the joint story-writing and return to one-on-one coaching with the focus on making sentences fit together, using only two sentences at a time.

Variations:

You can also write shared screenplays for movies and anything else you can imagine. As Explorers become more proficient, see if you can increase the number of participants in your story-writing teams. Eventually you may progress to a shared group or class story.

Obstacles/Opportunities:

Initially, you may have to carry much of the responsibility for making the story lines fit together. Be careful not to allow this to go on for very long. It is easy to over-compensate and, as a result of your efforts, produce a story that looks like an excellent collaboration. You have to continuously increase your demands for your partner to take responsibility for staying "connected." Only when they have assumed equal partnership can they progress to working independently with peers.

LEVEL V, STAGE 17, ACTIVITY 103

I Know Some Things You Don't

ACTIVITY HIGHLIGHTS

- ○ Understanding that our experiences result in a different base of information
- ○ Taking into account differences in the knowledge base between you and partners
- ○ Theory of Mind skills

Summary:

Some Explorers still have difficulty realizing that their listeners do not have access to the same store of information that they do. Their conversations reflect the errone-ous assumptions that you know who "Jack" is, or what the lunchroom in school looks like. This activity helps Explorers recognize when they can and when they cannot make assumptions about what other people know or don't know about their worlds.

Participants:

Two-person teams. You can have several going at once if you would like.

Getting Ready:

The only materials needed are a whiteboard and markers.

Coaching Instructions:

This exercise has four steps:

☐ STEP 1

Team-mates make a list of things they might or might not know about each other. "We know many of the same things. For example we all know that two and two equals four, right? But there are other things one of us knows that the others do not know. We are going to figure out some of these things."

☐ STEP 2

Each team-mate takes a turn adding some information to the list. They can add a general fact, some personal event or person, something they just imagined or thought up. Put the person's name next to their contribution.

☐ STEP 3

After you make the list tell the group members that you will now go down the "master" list, item by item and place each item into one of three lists, "We are going to make three lists. The first list is 'What do we know that is the same?' The second list is 'What does *(partner A)* know that *(partner B)* does not?' The final list is 'What does *(partner B)* know that *(partner A)* does not?' We are not going to figure out everything, because that would take too long." Begin by using general classes of information such as multiplication and skills such as tying your shoes. Group members can use a "Do you know _____?" format. The lists can be as long as you like, but what is critical is that you divide each list in two parts. One part is 'factual' information like mathematics – things that it is possible or probable that they could both know, and the other half is personal information, such as "the contents of my bedroom" – things that they probably could not both know.

☐ STEP 4

Teams practice determining the reasons why we should assume we do, or do not know the same things. This step is called "You probably know/don't know because _____." Team-mates try to guess what their partner knows or does not know, based on six criteria. Partners try to become as accurate as they can at guessing what their partner knows or doesn't know. Here are the six criteria:

1. General Information: "Most people know that _____."

2. Common Experience: "We both took the same subject in school."

3. Lack of Common Experience: "I am in a different grade and so I took a course that you haven't taken yet."

4. Personal Experience: "I have been someplace that you haven't."

5. Private Experience: "You don't know the people I know."

6. In My Mind: "It is something I just thought up. It's in my mind and not in yours."

Variations:

Once Explorers determine there are things that they both know and don't know, the next logical question is "Do you want to know?" Participants now return to the things that the other doesn't know and again work on two lists: "Things my partner might want to know because they are interesting or important to many people" and "Things that my partner probably doesn't want to know because they are unimportant or only interesting to me."

Obstacles/Opportunities:

This is another critical exercise that must be supported by everyone involved in order for it to work. Teachers, family members and friends have to begin stopping the Explorer in mid-stream and asking whether there is any way that they could know what she is talking about. They have to request that she consider that he might be leaving out some crucial information that the she knows but the listener couldn't possibly know.

LEVEL V, STAGE 17, ACTIVITY 104

You are Master, I am Novice

ACTIVITY HIGHLIGHTS

° Modifying your actions to effectively assist someone less capable

° Successfully operating in a "coaching" position with a less skilled partner

° Learning step-by-step project planning

Summary:

This activity is similar to the preceding one, in that it requires Explorers to consider that the person they are with has a different knowledge base than their own. However, now our focus is a bit different. Explorers have to take into account the difference in another person's level of skills. They have to learn to modify their ideas and communication to instruct someone who is a Novice or Apprentice and may be younger as well. This activity is also an introduction to empathy – placing yourself in another person's shoes.

Participants:

You can set up teams of two or three Explorers

Getting Ready:

Materials needed include a whiteboard and markers, a video camera and TV monitor.

17

Coaching Instructions:

There are four steps to this activity:

☐ STEP 1

In the first phase team members make an instructional video for a younger child who is just a beginner. Next, team members practice being a Coach by taking turns instructing each other in a skill that one has mastered and in which the other is just a Novice. In the third phase, we pick an actual younger child and have team members work together to teach her a new skill.

☐ STEP 2

Begin with the following instructions: "We are going to make a teaching video. Let's pick something that you know how to do really well." Find an activity or skill that team members are highly proficient in. "This video is for a child who is *(provide the age)* and who doesn't know anything at all about _____. The video has to teach her from the very beginning. Your first job is to decide where you will begin and to make a step-by-step plan of how you are going to do the teaching." Help the team make an outline of the steps they will use to instruct the Novice. Then work with them on the language and speed with which they will talk. Next work out the plan for visuals; where and how long the camera will focus. Finally, they can film the video and watch it together.

☐ STEP 3

In this step we ask the team members themselves to take the roles of "Master" and Novice. Find a skill or activity that one member is proficient in and another has no experience in. Members take turns being the Master and the Novice who has to learn from the very beginning.

☐ STEP 4

When team members are ready, tell them that they will be providing "live" instruction to a younger child who wants to learn a skill. Divide them into a Coach and Consultants who will observe and provide feedback to the Coach. Make sure that all team members get experience in both roles. Have periodic breaks where the Coach and Consultants meet to discuss strategy.

Variations:

Bring in a younger child who is not familiar with the activity and have her watch the instructional video. After she watches the video, ask the younger child to demonstrate what she has learned to do. After the younger child leaves, have the team members reflect and evaluate what worked and didn't work in their teaching video. Have them revise the video and try again. Do the same after the "live" exercise.

Obstacles/Opportunities:

This is an excellent exercise to pave the way for learning about patience with others. It is especially helpful for those Explorers with younger siblings. To be successful, the Explorer has to accept that the Novice cannot progress at a rapid speed. They must be aware of the rate in which they are providing instruction and learn to introduce new materials, based upon feedback from the Novice's performance. This is why it is crucial for everyone to have sufficient experience in both the Novice and Master roles.

Good Enough Solutions

ACTIVITY HIGHLIGHTS

- Learning "gray area" thinking
- Finding good solutions for problems that have no right or wrong answers
- Collaborating to jointly solve hypothetical problems

Summary:

This activity works on several major deficits of Executive Functioning. It combines working on what we call "gray area" problems – the type of problems that have no right or wrong answers – along with hypothetical problem solving and learning that you cannot always be perfect and sometimes "good enough" is just that, good enough! Team members work together to find "good enough" solutions to problems that have no right and wrong, or "black-and-white" answers. The types of problems are hypothetical. They could happen, but they are not actually happening at the time.

Participants:

You can try this exercise with teams of four.

Getting Ready:

The only materials needed are a whiteboard and markers.

Coaching Instructions:

Tell the teams, "We are going to try and solve some special type of problems. These are problems that don't have any one right answer. In fact there is really no perfect answer at all. We have to find some 'good enough' or 'best of the worst' answers that might help us. There will always be more than one of these." By now, Explorers have had enough experience with alternative answers that they should not be assuming there is one right answer. They may have more difficulty with the concept that these are the types of problems that have no right answer and might need practice on the concept of "good enough" and especially in the idea of "best of the worst," where there is no really good answer but you still have to find something to do. Feel free to make up your own hypothetical questions. Remember they must be realistic and cannot have any correct answers. You can use the hypothetical samples provided at the end of the exercise.

Variations:

If you want to take the next step, try working on problems for which there are no solutions such as "What is the sound of one hand clapping?" or "If a tree falls in the forest and there is nobody around to hear it, does it make a sound?"

Obstacles/Opportunities:

Don't be surprised if you find that a team member figures out a "right" answer for a problem that you thought had no correct answers. Don't stop and argue, just bow to his superior knowledge and move right along to the next problem.

Sample "Good Enough" Questions:

- What would you do to find your way out, if you were lost in the wilderness and didn't have a compass or a map?

- What would you do if you wanted to bake a cake and the recipe called for sugar but you just could not get any sugar?

- What would you do if it was 7pm and you realized that you had a big test tomorrow and you had forgotten to study for it?

LEVEL V, STAGE 17, ACTIVITY 106

Appreciating Alternatives

ACTIVITY HIGHLIGHTS
- Valuing your partner's strategies even if different than your own
- Accepting the value of alternative methods of problem solving
- Rapidly adopting alternative methods to supplement your own

Summary:

Now that Explorers have worked on problems that have no "right" answer, they are ready to learn how to communicate appreciation for team members' alternative solutions to hypothetical problems – an essential element in working together as part of a problem-solving team. This activity teaches Explorers to value the alternative solutions that other team members generate, even though there is nothing wrong with their own solution. Each person finds a different solution to a problem. Then they "switch" solutions and have to explain why their team-mate's method is the best.

Participants:

Divide Explorers into as many teams of two as you like.

Getting Ready:

You will still need only a whiteboard and markers.

Coaching Instructions:

There are two steps in this exercise:

☐ STEP 1

Choose a new problem that is somewhat general in nature like "What should we do to respond to the air pollution problem in our city?" Pick a problem that fits the age and intellectual level of the Explorers. Present the problem and ask each person to privately come up with his or her best solution and write it down, along with reasons to defend it as the best solution. Make sure that they are deriving different solutions. If they have the same solution, congratulate them and go to another problem, where you coach them to take different approaches.

☐ STEP 2

When they have finished and have two different solutions, take the finished product from each and tell them, "You both came up with a good solution. Now I want you to trade solutions. Make sure you understand your partner's solution and when you do, explain why it is the best solution to the problem." Have partners interview each other to make sure they understand the solution they will be using. Then have each explain to you why their new solution is a good one.

Variations:

Set up a small debate. Have different Explorers switch solutions and debate with each other. The object is to find flaws in your own original solution while defending the other person's solution.

Obstacles/Opportunities:

You may still come across Explorers who want to argue that their method is the better one, despite telling them that this is not the point of the exercise. This is an indication that they are not ready to work at this stage. It is time for you to re-group and determine a more realistic place to proceed.

17

LEVEL V, STAGE 17, ACTIVITY 107

Interests

ACTIVITY HIGHLIGHTS

° Developing knowledge about personal interests

° Learning to be curious about the interests of others

° Learning to share interests in a mutually enjoyable manner

Summary:

With this activity we return to the realm of developing a "Self." Our interests, among other things, make us unique. Second, we are working on one of the fundamentals of reciprocal conversations – sharing mutual interests. Finally, we are also laying the foundations for what we refer to as "mid-level" friendships based upon factors such as shared interests.

Participants:

This activity is suitable for a group or class. Divide them into teams of four.

Getting Ready:

Some medium for recording is needed.

Coaching Instructions:

There are four steps in this activity:

☐ STEP 1

For purposes of this activity, interests are defined as "Things I like to do." Make a table with one column for each team member. In the rows downwards, list different activities that each person likes to do. If the member indicates he likes it a lot put two pluses in the column. If he indicates that he just likes it, place one plus sign.

☐ STEP 2

When you are done listing activities and placing plus signs, take a different color marker and draw lines to link up interests that members share.

☐ STEP 3

Now give each team member a small journal. Have each member record his or her interests on the left-hand page and the team member who shares that interest on the same line of the right-hand page.

☐ STEP 4

Each time they meet, pick one area of interest and have team members observe who shares that interest and then conduct a short, structured conversation about that topic.

Variations:

Have team members co-write a short essay entitled, "Why we like to _____."

Obstacles/Opportunities:

While some Explorers have no shortage of interests, don't be surprised if others have great difficulty generating any interests at all, aside from one or two "obsessions." If this is the case, it may be time for some individual work with that person to generate a list of "Things I am willing to try, to see if I am interested in them." This entails making a contract with the Explorer to try out new activities, give them the proper time to get over the "shock" of their novelty and determine if he has a genuine interest or not.

LEVEL V, STAGE 17, ACTIVITY 108

Preferences

ACTIVITY HIGHLIGHTS
° Developing an awareness of personal preferences
° Learning to share preferences in a mutually interesting manner

Summary:

Like interests, preferences are part of the "stuff" from which our identity is created. We all prefer some things to others, whether that is a type of food, a style of music or a certain movie. Like interests, shared preferences are part of our normal conversational mix. They are another element in "mid-level" friendships.

Participants:

This can be done in a group or class. Once again, divide the Explorers into groups of four.

Getting Ready:

Choose your recording medium.

Coaching Instructions:

Keep away from clichés like "favorite color" which are really conversational dead-ends. Stay with preferences that can lead to interesting conversational topics like movies, music and food. Make it clear that preferences are different than opinions – the next activity topic. When we state a preference we are not trying to convince somebody that something is better. We are just telling about our own personal reactions to something. We might really like Chinese food. But by saying that we do not believe that Chinese food is better than Italian food we recognize that other people will have a reverse preference. We just happen to like the taste of it better. Some team-mates may need some time to make this distinction. As with

17

interests, place each member's preferences on the whiteboard in rows and link shared preferences with colored lines. Have members list their preferences in their Journals accompanied by the names of those who share the preference. Remember to start each meeting with a "preference" conversation as well as an "interest" conversation.

Variations:

As in the prior activity, teams of two can write an essay entitled, "Why we prefer _____."

Obstacles/Opportunities:

Once again, some Explorers have no shortage of preferences and are quite willing to tell you all about them. Others have a difficult time articulating more than two or three. This is a time for a person with a "preference shortage" to begin a Preference Diary and carry out experiments in observing and recording his preferences.

LEVEL V, STAGE 17, ACTIVITY 109

Opinions

ACTIVITY HIGHLIGHTS
° Developing personal opinions
° Learning to share opinions in a mutually interesting manner
° Validating other's opinions even if divergent from your own

Summary:

Opinions are a more delicate subject than preferences or interests, as they carry the implicit assumption that you believe one thing, or one way of doing something to be better than another. Opinions are an important part of our identity, of daily conversations and of what makes us human beings

Participants:

You can do the initial explanation and discussion of opinions with an entire group or class. Work in groups of two for practice.

Getting Ready:

Use a whiteboard and markers.

Coaching Instructions:

This activity has three steps:

☐ STEP 1

The first step is to define an opinion and provide many illustrations to distinguish it from a preference. For our purposes, an opinion is an idea you have about the best way to do something, or that one thing is better than something else. Everyone has opinions and most Explorers should have no problems expressing opinions they have about everyday things such as who makes the best hamburger in town, which sport is the most exciting, etc. The important thing about opinions is to be able to communicate about them in a way that respects your partner's opinions, even if they are the opposite of yours.

☐ STEP 2

Role-play several pairs of opinions, which are opposites and might lead to arguments. Instruct Explorers on how to express these opposite opinions in a manner that would be offensive as opposed to a way that would not be offensive. For example, "I think that country music is only for idiots" is a way of starting a fight. On the other hand, "I think that the best music is rock 'n' roll" is an opportunity to have an interesting discussion that does not have to become personal.

☐ STEP 3

More important than expressing your own opinion is being curious about your partner's opinions. Asking a person for his opinion in a genuinely curious manner is a great way to make him feel you think he is smart and knowledgeable. It is important for partners to practice asking others for their opinions and listening carefully without immediately responding with their own opinion unless asked for it.

Variations:

A prediction is a special form of opinion where we think we know what is going to happen in the future. Predictions tend to be fun to discuss and have less chance of sparking an emotional conflict. Make predictions about things in the near future. Then reflect on the predictions and see how each person did.

Obstacles/Opportunities:

The most dangerous opinions are those where we are critical of something, as this may be the very thing our partner thinks is wonderful! Work carefully with Explorers to coach them away from expressing negative opinions – that something is bad – at this stage of their development.

LEVEL V, STAGE 17, ACTIVITY 110

Emotional Reactions

ACTIVITY HIGHLIGHTS
° Ability to see emotions on a continuum
° Understanding that feelings come in "shades"
° Sharing emotional reactions with social partners

Summary:

This is the next step in developing our emotions vocabulary. It is also the next part of our conversation and "mid-level" friendship repertoire. Explorers practice expressing emotions in "shades" on a continuum, as opposed to yes/no, black/white entities.

Participants:

This exercise is suitable for a group or small class.

Getting Ready:

You will need a whiteboard and markers. Also, prepare handouts with the emotions vocabulary provided at the end of this exercise. Keep the positive and negative vocabularies on separate sheets.

Coaching Instructions:

Tell the group that they are going to practice understanding and sharing more subtle emotions. This time we are going to put emotions in shades. Draw lines and place shades of an emotion along a line to illustrate how emotions can be seen and exist on a continuum, even though they have different names. Various emotions may be represented at different places on a line. Begin with positive emotions. Make sure that each person can find plenty of personal memories for each emotion and can role-play each effectively. If they have no personal experience with a particular emotion you can also find segments from movies that illustrate the emotion. We have included a sample emotions vocabulary at the end of this exercise.

Variations:

Once Explorers have an adequate emotions vocabulary, we compare and contrast each other's emotional reactions to everything and anything from dogs to little brothers. Another related activity is to practice role-playing each of the feelings. You can play a "feelings" version of "Who Wants to be a Millionaire?" using multiple choice answers to questions like "Which emotion would you feel if your little brother is making too much noise and it's hard for you to listen to your TV program?"

Obstacles/Opportunities:

Remember to share the feelings vocabulary with all of the important people in each Explorer's life. Try and use the vocabulary as much as possible.

Sample Emotions Vocabulary:

Feel free to add more of your own!

Positive Emotions

A: Shades of Joy

Happy————————Joyful————————Ecstatic

○ *Happy:* "I am having a good time."

○ *Joyful:* "I am laughing and smiling a lot."

○ *Ecstatic:* "This is the happiest I ever felt. I hope it never stops."

B: Shades of Enthusiasm

Excited————————Enthusiastic————————Wild

○ *Excited:* "I really want to do something that will happen soon."

○ *Enthusiastic:* "I can't wait to do something."

○ *Wild:* "I am out of control with excitement. I can't stop thinking about it."

C: Shades of Pride

Pleased————————Confident————————Proud

○ *Pleased:* "I am happy with my performance."

○ *Confident:* "I know I did a really good job."

○ *Proud:* "I did something really special that I will remember."

Negative Emotions

A: Shades of Anger

Annoyed————————Irritated————————Angry————————Enraged

○ *Annoyed:* "Something is bothering me a little."

○ *Irritated:* "Someone is bothering me a lot – he is getting in the way of what I am doing."

○ *Angry:* "Someone is stopping me from doing what I want. Someone is invading me."

○ *Enraged:* "Someone is hurting me, or threatening me."

B: Shades of Scared

Nervous————————Anxious————————Scared————————Panicked

○ *Nervous:* "I am a little worried."

○ *Anxious:* "I am pretty worried and thinking 'what if.'"

○ *Scared:* "Something bad is happening and I want it to stop."

○ *Panic:* "I feel something terrible is happening and I need to get away right now."

C: Shades of Sad

Sad——Disappointed——Discouraged——Depressed——Hopeless

○ *Sad:* "I had a bad day, I am a little down."

○ *Disappointed:* "I didn't get something I wanted."

○ *Discouraged:* "I tried hard but it didn't get any better."

- ○ *Depressed:* "I feel sad and discouraged every day."
- ○ *Hopeless:* "My life will never get better."

D: *Shades of Frustrated*

Challenged————————Frustrated————————Overwhelmed

- ○ *Challenged:* "This is hard, but I can do it."
- ○ *Frustrated:* "I am making lots of mistakes. I don't know if I can do it."
- ○ *Overwhelmed:* "I give up. I can't do it. I feel like a failure."

LEVEL V, STAGE 17, ACTIVITY 111

It Can't Be Wrong. It's Mine!

ACTIVITY HIGHLIGHTS
- ○ Accurately distinguishing facts and perceptions from subjective ideas
- ○ Validate the opinions and views of social partners
- ○ Convey interest and appreciations for partner's feelings and ideas

Summary:

Before we leave the stage of sharing ideas, we want to make absolutely sure that Explorers can distinguish their own personal, subjective "ideas" from the world of external facts and perceptions. In this activity we teach that internal feelings, interests, preferences and opinions "belong" to the person who expresses them and cannot be judged right or wrong by another. This is in contrast to external facts and concrete objects, which exist in a more "black-and-white" world. An idea, feeling, or preference belongs to me. A fact or description belongs to everyone.

Participants:

This activity is suitable for a group or small class.

Getting Ready:

You will need a whiteboard and markers.

Coaching Instructions:

Provide members with plenty of statements and have them agree or disagree about whether they are ideas or facts. For the purposes of this exercise, ideas are defined as the following eight "idea" forms: Creation, Joke, Strategy, Fantasy, Interest, Preference, Opinion, or Emotional Reaction. See if, as a team, they can be right every time, even if you try and trick them. Have participants practice making statements of each different type and then mix them up without warning their partners. The group's job is to distinguish whether the statement is an idea or a fact. If it is an idea, have them identify which of the eight idea forms it is.

Variations:

Make up "facts versus ideas" quizzes. Make an idea quiz that tests Explorers' ability to distinguish the eight idea formats.

Obstacles/Opportunities:

Remember, facts that I get wrong such as "two and two equals five" still belong in the "facts" category. I am just mistaken about their truth.

17

STAGE 18: WHAT'S INSIDE?

Goals and Objectives

Explorers are now aware of the importance of minds. Next they will explore the complex terrain of the mind and learn that what we see does not always correspond with what lies beneath the surface. In Stage 18, Explorers come to grips with deception and pretense. These are inescapably part of our system of humor, but they are also the cause of much hurt and victimization. They also explore the way we can use our minds to carry ourselves back to the past and into a potential future.

Activity Summary

The stage begins with several activities that explore the implications of pretense and deception. Explorers practice a number of different forms of playful pretense and deception and work to distinguish these from their more harmful variants. Following this, we transition into the mind's ability to live both in the past and future as well as the present. Explorers share important life stories with one another and together speculate on their futures. In this context we address the skills of anticipating and preparing for setbacks and setting future goals. At the close of the stage we explore the mind a bit more deeply. We examine the world of other people's intentions. We teach the internal Self Talk methods to cope with teasing. Finally, we examine what it is like to walk in other people's shoes and end the stage with a comprehensive exercise on empathy.

Critical Tips

- Be careful to discourage sarcasm. It is a dangerous form of communication that typically backfires.

- Repeatedly emphasize the difference between cruelty and shared pretending.

- Understanding the appropriate methods and context for playful deception will take a good deal of effort, but it is well worth it. Like it or not, Explorers live in a world where this type of humor is prevalent.

LEVEL V, STAGE 18, ACTIVITY 112

Should You Believe?

ACTIVITY HIGHLIGHTS

° Learning verbal and non-verbal contradictions in communication

° Discrepant information can be conveyed by different "channels" of communication

° Learning the difference between "inner" and "outer" emotions

Summary:

This activity exposes Explorers to the problem that our verbal and non-verbal channels of communication can contradict one other. In this activity we practice observing and reacting to non-verbal and verbal communication that doesn't fit together.

Participants:

Small groups can have fun with this activity.

Getting Ready:

A video camera and monitor are quite helpful.

Coaching Instructions:

Tell the Explorers, "Sometimes our emotions and our words don't fit together. When that happens, how can you tell how I really feel?" Explorers practice using different communication channels to deliver contradictory messages. They try to judge what the sender of the message is "really" intending. They are provided with four different ways that they can interpret contradictions:

° A smile tells you the person is joking and that the negative emotion is really not the way they feel. For example, "I hate you so much!"

° A pretend voice tells you the person is just joking. For example a big boy can use a squeaky baby voice to say "I'm so scared."

° When a person hesitates in agreeing to something, "Well I...guess you can come over," they probably do not really want to do what they are agreeing to.

° When a person is being sarcastic (using a facial expression of contempt) "Oh, you're sooo smart! You must be the smartest person in the world!" They are probably really feeling the opposite of their words.

Provide numerous demonstrations of these four formats and see if you and the group can come up with any more signals that tell you what to pay attention to. Try to figure out what your partner is really trying to communicate.

Variations:

Have teams make videotapes of contradictory expressions and see if they can stump family members with them.

Obstacles/Opportunities:

Some Explorers may take this exercise as an opportunity to practice sarcasm. Others already use sarcasm to their own detriment. While some people may use sarcasm to great effect, we discourage it. Individuals we work with are confused enough already in their conversational environments without creating even more complexity and opportunities for misunderstandings.

LEVEL V, STAGE 18, ACTIVITY 113

Pretend Feelings

ACTIVITY HIGHLIGHTS

° Distinguishing deep from superficial emotional expression

° Building the desire to know inner feelings and not accept superficial expressions

Summary:

In this activity, Explorers experience what it is like to pretend that you have a feeling you don't really have. Our clients are often victimized because they cannot read the cues of people who are being deceptive. These activities are useful in exposing Explorers to the many ways people can alter what they really think and feel, and teach them to look beneath the surface. On the other side of the coin, it is critical for Explorers to know that often our most important feelings are those we keep within us.

Participants:

This activity is suitable for small groups or classes.

Getting Ready:

No materials are needed.

Coaching Instructions:

This exercise has three steps:

☐ STEP 1

In the first phase, partners simply practice feigning an emotion that is not what they are feeling inside. One example is the game of "Hey you!" where partners practice feigning anger at each other:

- "Hey you! You can't play the radio!"
- "Hey you! I'm getting tired of you doing all that smelly cooking!"
- "Hey you! I'm mad that you broke my car!"

- "Hey you! You're breaking the law!"

☐ STEP 2

In the second phase, partners each work on a poem that explores what it would be like to have different feelings using the following format:

- If I felt _____ I would _____ *(some action)*.

☐ STEP 3

In the third step, partners pretend to be a stranger, trying to convince someone that they are really something they are not.

- "Hi! I know you from school. Why don't you come in my car for a ride?"
- "Hey! I'm a friend of your mom. I'm scared of robbers and I really need you to let me into your house."
- "Hey! I'm the police. You need to come with me right away or you will be arrested!"
- "Hi! I'll be your best friend if you just put this rock on your head and spin around ten times. Everyone will think you are really cool if you do it!"

Variations:

You can practice many different role-plays where one of the partners is trying to deceive the other by feigning a particular emotion. Try to think of some more activities where partners can practice feigning emotions. We are sure you will come up with many.

Obstacles/Opportunities:

The point of this exercise is to help Explorers understand when someone is being deceptive, so they are not victimized. We actively discourage their use of this type of deception. There is a time and a place for playful deception and we will be practicing this shortly.

LEVEL V, STAGE 18, ACTIVITY 114

I am Only Joking

ACTIVITY HIGHLIGHTS

° Distinguishing pretense from reality

° Understanding the appropriate context for playful deception

° Communicating "I am only joking" through effective non-verbal cues

Summary:

The purpose of this activity is to firmly cement the difference between the world of pretense and that of reality. It also teaches Explorers how to use deception in a playful manner. In this activity partners are allowed to make outrageous statements as long as they use the proper "This is a Joke" tone of voice and facial expressions and know themselves that the statement is not real.

Participants:

This is an individual activity, which can be conducted with any number of Explorers.

Getting Ready:

All you will need are paper and pen, or a computer.

Coaching Instructions:

There are two steps to this activity:

☐ STEP 1

"We are going to write some poems called 'Lie' poems. In this poem we make up stories about things that we can do, or things that we did that are clearly true." Show partners the format:

> I _____ *(past action)*
> But not really.
> I can _____ *(ability or permission)*
> But not really.

☐ STEP 2

Now we practice telling each other "lies" without the "not really" additions. Make sure that participants use voice and facial expressions that clearly communicate that they are not being serious.

Variations:

There are many poetic variations you can use. You can also use jokes and story telling – tall tales and fables that the partners write and tell, as long as they are distinguishing between fantasy and reality.

Obstacles/Opportunities:

If an Explorer has problems with distorted thinking, he may not be able to successfully perform this activity without a great deal of support. Yet, like most of our illus-

18

trations, those Explorers are the ones with the greatest need for this exercise, who will benefit the most if you are patient and proceed slowly and carefully.

LEVEL V, STAGE 18, ACTIVITY 115

Absurd Facts

ACTIVITY HIGHLIGHTS
° Sharing playful absurdities
° Using contradictory verbal and non-verbal communication for humor

Summary:

In this exercise we explore another playful side of deception. We explore ways we can be playful and tease our friends, without being cruel and hurtful. Explorers now adopt a "mock serious" expression. Yet, through the absurdity of what they are saying, they communicate clearly that they are being humorous. With mastery of this more subtle form of "double" communication, they can safely participate in humorous activities that we all enjoy. In this activity we play one such game called "Pretend Facts."

Participants:

This is a good activity for a small group.

Getting Ready:

No materials are needed for this exercise.

Coaching Instructions:

Tell the Explorers, "We are going to play a new game called 'Pretend Facts.' In this game we make up a fact that is totally absurd and we try, with a serious expression to convince our partner it is true. But, at the same time, we are going to give our partners clues that we are only joking. Remember how we used our faces and voice tones to show we were joking in the last exercise. Well, another way we communicate we are joking is that we use a very serious expression, but the things we say are so ridiculous, they could never be true." Give the group some examples at the end of the exercise and then let them try out the format. We have provided some examples to give you the feel.

Variations:

To make it even more fluid, have a team-mate listening to the pretend fact, pretend that he believes it and add something to it as an enhancement. For example,

"Women like to grow beards!" "Yes. I know that. And they go to special Beard Parlors to get their beards trimmed." See how many "rounds" the partners can go.

Obstacles/Opportunities:

Some readers may wonder why we spend so much time on "playful" deception. There are several reasons. The first is that this is one of the most confusing aspects of communication throughout the entire lives of our clients. These activities are a great way to understand subtle, non-verbal communication. Second, people do a great deal of this in their social conversations.

Pretend Facts:

- The capitol of New York is Moscow. Really it is!
- A city in Texas is St. Louis.
- Cucumbers are square.
- Apples are triangular.
- Women like to grow beards.
- My friends like to make a big volcano.
- There are a total of 37 people who live in Houston, Texas.
- There are many science projects in the farm.
- There are 243 days in the year.

LEVEL V, STAGE 18, ACTIVITY 116

Imagine the Future

ACTIVITY HIGHLIGHTS

- Authentically expressing personal dreams and goals
- Using poetry for expression of hopes and dreams

18

Summary:

Now we leave pretense and deception behind and move to use the past and the imagined future in the exploration of the Self. As relationships mature, people define their friendships by the perception that they have a shared past and a shared future. This activity prepares the way by providing Explorers with the experience of defining themselves through their own past experiences and future dreams.

Participants:

This is an individual activity. So any group can participate.

Getting Ready:

You will need a computer or paper and pen.

Coaching Instructions:

Instruct members that they are going to return to the poetic format again to write past and future poems. At the end are some formats that you can use.

Variations:

Past and future stories are just as much fun.

Obstacles/Opportunities:

This type of exercise reinforces the sense that we are dynamic entities, changing over time, in just the same way as the rest of the world around us does not remain static.

Past and Future Poem Frameworks:

° When I was little I _____, but now I _____.

° I used to be _____, but now I _____.

° When I was little I couldn't _____, but now I can.

° I used to believe _____, but now _____.

° Now I am just _____, but someday _____.

° I could not _____ now, but someday I will _____.

LEVEL V, STAGE 18, ACTIVITY 117

Could Something Go Wrong?

ACTIVITY HIGHLIGHTS

° Learning to prepare for undesirable outcomes

° Preparing alternative contingency plans

° Learning to analyze and troubleshoot plans that do not work

Summary:

One of the most important uses for future thinking is to aid in anticipating and preparing for possible circumstances that can disrupt even the most thoughtfully made plans. One of the biggest problems of Explorers is having few coping resources when something is planned and doesn't go as expected. In this exercise, Explorers get to make good plans and then analyze – troubleshoot – in advance, what could happen to disrupt them and how they would help each other handle it. Thus, they are prepared for the inevitable "Murphy's Law."

Participants:

This activity is suitable for a small group or class.

Getting Ready:

You will need paper and pen or a computer.

Coaching Instructions:

This activity has five steps:

☐ STEP 1

Explorers are asked to jointly choose and then plan an event. This could be a small party, a visit to an amusement park, the zoo, or any equivalent activity. They make detailed plans which cover all the bases of "Who, What, When, Where and How:" Who is going? Who do we need to help us? What are we going to be doing? What do we need to bring, buy, obtain? When do we go? When do we need to do different things to prepare? Where are we going? How are we going to get there, pay for it, get home, etc. If you want, you can also add "Why" – Why do we want to go?

☐ STEP 2

Once the plan is made to their satisfaction, it is time for advance troubleshooting. Now the problem becomes one of determining what could go wrong and what we will do if it does. Explain to group members that there are two reasons for this "what could go wrong" preparation. The first is so that we can prevent some of the things from actually going wrong. Use the example of a NASA astronaut's pre-flight checklist. The other reason is to "inoculate" ourselves in case something does go wrong, so we do not panic. You can return to the NASA example and explain how astronauts spend hundreds of hours simulating all kinds of problems and emergencies that could happen in space. That way, if something does go wrong, the astronaut will not panic. He has been "inoculated" for the stress.

☐ STEP 3

Team members discuss the types of things that could go wrong, how they would feel if the specific thing went wrong and finally how, as a team, they would help each other to deal with the problem. Do not accept improbable scenarios.

☐ STEP 4

For each "what if" that the group accepts as plausible, they have to find a way of coping with it. The group should actually carry out their plan and congratulate themselves for such good preparation and troubleshooting.

☐ STEP 5

Now comes the really important part. The group should practice their "what could go wrong" plans for several months, until they become a regular habit. After the event, they should review their lists and see if they were able to cover all the bases.

Variations:

An excellent variation is to examine the flip side of future events – unexpected things that could go "right" and make the experience even more enjoyable.

18

Obstacles/Opportunities:

Some Explorers are already experts in what we refer to as "Pessimistic Projection." They immediately see how a plan is going to fail or they are not going to get what they want. They will need some advanced practice in positive Self Talk.

LEVEL V, STAGE 18, ACTIVITY 118

Accidental or Deliberate?

ACTIVITY HIGHLIGHTS
- Considering the intentions of someone along with their actions
- Learning to determine if an action was accidental or deliberate
- Taking different actions depending upon intent

Summary:

Once we begin to be aware of the existence of "inner" and "outer" worlds that may not necessarily match, we discover that "why" people take an action is as important as the action itself in determining our response. Figuring out whether an action is deliberate or accidental is an important function in all of society, even in our courts of law. In this exercise, we explore the concept of a person's intentions and then practice how to determine intentions and how to react depending upon that determination.

Participants:

You can do this activity with a small group or class.

Getting Ready:

Participants should understand the "inner/outer" distinction, as it pertains to emotions and ideas.

Coaching Instructions:

There are three steps in this exercise:

☐ STEP 1

The first step is to make sure that all participants understand that people can do the same action for different reasons. Use as many examples and role-playing scenes as necessary to clearly get this point across. It is helpful for group members to think of as many intentions as possible for undertaking a number of specific actions.

☐ STEP 2

Now we discuss how we can sometimes tell the intentions of a person. The obvious way is to ask the person why they did something. But sometimes we cannot trust what the person will tell us, because we don't know her very well. In that case, we have to play "Intention Detective." Sometimes we can tell someone's intentions by the behavioral clues she leaves us before and after the action. Use the example of someone who does something that bothers you or hurts you. The question is whether it was an accident, or whether she did it on purpose. First we can play detective and examine "clues" from our shared history:

1.   Does the person have a history of taking negative actions against you?

2.   Are you in a conflict with the person?

3.   Just before the action took place, was the person communicating in a negative manner?

4.   Did it appear that the person was trying to impress a group of friends?

The second type of clues come from the person's behavior just after the action:

5.   Did the person appear surprised right after the action? *(Make sure that all group members recognize the facial expression of surprise.)*

6.   Did the person appear embarrassed? *(Again, make sure that members can recognize embarrassment.)*

7.   Did the person apologize with a sincere tone of voice? *(Help members distinguish between sincere apologies and sarcastic or deceptive ones.)*

Now you can role-play scenes where negative actions occur. Have team members work together to play "Intention Detective" and analyze the behavioral clues leading to your conclusion.

☐ STEP 3

The final step is simple; it is to discuss the different ways of reacting when you believe that a person has been hurtful on purpose as opposed to by accident. Remember to emphasize that even if they have been a good "Intention Detective" and concluded that the act was deliberate, it doesn't mean that they are right. It is always best to wait a while, think about it and talk to people you trust before taking any actions.

Variations:

In this exercise we only cover accidental and deliberate intentions. It is important to examine other types of intentions, especially ones where the person is nice to you because they want to use you or get something from you as opposed to trying to be your friend. Many of our group members are easily victimized by someone offering just a bit of kindness or friendliness, never stopping to play "Intention Detective."

Another very important variation is an activity we call "Readout or Signal." When you look at another person's face, you need to know whether what you see is a deliberate communication or a "readout" of what they are feeling and not necessarily wanting to communicate to you. One is intentional and the other is not. You

18

293

respond to a signal differently than you respond to a "readout." How can you tell the difference?

Obstacles/Opportunities:

Some of the people we work with have been hurt so badly by their peers that they enter into this exercise firmly believing that every negative peer action is a deliberate attempt to hurt them. They are showing a classic post-traumatic response and may need psychotherapeutic treatment to help them accept that at least some peer actions are accidental.

LEVEL V, STAGE 18, ACTIVITY 119

Teasing

ACTIVITY HIGHLIGHTS

° Become less sensitive to teasing

° Using Self Talk to cope with teasing

° Learning the best responses to being teased

Summary:

Being teased and put down is one of the major problems reported by our clients. There are two types of problems related to teasing. The first problem is the failure to distinguish gentle, friendly teasing from its meaner cousin – the difference between laughing with me and laughing at me. The second is how we react to being teased in a cruel way. This activity introduces the different forms of teasing and helps develop methods of managing responses so that they do not encourage the "perpetrator" to continue.

Participants:

This activity is suitable for a group or class.

Getting Ready:

No materials are needed.

Coaching Instructions:

First, we distinguish between "cruel" teasing and "gentle" teasing. Someone who cares for you such as your parents or a good friend does gentle teasing. The facial expression of a gentle teaser is inviting or friendly. The facial expression of a cruel teaser is contemptuous or hostile. They also have different voice tones. Make a short videotape of the non-verbal elements of both types of teasing. Try and use garbled words so that partners focus on just the facial and voice elements and not the content. Have each person practice both types of teasing expressions. Make videos of them and use them for feedback. Once everyone is reasonably proficient in distinguishing the two forms of teasing it is time to practice methods for handling the cruel variety. There are six steps to effective management:

☐ STEP 1   TEASING TRIGGERS

Learn your "teasing triggers." These are the subjects that make you react quickly when they are brought up. Everyone has different teasing triggers. Each person needs to find his three biggest ones. Bullies try to find your teasing triggers. Once they find one, they think they have won.

☐ STEP 2   INOCULATION

We call this step "Inoculation" against your teasing triggers. Explain the process of "Inoculation" in a simple manner. If you practice hearing something over and over, you will not react when it really happens. It is like strengthening the muscles in your stomach so that when someone hits you there it does not hurt very much. Practice role-plays where one is a cruel teaser and uses the identified teasing triggers of the other person. Now you can practice simple Self Talk phrases like "That is not true about me, " "If I get upset, he wins," "I won't give him what he wants." The latter phrase is highly effective in orienting the person to not emotionally reacting to the cruelty.

☐ STEP 3   TEASING MAGNETS

Learning if you are a "teasing magnet." Some of us engage in specific actions, or have some aspect of appearance or manner, that sets us apart from others and makes us an easy target for bullies. We call these "teasing magnets." Help each person identify their teasing magnets and work on realistic adaptations.

☐ STEP 4   DO YOU PROVOKE OTHERS?

Another type of trigger occurs when we interact in what starts out as gentle teasing and quickly escalates to the cruel variety. At this stage we believe that Explorers are not ready for the subtleties involved in carrying out any form of sarcasm or teasing and we ask them to refrain from it until Coaches believe they are ready.

☐ STEP 5   CHOOSING THE RIGHT RESPONSE

The first thing we always try is avoiding the cruel teasers. If avoiding does not work we fall back on ignoring and walking away. With a bully this will not work and we have to be prepared to respond in a more powerful way. We need to experiment and find the method that works best for each of us. Three effective choices are:

1.   Quietly nodding agreement in a sarcastic manner, followed by non-verbally communicating how boring his behavior is – rolling your eyes, shaking your head in disgust and using a "half smirk."

2.   Actively taking control. Bullies tease because it makes them feel powerful. We role-play how you can walk over to a persistent bully and tell him it's time to start teasing. The next step is to supply the bully

18

with the "teasing script" and then insist that he begin his teasing "work" right away.

3. Use simple quick comebacks followed by quickly walking away. The comebacks we chose do not fight cruelty with cruelty. Rather they point out the foolishness and immaturity of the teaser to spend his time acting like this. Examples of comebacks are: "Well there you go again. Showing off your immaturity." "Don't you think it's time you grew up?" "Is that the only thing your brain can come up with?"

☐ STEP 6   CAPABLE EXECUTION

These methods will only work if executed with the correct form. We have to spend considerable time practicing both the timing of responses and the proper voice tone and body language. Extensive coaching and role-playing is essential.

Variations:

Some Explorers are not just victims of cruelty but are unwittingly or purposely cruel themselves. It is important not to bypass this and assume that they are never at fault or never precipitate incidents that lead to cruelty. Make sure to sensitize each person to his or her potential contributions to cruel teasing.

Obstacles/Opportunities:

Adults have to be careful not to recommend that school children use the clichéd method for dealing with teasing – "Ignore them and if they persist, tell an adult" – which has been proven over and over not to work with bullies. However, we have to be careful in distinguishing between "cruel" and "dangerous" bullies. Some children, unfortunately, are in settings where their physical safety may be in jeopardy. There is a difference between being teased and being threatened and everyone needs to be acutely aware of the distinction. This is one case where imme- diately informing adults is the best course of action. Some Explorers also need to learn when they are sounding or acting in a threatening manner. They may need extensive practice in making the distinction between gentle and cruel teasing. Do not rush through this!

Who Am I Now?

ACTIVITY HIGHLIGHTS

° Practice in taking on different identities

° Putting yourself in another's shoes

Summary:

This activity is another step in preparation for empathy. We ask Explorers to pretend that they are someone entirely different from themselves. Then they are interviewed and asked to stay "in character" and develop a scenario that is consistent with the identity they have chosen.

Participants:

This activity is best done in small groups.

Getting Ready:

Participants should have completed the prior "deception" activities.

Coaching Instructions:

Take turns interviewing each other under an assumed identity. Each person takes turns being the "Pretender" and the "Interviewer." A sample interview is presented at the end of this exercise.

Variations:

Explorers can write essays, describing a day in their life, pretending to be someone from another culture, another sex, another age or some other variable that is very different from their actual life situation.

Obstacles/Opportunities:

This is a great opportunity to become sensitive to the differences in knowledge, practices, beliefs and lifestyles of different cultures and people. We want to provide as much experience as possible in walking in another's shoes.

Who Am I?

"I am a painter. I paint houses."

"Where do you live Mr Painter?"

"I live in San Francisco, California."

"How old are you?"

"I am 30 years old."

"What do you do for fun?"

"I like to go to Hollywood."

18

297

Empathy

ACTIVITY HIGHLIGHTS
° Understanding the meaning of empathy
° Practicing the basic elements of empathy

Summary:

There is no one exercise that can teach a person a skill as complex as empathy. A number of activities up to this point have exposed explorers to the different elements of empathy. This activity is a more concrete attempt to teach empathy. It won't work on its own. But, it is quite helpful when integrated with the concepts we have been working on up until now.

Participants:

This activity can be done with a group or class.

Getting Ready:

Study the five steps we have outlined below.

Coaching Instructions:

Begin by having a short discussion about empathy. Ask Explorers to share their definitions and provide examples. Now explain that you are going to break down the concept of empathy into five steps. The group will practice each step separately prior to putting them all together. The first three steps are:

☐ STEP 1

Understand the other person's emotional reaction.

☐ STEP 2

Understand the experience that triggered the emotional reaction for them.

☐ STEP 3

Remember a similar emotional reaction that you had and a similar experience that triggered it by thinking of a similar "class" of experience. This is an important place to stop and teach that similar does not mean identical. Explorers may have to learn about general "classes" of experiences. Make sure that everyone is able to correctly classify any episode with negative emotions into one of the following classes. They should all practice remembering and recording several poignant memories that fit into each of the classes presented below. The different classes to learn about include the following:

- Losses
- Rejections
- Disappointments
- Scary situations
- Physical pain

- Failure

- Shame

- Helplessness

Explorers should practice placing different stories into the same class, even though they do not have identical details and elements. Now move onto the fourth and fifth steps:

☐ STEP 4

Communicate that you know the emotion they are feeling.

☐ STEP 5

Communicate that you have had a similar experience.

After Explorers have mastered all five steps, something that can take quite a while, move onto empathy discussions. Talk about experiences in our lives that resulted in fear and sadness and practice empathizing. Following this, you can conduct empathy role-plays. Make sure that you conduct each step of the role-play slowly and with enough periods when you pause and stop the action so that partners have a chance to go through all of the empathy steps without feeling rushed.

Variations:

You can also work on hypothetical empathy questions. Here are three sample questions. Feel free to construct your own:

1. What would you do if a girl in your class came to school one day and sat down next to you during lunch and had tears in her eyes and told you that her mother had cancer and was dying?

2. What would you do if your dad came home from work and told you that he had been fired from his job?

3. What would you do if a boy much smaller than you, a four-year-old, started to fight with you every day and you told his teacher and he was punished and the next day he came over and started fighting again and you told his teacher and he was punished again and the next day he started fighting again and both his teacher and his mother told you that they didn't know what to do anymore, because punishing him doesn't seem to stop him? And the next day he came over to you again and tried to fight with you?

Obstacles/Opportunities:

We prefaced this exercise by saying that empathy cannot be learned from one exercise alone. It is a highly complex skill that builds on the foundations of many prior skills and experiences. This exercise can serve as a culmination of the work that has come before it.

18

STAGE 19: CONVERSATIONS

Goals/Objectives

We have been working on conversational formats ever since Level I, so why is Stage 19 called "Conversations?" It is because in Stage 19 we reach the culmination of our work on conversation. In this stage conversations are finally viewed as pure exchanges of minds. From this stage on, they are the most important means for sharing our experiences and our selves. Now we explore both the reasons for conversations and the means for conducting them in a mutually satisfying manner.

Activity Summary

We begin with an activity that explores what it really means to have a conversation and attempt to distinguish it from other forms of verbal exchange. This is followed by several exercises that focus on the mechanics of interesting reciprocal conversations. In the process we get to practice all the ways one can engage in a conversation incorrectly, as well as how to succeed. While this is clearly a stage requiring some degree of language proficiency we are careful to address the importance of the non-verbal components of conversation.

Critical Tips

- Make sure that Explorers have enough intrinsic reasons for engaging in conversation before starting this stage. The single most important reason is a genuine curiosity about the workings of your partner's mind.

- Do not neglect the importance of non-verbal elements of conversation.

- Understanding the elements of a good conversation does not necessarily mean you know how, or even desire to have one.

- Conversations are not always about agreements.

- Be sure to emphasize the high frequency of conversational misunderstandings that are inevitable, even for the most proficient communicators.

LEVEL V, STAGE 19, ACTIVITY 122

Conversation Functions

ACTIVITY HIGHLIGHTS
° Distinguishing authentic conversations from "un-conversation"
° Understanding the different reasons why we have conversations
° Learning to prefer real, reciprocal conversations to un-conversations

Summary:

It is not enough to know how to have a conversation. Equally as important, or maybe more so, is to know why we have conversations. Real reciprocal conversations take considerable effort to do correctly and unless we obtain enough payoffs, why should we do all the work? We start out with some fun: figuring out different ways to have un-conversations.

Participants:

This activity is suitable for a group or class.

Getting Ready:

Construct ten cards, each representing a function of conversation listed at the end of this activity. You will also need a simple game board of your choosing and sufficient game markers.

Coaching Instructions:

There are two steps in this exercise:

☐ STEP 1

"We are going to start by having some fun. We are going to learn about 'un-conversations.' We are going to practice four types of un-conversation. These are things that superficially look like a conversation but are really its opposite. They are: Monologues, Interrogations, Lectures and Disconnected Dialogues." Descriptions of un-conversations are provided at the end of the exercise description. After defining the four types, practice each type of un-conversation. See if each person can come up with some new un-conversation variations.

☐ STEP 2

Now we explore the reasons for authentic conversations. "You know a lot about how to have a conversation and you also have learned a lot about why we have conversations, but you may not realize how much you know." Have partners guess all the possible reasons why we have conversations and see if you can steer them onto the right track. "Yes you are all right. To say it in another way, the reasons we have conversation is to share each other's minds. Here are the functions of conversations, the reasons why we have them *(lay out the ten cards)*. We are going to play a game in which we practice conversations." Demonstrate how they will use the cards to play a board game. When a partner lands on a specific space, she has to pick one of the cards and have a brief conversation using the function that is shown on the card. If she cannot do this she must move back to her previous space.

Variations:

Just for fun make up some "Un-Conversation cards" and slip them into the deck. See what happens. An important variation is for partners to practice "stopping the action" to guess, or be curious about which function they are using, as well as stopping the action if they observe an un-conversation.

Obstacles/Opportunities:

It is always important to re-emphasize that conversations are mostly about learning what is in another person's mind for no particular endpoint except your curiosity and desire to know them better. Make sure that everyone can distinguish between real conversations and their "un-cousins."

Four ways to have an Un-Conversation:

Monologues are when you are talking and have no interest in whether the other person talks or not. You just like hearing your own voice and having an audience.

Interrogations are when you ask question after question and treat the person like a human computer, as if they exist only to answer your questions.

Lectures are when you tell someone how to do something you believe they are doing incorrectly. You do not want to hear the other person's point of view. You just want them to listen to you and do what you say.

Disconnected Dialogues are when two people are talking to each other and if you don't listen carefully it appears they are having a conversation. But if you stop and listen, you will find that what one person is saying is not connected to what the other person is saying. Disconnected Dialogues are really disguised Monologues. Both people are talking just to hear their voice and are not interested in what the other person has to say.

Some of the Functions of Conversation:

° Sharing and co-creating humor.
° Developing strategies.
° Creating fantasies.
° Sharing interests.
° Comparing and contrasting preferences and opinions.
° Sharing emotional reactions.
° Collaborating to solve problems.
° Making plans.
° Remembering great experiences you shared.
° Dreaming about the future.

19

LEVEL V, STAGE 19, ACTIVITY 123

Conversation Enhancement

ACTIVITY HIGHLIGHTS
° Learning methods to enhance an ongoing conversational topic
° Distinguishing between conversation enhancements and interruptions
° Becoming aware of interruptions and topic changes that disrupt conversation
° Using frequent self-monitoring to maintain conversational coherence

Summary:

This exercise is similar to one we did in Level IV, when we taught how to distinguish between ways of enhancing each other's perceptions as opposed to ways of "interrupting" the topic. This exercise accomplishes the same purpose, but with ideas and not external perceptions.

Participants:

This exercise is suitable for a group or class.

Getting Ready:

Use the game board and markers from the previous activity. Make enough "Enhancement" cards, "Disconnection" cards and "New Topic" cards to play the game. Make five "Connection" cards for every New Topic card. Shuffle them together so they will appear randomly in a deck.

Coaching Instructions:

This activity has five steps:

☐ STEP 1

If group members have completed Level IV activities, they are reminded of the "Enhancing or Changing" exercise that they played. Whether they have done it or not, the game is reviewed.

☐ STEP 2

After Explorers demonstrate their competence, we move to the current activity. "Now we are going to play a new version of the game. We will have three sets of cards: Connection cards, New Topic cards and Disconnection cards. When you draw a Connection card, you must make a connection with your partner's topic. If you draw a New Topic card you can change the topic. I will use the Disconnection card to signal you, when you thought you were connecting but you wind up changing the topic. If that happens, you have to move back three spaces."

☐ STEP 3

Now start the game. Instead of rolling dice to move, players pick a card requiring them to either change topic or connect with the current topic.

☐ STEP 4

The next phase of the game requires players to not only make connections, but to make sure that the connections are interesting to their partners. Explain that there are two types of "making connections" with a partner. The first type is if what you say "fits" with what your partner has just said. The second part, which is our new definition of "enhancement," is when you connect with your partner in a way that fits but is also fun, or interesting to him. Practice both types of connections.

☐ STEP 5

Now add a third level of the game by specifying methods for enhancing conversations. Remind Explorers that enhancements are interesting and fun connections. Cards should indicate the following:

- Enhance your partner's topic by being curious.
- Enhance your partner's topic by being funny.
- Enhance your partner's topic by sharing his emotion.
- Enhance your partner's topic and use only three words at most.
- Enhance your partner's topic by using a compliment.
- Enhance your partner's topic by adding your own experience.

Variations:

Try using these cards with games that Explorers already play, like Monopoly.

Obstacles/Opportunities:

As we have repeated many times, while our activities are fun and a good arena for practice, complex skills like "Conversational Enhancement" will only become part of a person's repertoire if practiced on a daily basis. There is no substitute for practice and for application in as many settings and with as many people as possible.

19

LEVEL V, STAGE 19, ACTIVITY 124

Conversational Tennis

ACTIVITY HIGHLIGHTS
° Remaining aware of the interest of the other person in a conversation
° Working to keep a conversation going

Summary:

This activity emphasizes the importance that both participants in a conversation take responsibility for coordinating the topic. "Conversational Tennis" requires that both partners carefully maintain a balance of regulation and excitement in order to win.

Participants:

At least three people are needed for this game – two players and a judge. There can be more than one group playing at a time.

Getting Ready:

Each team needs a pencil and score sheet.

Coaching Instructions:

There are three steps in this activity:

☐ STEP 1

Explain the game of tennis (or "catch" as an alternative). Explain that the object of our version of the game is not to beat the other person but to keep the "ball" in play. We want to hit the ball over the net so that our partner can hit it back to us. The longer you can keep the ball from being "dropped" the better you are doing. In this game we do not use a real ball. Instead we use a "conversation" ball. If the conversation ball is kept in play long enough, then your team wins. The way you keep the conversation ball in play is by making enhancements of your partner's topic. You also get to "serve" the ball by choosing a topic, or changing the topic. But a good serve is one that your partner is interested in and is able to respond to well. Review enhancements from the prior exercise before proceeding.

☐ STEP 2

Interests should be reviewed based on the "Interests" activity completed in Stage 17. Make a score sheet for keeping track of earned points.

☐ STEP 3

One team member is selected to serve first and begin the topic, a second to receive and a third to be the judge. Each person chooses a card from a deck. When she turns over the card, she shows it to everyone. The card will instruct the partner to do one of the following: 1. an Interesting Enhancement, 2. a Boring Enhancement, 3. a Disconnection, or 4. an Interesting Topic Shift. Each time there is a Disconnection it is automatically time for a new serve – an introduction of a new topic. The judge provides feedback about how well the partner matched the instruction and keeps the overall score for the team.

Variations:

You may decide to begin this exercise on a computer with the partners seated on either side of the Coach. Explorers can then have the added visual feedback of examining their statements in relation to those of their partner. See if you can play "Conversational Tennis" with a larger group.

Obstacles/Opportunities:

Whenever we do a team activity, the possible "specter" of blame and need to win arises. If this does happen, stop the action and emphasize again that this exercise is not about winning or scoring the most volleys, it is about supporting each other as team-mates and helping each other to do the best you can do.

LEVEL V, STAGE 19, ACTIVITY 125

Conversation Rhythms

ACTIVITY HIGHLIGHTS
° Practicing conversational rhythm and timing
° Effectively using non-verbal skills for successful conversation

Summary:

Conversations have their own rhythm and timing that is not necessarily defined by the words we speak. Research tells us that proficiency in the non-verbal part of conversation is critical. This exercise teaches Explorers to be sensitive to the non-verbal rhythms of conversation. Explorers practice "word-less" conversations. In addition they practice each of eleven non-verbal skills that enhance conversations. Initially they practice each skill separately. Eventually, they learn to combine the elements into a fluid non-verbal "symphony."

Participants:

Make up teams of three, with one person acting as an observer.

Getting Ready:

It helps to use a video that illustrates all eleven of the non-verbal skills of conversation. The tape should be broken out in short segments. The video should begin by demonstrating each of the elements on its own and then show how to gradually integrate them. You can purchase a video from our website, or make your own. If you can't get a video, just go ahead and demonstrate the elements yourself.

19

Coaching Instructions:

Begin by explaining that a big part of a conversation actually goes on without any words. We are going to work on some of the non-verbal parts of a conversation and then put the elements together in practice non-verbal conversations. The elements are listed at the end of the exercise description. Begin by looking at the video and practicing each one of the elements on its own. Now start integrating two and then three elements at a time in "practice" conversations. Eventually we want to combine all of the elements in a fluid manner. Do not be surprised if this takes several months of practice.

Variations:

Team members make their own movie where they do a short "play" without using any words. Another great activity is to study some of the films of Charlie Chaplin and have partners analyze the different ways in which he was able to conduct complex conversations without speaking a single word.

Obstacles/Opportunities:

Many people and especially those in the Autism Spectrum learn significantly better when we break down complex skills like this into smaller pieces, master each piece and then put them back together in a systematic fashion.

Eleven Non-verbal Conversation Skills:

1. Maintain a personal space that keeps your partner comfortable.

2. Provide a conversational space to allow your partner to contribute equally. ("Conversational space" refers to two things: to body language, how closely does one sit or stand to one's listener and whether one's body is correctly oriented to him or her; and also to the opportunity one should give to allow one's listener to respond.)

3. Communicate without words that you have something funny to say.

4. Communicate without words that you have something important to say.

5. Look to your partner expectantly after speaking, to indicate that you can't wait to hear what he has to say.

6. Use your facial expressions, body orientation and voice to indicate interest in what your partner is saying.

7. Use voice intonation, head nods and facial expression to indicate that you are following what your partner is saying.

8. Express curiosity non-verbally, while you are listening.

9. Express surprise non-verbally while listening.

10. Signal understanding and enthusiastic agreement without words.

11. Communicate respectfully, without words either through body language or facial expression, that you are getting tired of the topic and wish your partner would talk about something else.

(See if you can think of some more!)

LEVEL V, STAGE 19, ACTIVITY 126

Understandings and Misunderstandings

ACTIVITY HIGHLIGHTS

° Understanding conversational breakdowns

° Viewing conversational breakdowns as constant occurrences

° Taking responsibility for monitoring accuracy and repairing misunderstandings

Summary:

George Bernard Shaw once said that "The greatest problem of communication is the illusion that it has been accomplished." To paraphrase Shaw, the one sure thing we can count on in communication is that, despite our best efforts, it is bound to break down. This exercise addresses the issue of misunderstandings. We want our social partners to learn that they have to be constantly on their guard for misunderstandings, expect them as a part of any conversation and know how to manage them when they inevitably occur.

Participants:

This exercise is best done in teams of two.

Getting Ready:

Explorers should already be taking some responsibility to monitor the accuracy of communication.

Coaching Instructions:

Begin by emphasizing that misunderstandings are a normal part of communication. No matter how hard you try to be clear and no matter how hard you try and listen, your partner and you will sometimes misunderstand one another. This exercise has three steps:

19

☐ STEP 1

The first step is to make sure that we know what a misunderstanding is. Explorers practice purposely misunderstanding each other. There are several different types of misunderstandings to be practiced:

1. Misunderstanding who your partner is talking about, "To whom is she referring?"

2. Misunderstanding the intent of the speaker, "Was she trying to put me down?"

3. Misunderstanding the topic.

4. Mishearing important words.

5. Not knowing some information your partner thinks you know.

Now practice intentionally doing as many variations of these five types of misunderstandings as you can think of. Keep practicing until the Explorers can recognize all five.

☐ STEP 2

The second step demonstrates how a speaker and listener may carry on a conversation without realizing that they are misunderstanding each other. In this step we introduce the concept of the "subtext" of a conversation. A subtext is the words we say to ourselves to interpret what the speaker is really trying to say to us. We are all aware of the subtext of our conversations and the only way to know your partner's subtext is to ask about it. Practice making cartoons where there is a conversation going on between two people and at the same time there are "thought bubbles" that share the subtext. You can use them to illustrate any of the misunderstandings.

☐ STEP 3

In the third phase, we practice ways to reduce misunderstandings. Reflection is one key tool. When we reflect we put our partner's words into our own words and respond in question form to make sure we understood correctly. We usually begin to reflect with something like "So you are saying that _____?" Practice "translating" the speaker's words into your own words.

Another key tool is more straightforward – asking the person to rephrase what he has said or even more directly asking him what he meant. Practice asking for rephrasing in a respectful and positive manner.

The other side of minimizing misunderstandings is to check whether your message was received as intended. The corollary to reflecting is paraphrasing, saying something in a slightly different way to help your partner understand it better. The more straightforward approach is called "monitoring." When we monitor we use different methods to find out if our partner understands us as intended. One form of monitoring is checking your partner's non-verbal cues. As practice, you can conduct staged conversations where one partner begins to look confused. A more direct form of monitoring is to ask your partner more directly if he is confused or if he would like more clarification.

Variations:

You can also practice role-plays where one changed word or one different voice inflection changes the entire meaning and creates a major misunderstanding. A more advanced form of reflective listening includes adding the emotion you believe the other person has expressed, for example, "That must have been frustrating," to check out that you have correctly perceived that emotion.

Obstacles/Opportunities:

Occasionally one of our clients will get to this exercise and refuse to participate, stating that they have no trouble misunderstanding others. They always understand everything. If this feeling is expressed, the person is either in a great deal of denial, or you have moved too quickly to this stage and it's time to move back to less verbally-oriented activities.

LEVEL V, STAGE 19, ACTIVITY 127

Boring

ACTIVITY HIGHLIGHTS
° Becoming aware of common conversational "turn-offs"
° Increasing frequency of checking on listeners' reactions to you
° Learning to observe non-verbal cues to determine whether listeners are bored

Summary:

You may have noticed that we spend a good deal of time teaching people how to do things the wrong way. This is not because we are perverse. It is because we know that one of the best ways to teach someone how to do a skill correctly is to demonstrate very deliberately the ways it is done incorrectly. This was so that the person can recognize it for herself. In this exercise we teach Explorers the different ways that they can be boring if they wish. We also practice ways to monitor listeners for signs that we are boring them.

Participants:

This exercise is best done in teams of two or three, rotating the roles among team members.

19

Getting Ready:

Make up some "Boring" cards to serve as visual cues when the speaker is starting to be boring.

Coaching Instructions:

There are three steps to this exercise:

☐ STEP 1

First practice all the things you can do to be boring. Demonstrate five ways that are almost guaranteed to bore a peer in conversation. Make sure that everyone understands and thoroughly practices each of the following methods. We want to make sure that they have ample experiences on both ends of the conversation:

- You perform a Monologue and don't act interested in what your partner has to say.
- You keep on talking and don't find out if the listener is interested in your topic.
- You go on and on, as if fascinated, about irrelevant facts and small details, without knowing if the listener shares your avid interest.
- You ask your partner a general list of questions about himself, as if you are filling out a questionnaire.
- You talk in a monotone, with no enthusiasm.

☐ STEP 2

After practicing being boring, make sure to practice how you could change the conversation so that it would not be boring.

☐ STEP 3

Now practice how to read the non-verbal cues that signal your partner is getting bored. Again, practice being on both sides of the conversation – the boring person, and the partner who is getting bored. The non-verbal cues to practice are:

- Starting to look at other things around you.
- Fidgeting.
- Fiddling with some objects.
- Facial expressions which communicate that the person is getting annoyed
- Getting up and walking around while you keep talking.
- Yawning.

Variations:

Find more expressions of boredom and practice them. Make your partner uncomfortable.

Obstacles/Opportunities:

As we discussed before, we love to practice both sides of a skill. We find that people actually learn more from the "getting it wrong" part than the "getting it right." It is easier to learn how to do a skill. It is harder to monitor yourself to be aware of when you are not doing it.

In Demand

ACTIVITY HIGHLIGHTS
° Learning different methods for communicating interest to a speaker
° Learning to make other people feel valuable

Summary:

The first thing that any conversation expert will tell you is that one surefire way of getting people to want to be around you more is to make them feel that what they have to say is important and interesting to you. While we have practiced good listening skills in prior activities, this exercise isolates actions that leave your partners feeling that they want to talk more with you.

Participants:

Divide Explorers into teams of three, rotating the observer.

Getting Ready:

No special preparation is needed.

Coaching Instructions:

Tell the teams, "We are going to practice three different forms of making your partner feel that you find him interesting:"

■ **METHOD 1**

Of course the first and most obvious method is to communicate that you find someone interesting at the time of the conversation. Practice many verbal and non-verbal ways of showing you are really interested in what your partner is talking about.

■ **METHOD 2**

A surefire way of communicating that you find your partner interesting is to show that you remember something they talked about by making a point of bringing it up at a subsequent meeting. Have each partner begin a conversation by recalling a topic brought up during a previous meeting. Practice starting the conversation by saying "I've been thinking about what you said (the other day) and _____."

■ **METHOD 3**

Another great method to make your partner feel important is to take some action following the conversation, based upon something your partner indicated he was interested in. Practice communicating that you are aware, from a prior conversation, of a special interest of your partner and that you left the conversation and did some additional research, or found something that related to the interest area and brought it back just for your partner, "I know you like basketball. So, when I saw this article on the NBA in the newspaper, I cut it out. I thought you'd be interested in it."

19

Variations:

Practice initiating a conversation based on a remembered need or concern of your partner. Choose the topic specifically based on a past conversation in which she was told about some difficulty, problem or concern.

Obstacles/Opportunities:

Make sure that Explorers understand that even though we want them to use these skills, they should not expect that everyone around them will do so. This is a continuing theme that we must reinforce. We are teaching skills that will work in the real world, but that does not mean that everyone in the real world uses them, or is especially good at relationships. These are the skills that "Relationship Masters" use. Remind explorers that they should not go around lecturing or providing unsolicited feedback about other people's conversational deficits.

STAGE 20: ALLY

Goals and Objectives

By the end of Level V, the concept of friendship has undergone another revolution. Friends now understand and value peers who demonstrate consistency, loyalty and trustworthiness. Friends must prove themselves as allies, ready to support and stand up for their buddies whenever called upon to do so. The other side of friendship is explored in an exercise on loneliness. In this stage Explorers learn about the need for regular friendship maintenance to avoid loneliness. They face the fragility of friendship and the need to be careful to manage conflicts productively.

Activity Summary

The stage begins with Explorers learning more advanced techniques for stress and mistake management. Without a sophisticated ability for emotional regulation, friendships may be initially gained, but then quickly lost through arguments and hurt feelings. Next, we explore the critical concept of "Ally." Explorers develop a contract with a peer to become mutually supportive and protective. The stage continues by addressing two skills necessary for maintaining a friendship at this level: how to take sole responsibility for inviting a friend over and managing the inevitable conflicts that occur even between the best of friends. The close of this final stage provides several activities geared to developing close friendships based upon mutual trust and regular caring and concern.

Critical Tips

- Don't be surprised if some Explorers do not understand the need for an ally.

- Similarly some of your group members will claim that they never feel lonely, even if they are isolated from others.

- Be careful to explore friendship choices to make sure that your Explorers are not setting themselves up for failure.

- This stage should serve as an important reminder to us all of how hard we must work to develop and maintain a good friendship and how easy it is to damage or ruin one if we are not careful.

LEVEL V, STAGE 20, ACTIVITY 129

Stress 2.

ACTIVITY HIGHLIGHTS
° Understanding the concept of "Emotion Regulation"
° Understanding "fight–flight" stress reactions
° Learning the destructive effects of negative Self Talk during stress
° Determining your unique "emotion triggers"
° Learning constructive Self Talk for managing stress
° Finding your most effective "self-soothing" methods

Summary:

Many Explorers experience relationship problems due to their difficulty regulating their emotional state. Frequent episodes of anger and rage are immediate turn-offs to peers and exhausting to family members. This exercise focuses on ways that our partners can become more aware of their emotional impact on others and more proficient in emotion regulation.

Participants:

These exercises are suitable for any ongoing group with a trained facilitator.

Getting Ready:

This is a multi-part exercise that should be done systematically, over a period of several months. Explorers should already be well-versed in describing their emotions. They should also recognize that emotions occur within them and are not external events "caused" by someone or something outside of themselves.

Coaching Instructions:

There are seven steps to this exercise:

☐ STEP 1   EMOTION REGULATION

Begin by providing Explorers with an introduction to emotion regulation. "Emotions are positive information. We do not want to control or stop our emotions. However, we do want to manage them so that they do not harm others or ourselves. For example, too much rage or panic can have terrible effects on our bodies. Anger and hostility can drive people away and lead to escalating situations." Use the thermostat analogy to help partners understand the concept of "regulation."

☐ STEP 2   FIGHT–FLIGHT REACTIONS

Discuss "fight–flight" reactions. A special type of emotional reaction is wired into our brains. Fight–flight reactions are immediate responses to threatening situations that do not involve any thought or decision-making. Fight–flight reactions are very important in crisis situations, where there is no time to think, such as when you suddenly notice that a big tiger is running towards you. Unfortunately, our bodies sometimes trigger panic or rage when such reactions are not needed and this can cause some real problems for us. Explorers should try and provide examples of their own fight–flight reactions and the types of crisis situations where they might be very helpful, as well as those in which they would present an obstacle.

☐ STEP 3   HIGHER LEVEL REACTIONS

Now discuss "higher level" reactions. A second type of emotional reaction does not occur automatically. Higher level emotions are the result of the way that we have learned to talk to ourselves about a situation. For example, "One of your friends makes a joke about a time when you slipped on a banana peel and dropped a whole tray of food, but nobody was hurt. How would you react to that friend?" Have Explorers discuss the different types of reactions they might have to this event. "You might be angry at your friend, you might be scared that your friend would tell others who would put you down, or you might laugh along with your friend. Your reaction depends upon how you 'read' your friend's intentions, and how you talk to yourself about what is happening."

☐ STEP 4   EMOTION TRIGGERS

Now begin a discussion of "emotion triggers." Triggers are the things that are directly related to the type of emotional reaction we have. The triggers for fight–flight reactions are perceptions that we are being threatened or that someone or something is trying to harm us. The triggers for higher level reactions are the types of things we say to ourselves to interpret the situation. Some triggers are universal, such as a tiger running towards you. But most triggers are different for each person. It is very important that you know what your triggers are. Knowing your triggers allows you to recognize one early on and act before it is too late.

☐ STEP 5   STRESS REACTIONS

Focus on methods for dealing with emotional "meltdowns" and panic reactions – what we will hereafter call "stress reactions." There are four steps to effectively dealing with stress reactions: 1. recognizing your triggers, 2. recognizing that a stress reaction is starting, 3. temporarily withdrawing, and 4. effective selfsoothing. All four steps are summarized at the end of this exercise.

☐ STEP 6

Explorers examine the role of constructive and destructive Self Talk in dealing with higher level reactions. There are a number of steps to effectively manage higher level reactions. The first is the same as in stress reactions – know your typical triggers. We want Explorers to spend as much time as necessary to understand each type of trigger and find examples in their own lives of each of these triggers. It is important to spend time role-playing real and contrived situations. There are three general types of triggers: Sensitive Areas, Catastrophizing and Over-generalizing, and Misinterpretation. Each is described at the end of the exercise. Each type of trigger has its own constructive alternative.

☐ STEP 7

The last phase of the exercise involves applying this information into real-life situations. Explorers make lists of their assumed triggers and typical reactions. Next

20

they construct "Stress Diaries" which chronicle their emotional reactions for a period of several weeks. The Stress Diary should include the following information: the type of emotional reaction, the presumed trigger, how the partner tried to manage it and the results of their efforts. Stress Diaries take a good deal of effort by Explorers to become accurate and useful. Triggers have to be continually modified and re-assessed. Stress management methods have to be tried out, with many discarded along the way. But they are more than worth the effort involved, as they can become a life-long tool for emotion management.

Variations:

Explorers can become proficient at making predictions about typical triggers and "inoculating" themselves in advance by preparing for how they will manage the trigger event. Being able to predict an event, even a very unpleasant one, provides us with the illusion that we are not helpless victims and typically will lessen or prevent the onset of a full-blown stress reaction.

Obstacles/Opportunities:

Remember, just because one method of stress management has worked for you or a particular Explorer, there is no reason to assume it will work for someone else. Explorers have to learn to function like good scientists, developing hypotheses and then testing them out. Be careful not to replace negative Self Talk with over-optimistic Self Talk. If an Explorer failed a test, there is no realistically positive way to interpret it. However, he can learn to use a neutral interpretation rather than a catastrophic one. For example, a response to failing a test can be, "That was unfortunate, but it is not the end of the world. I can learn from my mistakes and do better on the next test."

Managing Stress Reactions:

Recognizing your triggers is the best way to manage a fight–flight reaction, because it is the only way you may be able to prevent it in the first place. If you wait too long, "stress chemicals" are released into your body, you go into a physical stress reaction and you can no longer prevent it. Coaches should discuss their own fight–flight triggers and lead a discussion where all Explorers discuss their own triggers.

Sample Triggers:

- ° I have to wait for something I really want.
- ° Somebody messes with my things.
- ° Someone makes fun of my clothes.
- ° Someone breaks a promise made to me.
- ° I get blamed.
- ° My teacher makes me do something I don't want to do.
- ° I feel rushed.
- ° My parents take the side of my brother and sister.
- ° There is too much noise.

   ° People criticize me.

   ° I'm picked last for the team.

   ° Somebody who I thought was a friend doesn't invite me to a party.

   ° People make fun of me when I make a mistake.

   ° My work didn't turn out as perfect as I wanted it to.

   ° I know that I'm right and nobody will listen to me.

What if it's too late?

If the stress reaction is already starting, you have to recognize that it is happening in order to do something about it. It is important for the Coach to point out that, while Explorers may externally show the reaction in different ways, some people become panicked, others loud and raging and still others silent but feeling like a volcano inside. Discuss each person's characteristic ways of showing the stress reaction. Remember that no one way is better or worse. Videotaping role-plays using each person's characteristic triggers and stress reactions can be quite helpful.

There are two things you can do if you recognize that a stress reaction has begun. The first is to temporarily get away from the person or situation that has triggered the reaction. We call this "taking a break." Regardless of the way that someone shows the stress reaction, the physiology of a fight–flight reaction is going to be the same for everybody. The adrenalin and norepinephrine that are released in the body will cause changes in heart rate, breathing and thinking. People become more rigid, less logical and more perseverative. Even if you are very good at relaxing, it will usually take at least twenty minutes for the stress chemicals in your body to break down enough so that you can calm down and think rationally. You should never argue with someone or try and solve a problem during a stress reaction. The best thing to do is to temporarily remove yourself from other people until you are calmer.

Self-soothing

Now, once you have temporarily removed yourself from the situation, you want to calm down enough to return and resolve it. That is why we call it "taking a break." We expect that most of the time you will return from your break and productively deal with the problem that caused the reaction. You never want to end a stress reaction by running away from the problem, unless it is a real physical danger such as a tiger. You always want to be able to return to it when you are feeling calmer and better able to manage it. To do this, you need to know which stress management methods work best for you. There is no one good stress management method. What soothes is different for everyone. For some people taking a walk is helpful. Other people meditate and still others listen to music. Explorers discuss the different methods of stress management they have tried and compare what has worked and what has not. If they have not had success in the past, they should spend time working on plans to try out new methods and report back on the results.

20

Three Types of Self Talk Triggers:

1. *Sensitive Areas:* Most of us are sensitive about certain topics. It could be a part of your body, your weight, your hair, a problem you are having, and something you are not good at. When these sensitive areas are brought up, you are likely to respond in a "defensive" manner.

2. *Catastrophizing and Over-generalizing:* Like the previous mistake example, some of us immediately catastrophize, or over-generalize in our response to a problem.

3. *Misinterpretation:* A third trigger comes from misinterpretation. We don't stop to check out someone's intention or motivation but immediately jump to the conclusion without gathering information. We make assumptions that can turn out to be disastrous.

LEVEL V, STAGE 20, ACTIVITY 130

Mistakes 2

ACTIVITY HIGHLIGHTS
° Learning to view mistakes as learning opportunities
° Becoming aware of different forms of negative Self Talk
° Learning constructive Self Talk skills to be used when encountering mistakes and setbacks
° Learning to set realistic performance expectations

Summary:

Some Explorers do not know how to be their own "Allies." Many go through life as if they could avoid all mistakes and are tortured when they make a mistake. Others avoid even thinking about their mistakes and thus are condemned to repeat them over and over again. Regardless of the response, when a mistake occurs Explorers have few resources for managing it productively. This exercise provides a more sophisticated format for learning about mistakes. Explorers see that mistakes are a natural part of life. They learn constructive ways to use mistakes as opportunities.

Participants:

This activity is suitable for all groups and classes where there is a facilitator.

Getting Ready:

Explorers should already have had extensive practice in being aware of and managing their Self Talk. They should be aware, from the previous exercise, of the extent to which our Self Talk responses control the way in which we perceive and react to the events in our lives.

Coaching Instructions:

This activity has four steps:

☐ STEP 1

Begin by discussing the importance of mistakes. Mistakes are framed as inevitable and more important, they are essential for a good life. Without making mistakes we would hardly learn anything important. Use many examples from your own life and foster the group to discuss how they have learned from their own mistakes.

☐ STEP 2

Now focus on how the way we talk to ourselves about a mistake results in the mistake either being destructive or constructive. Identify the destructive types of Self Talk following mistakes. Destructive responses tend to over-generalize and catastrophize.

Over-generalizing – This mistake means:

- I am stupid, or
- I have failed.

Catastrophizing – This mistake proves:

- I can never be any good.
- I will never graduate from school.
- I will become a homeless person.

Have Explorers practice making minor mistakes and then over-generalize and catastrophize their responses. Have the group make up their own over-generalizing and catastrophic Self Talk. This can become quite humorous and by itself begins to take the edge off of mistake-making.

☐ STEP 3

Now Explorers work on constructive responses. First present three different ways that mistakes can provide helpful information: Signal Mistakes, Missing Information Mistakes and Risk-taking Mistakes. Descriptions of these three are provided below. Explorers practice role-playing making different kinds of mistakes and choosing which of the three categories to place the mistake in. Along with categorizing, practice the constructive Self Talk that goes with each of the three. For example, after identifying a Signal Mistake the Explorer can say something to the effect of, "I'm glad I got that signal in time, before a really big problem occurred." In response to an Missing Information Mistake, a constructive response would be, "Now I know what information I need to get before the next time I am in this situation." Finally, for a Risk-taking Mistake, Explorers can respond with, "Even though

20

it didn't work out exactly the way I wanted, I am still proud of myself for having the courage to take a risk."

☐ STEP 4

Explorers should keep a Mistake Diary where they track their mistakes and put them in categories. They record their constructive and destructive Self Talk and what they have learned from each mistake. They should discuss their mistakes regularly with each other in their group and help each other "reframe" the mistake in a more productive way.

Variations:

The "mistakes quota" is a great variation for Explorers who over-generalize. Ask the Explorer to think about all of the areas of life where mistakes are always going to occur no matter what you do (i.e. batting averages). Now ask the Explorer to predict a reasonable quota of mistakes for different tasks. Adjust the quota as necessary. When that quota occurs they learn to congratulate themselves for being a success at accurately predicting and limiting their mistakes. They are only allowed to feel bad if they do more than that number. Another crucial activity is to ask Explorers to allow for mistake quotas for the people around them. In other words, they provide a quota for mistakes that people make affecting them and practice not getting angry at that person until they have exceeded their quota. This is a great way to teach tolerance for others.

Obstacles/Opportunities:

Explorers with highly perfectionist qualities will have the most difficult time with this exercise. Yet this activity may hold the greatest opportunity for them to overcome this tendency and learn to live in a "less-than-perfect" world.

Different Types of Mistakes:

1. *Signal Mistakes:* Sometimes a mistake is a helpful alarm that something needs to be taken care of. Certain types of mistakes are telling us we are tired, that it's time for a break, etc. Partners can identify the mistakes they make that are signals to take new actions (i.e. spelling errors, running into people, taking a break).

2. *Missing Information Mistakes:* Making a mistake when trying to use good judgment but not having enough information. An example is that you take a test and fail because the teacher gave you the wrong information to study. Or you are in a social situation and you make a joke about something without having enough information about whether it will offend the listener.

3. *Risk-taking Mistakes:* Sometimes when you take a courageous risk you will make a mistake. But you should congratulate yourself for having taken the risk. You can predict that there is a possibility that the risk

may lead to mistakes, but you choose to take the risk anyway. Making the mistake does not keep you from taking future constructive risks.

LEVEL V, STAGE 20, ACTIVITY 131

Friends have Fights

ACTIVITY HIGHLIGHTS

° Understanding and eliminating use of the major destructive elements of conflicts

° Learning and using the six steps in making a constructive complaint

° Learning to repair conflicts before they escalate, so friendships are not damaged

Summary:

Even the closest of friends have periods when they are irritated or upset with one another. Conflict is a fact of life for all of us. For friendships to endure, we must have the desire and skills to minimize the damage we do and also to repair the damage that is inevitably done. Minimizing initial damage requires the perspective that winning a conflict with a friend at all costs can result in actually losing the friendship. It also requires skills in addressing your own complaints and responding to a partner's complaints without escalating negative feelings. Repairing damage requires that we learn to calm down if we are upset and then move away from blaming and instead focus on acknowledging our own part in whatever caused the upset.

Participants:

This exercise is done in pairs. It can be conducted in a small group with several pairs.

Getting Ready:

Participants must be willing to acknowledge the inevitability of conflicts. They also need to learn that a conflict is not a "fight" but rather a disagreement, where two individuals want different things to happen.

Coaching Instructions:

Explain that a conflict is a natural part of any relationship. Next, identify the major destructive elements of conflicts. There are seven destructive elements, which we call "flamers," which serve to "enflame" and escalate conflicts:

1.   Need to win at all costs

20

2.   Personal criticism

3.   Blame ("It has to be someone's fault")

4.   Put-downs

5.   Contempt

6.   The silent treatment

7.   Aggression or threats (against objects or persons)

Make sure to practice each of these "flamers" and carefully discuss why each one should be avoided. After carefully reviewing and practicing each "flamer" identify constructive alternatives to each one. Constructive alternatives allow friends to have conflicts that do not "burn down" the friendship. You will need to provide extensive practice in role-playing each of these alternatives. We have listed them at the end of the exercise.

Next, practice the steps of making constructive complaints. Below are some typical peer conflicts that you can use for role-plays and discussion. Feel free to create your own.

Variations:

Construct a multiple choice "Conflict Quiz" with items that reflect both positive and negative ways of conducting a conflict. Practice "getting conflicts wrong" by having Explorers deliberately insert inflammatory elements into their conflicts and discussing the effects of "fanning the flames." Learn about the following different kinds of conflicts and help Explorers develop different approaches to each one:

- Differences of opinion.
- Debates.
- Different things you each want to do.
- Your partner's behavior is annoying or irritating to you.
- Your partner is doing something to hurt or attack you.

Obstacles/Opportunities:

Explorers with severe emotion regulation problems can become very upset even during role-plays. They may first have to work more on emotion regulation prior to doing this exercise.

"Flamers" and Constructive Alternatives:

Flamer	Constructive Alternative
Need to win	Win–win positions or compromise
Personal criticism	Making complaints without personalizing
Blame	Blameless, no-fault conflicts
Put-downs	Positive statements to "soften" the conflict

Contempt   Acknowledging your faults ("I have problems too")

Silent treatment   Discussing the problem when you are both calm

Aggression/threats   Assertion

Steps in making a constructive complaint:

1.   Use "softened startup." Begin with a positive statement about your partner. Don't just plunge into the negative. Try to start with an "appreciation."

2.   Briefly state your complaint without making it a personal criticism of the other person. Keep it to as few words as possible. Avoid any blame or personal criticism. Avoid words like "always" and "never." It helps to just stick with your own feelings, rather than making statements that sound like lectures or "truths."

3.   Make a specific request for something that is within your partner's power to provide.

4.   Carefully listen to your partner's point of view and let him or her know you acknowledge that his or her position is valid.

5.   Be prepared to acknowledge valid points that your partner makes.

6.   Be prepared to find a win–win position where each partner has to compromise and find a middle ground.

Sample Peer Conflicts:

° After school, you are sitting in the library doing a library project. Your friend comes over and asks you if you would help him with his homework in another subject. You tell your friend that you need to finish your project, but he still asks you to help him.

° You and your friend just finished playing your favorite board game. You had fun playing the game and you would like to play it again, but your friend says she doesn't want to play this game anymore and it is her turn to pick one. She picks one that you really don't like too much.

° You and your friend make plans to go to a movie on Saturday afternoon. But then on Friday night a girl that you really like calls you and invites you to a birthday party on Saturday afternoon. Your friend is not invited. You would like to go to the party, but your friend still wants you to go to the movies with her.

° You were putting together a puzzle during your lunch break. You've worked very hard at the puzzle and it's almost finished. Your friend comes over, picks up some puzzle pieces and wants to do the puzzle with you. You tell your friend that you really want to finish the puzzle by yourself and you ask

20

him to give you back the pieces, but he doesn't want to give them back to you.

  ° You are looking forward to playing with your friend at recess, but your friend asks some other kids to come over and play with you.

  ° You are playing basketball with a friend who keeps hogging the ball.

  ° Two kids who sit behind you in class keep talking and you can't hear the teacher.

LEVEL V, STAGE 20, ACTIVITY 132

How to Kill a Friendship

ACTIVITY HIGHLIGHTS
  ° Learning to use critical friendship maintenance actions on a regular basis
  ° Understanding the fragility of a friendship and need for constant effort to protect it.
  ° Learning various actions that can destroy a friendship

Summary:

Friendship is a very precious commodity. Friendships are fragile entities that will wither away, or be destroyed without the proper care and respect. This exercise illustrates the importance of maintaining existing friendships. We make a list of all the different ways that you could lose a friend and learn to be sensitive to when you are acting in these destructive ways. Then we practice the constructive "friend-keeping" alternatives.

Participants:

Small groups can enjoy this activity.

Getting Ready:

Make sure that all participants have sufficient motivation to do the "work" necessary for friendship maintenance.

Coaching Instructions:

Begin by seeing if each person can generate her own group list of ways to ruin a friendship. Then compare lists and develop a group-generated "master" list. Remind members of the different ways that they have already learned to be "destructive versus constructive." Once you have a comprehensive list, it is time to begin practicing the enactment of each of these friendship "killers" as well as the ones we have provided at the end of this exercise. First, practice all the "killers" and make sure that everyone is highly skilled at recognizing when they are doing them and are having them done to them. The final "killer" list can include all of the examples listed at the end of the exercise description, and more.

Variations:

Of course the natural variation is to summarize the different ways of keeping a friendship – "constructive alternatives." As before, make a comprehensive list of friendship "keepers" and then develop skills in each one. We have provided a sample list to start you off.

Obstacles/Opportunities:

Many people with relationship problems do not fully understand the degree of ongoing effort required to maintain a friendship. This exercise once again reinforces the need to give a lot if you desire to obtain a lot.

Sample List of Friendship "Killers:"

- ° Invite her over and then ignore her.
- ° Choose the games that most distract you when you are together.
- ° Talk about facts that only you are interested in.
- ° Ignore him when you are too busy doing something else.
- ° Talk in Monologues.
- ° Walk away from her when there is something more interesting to do.
- ° Don't bother calling him. Wait until he calls you.
- ° Only invite her over, if she agrees to do what you want to do.
- ° Use as many "flamers" as you can during a conflict.
- ° Don't ever try and repair a conflict if you do not win. Don't ever forgive him, no matter how much he apologizes.
- ° Criticize her and give her lots of lectures about how she is doing things the wrong way.
- ° Brag about how much better you are in things than he is.
- ° Put her down for things she doesn't do well.
- ° Talk badly about him, or embarrass him in front of other people.
- ° Talk to other people about personal things he asked you not to tell.
- ° Don't bother to learn important things about him.
- ° Get angry at her if she spends time with any other friend but you.

Sample List of Friendship "Keepers:"

- ° Finding out his interests.
- ° Being an Ally.
- ° Showing appreciation.
- ° Keeping away from your distractions when she is over.
- ° Keeping conflicts constructive.
- ° Calling him to show interest.
- ° Learning about the things that are important to her.

20

Friend Maps

ACTIVITY HIGHLIGHTS
° Learning to maintain a mental map of friends' inner lives
° Increasing motivation for ongoing knowledge of friends

Summary:

One of the defining characteristics of someone we call a friend is the fact that she takes the time and effort to get to know us. Of course "getting to know" means something different at different ages. At the Ally stage, "getting to know" usually entails finding out about your friend's interests, preferences, likes, dislikes, strengths and weaknesses. It also means learning about your friend's other friends, as well as her enemies and adversaries. Making a "Friendship Map" is only an initial stage. Equally important is keeping the map updated, as all of us change constantly.

Participants:

Ideally, this activity is conducted with small groups who have developed a degree of friendship. Alternatively a group can do this exercise with each person choosing an "outside" friend to make a map of.

Getting Ready:

Provide each person with a small journal or composition book to record his or her map.

Coaching Instructions:

Hand out the composition books and explain that each member is going to pick one friend about whom she will construct a "Friendship Map." These will not be real maps, but rather a map of "your friend's mind – what she cares about and thinks about." Begin the assignment by presenting the questions listed at the end of the exercise description in a "quiz" format. Following the quiz, members must find out whether their responses were accurate. If the friend they chose is in the group, they can do this immediately. If it is an outside friend, they must report their results back to the group at a later meeting. We have provided some sample questions for the quiz and follow up at the end of the exercise description. Feel free to add your own.

Variations:

Group members can practice interviewing each other, so that each person knows how not only to elicit the information in an inviting manner, but also to provide it.

Obstacles/Opportunities:

Some members may not be able to answer these questions about themselves. If this is the case, "stop the action" until each person can answer these map questions about herself. Some participants might be embarrassed or defensive about interviewing an "outside" friend to verify the information. If this is the case, rehearse ways that the information can be obtained gradually, over a period of several weeks, without seeming like an interrogation.

"Friendship Map" Questions:
- ° Who are her other friends?
- ° Who are his enemies?
- ° What does she like to do for fun?
- ° What is his favorite place to go?
- ° What is her favorite TV show?
- ° What achievement is he most proud of?
- ° What does she hate doing more than anything else?
- ° What kind of music does he like?
- ° What kind of food does she like?
- ° What are some things that he does well?
- ° What are the things that are hard for her to do?

(Add a few more questions of your own.)

LEVEL V, STAGE 20, ACTIVITY 134

Ally Contract

ACTIVITY HIGHLIGHTS
- ° Understanding the critical concept of friends as "Allies"
- ° Understanding friendship as a mutual contract to support one another
- ° Developing relationships with Allies you can trust

Summary:

One element that clearly distinguishes this "mid-level" stage of friendship from earlier types of friendship is the knowledge that a friend should function as a reliable Ally. An Ally is someone you can count on, someone who always takes your side (except when the two of you are having a conflict). An Ally will stand up for you if someone is trying to hurt you.

Participants:

This activity is best done within a group where individuals have developed some degree of trust.

20

Getting Ready:

Make sure that each person has someone with whom they can form an "Ally Contract."

Coaching Instructions:

There are three steps in this activity:

☐ STEP 1

Begin by explaining the concept of an Ally. In teaching about Allies we cover four major points:

1. An Ally will always be on your side if other people are trying to hurt you or put you down.

2. An Ally will always stop and make time to help you if you really need them.

3. An Ally will always try and cheer you up if something bad happens.

4. An Ally is a friend who never says bad things about you to someone else.

☐ STEP 2

Next perform some "Ally" role-plays, illustrating each of the four points:

1. A bigger person is acting in a hurtful manner and the Ally comes to your side.

2. You urgently need the help of your Ally and she stops what she is doing to help you.

3. A negative event happens (such as failing a test) and your Ally tries to cheer you up.

4. You are an Ally and a person you wish to befriend starts putting down your Ally.

☐ STEP 3

The last step consists of each person making an Ally Pact. This is a contract between two persons who agree to abide by all four of the Ally principles. A sample contract is provided at the end of this exercise.

Variations:

Construct an Ally Quiz. Make up questions and then ask, "Is this what an Ally would do?" View movies where children act as Allies and stand up for each other. *My Bodyguard* and *The Sandlot* are two exceptional examples that merit viewing and discussion. Review and discuss famous real and fictional Allies such as Batman and Robin, Sherlock Holmes and Dr Watson, etc. Have each partner create a fictional Ally and write a poem and story about them and their Ally and what would be different if they had one.

Obstacles/Opportunities:

Knowing you have an Ally is a great basis for feeling you will be able to stay calm in the midst of teasing and put-downs. The largest obstacle in this exercise is when someone has no one with whom they can form an alliance. If no one else is available they can make a modified contract with a Coach.

Ally Contract:

Between _____ and _____ Date: _____

From this day on, we promise to be Allies to each other. We commit to the following:

1. I will always come stand by your side if anyone tries to hurt you or put you down.

2. You can always call me, at any time, if you need help. I will always give help if there is any way that I can.

3. I will always try and cheer you up when you are feeling down.

4. I will never put you down or say anything bad about you to another person.

20

LEVEL VI: PARTNER

Introduction

Summary

By the close of Level V, friendships are based on the Partner's desire to form enduring, sometimes lifelong partnerships, from which she will derive her own unique identity and sense of "place" in the environment. Level VI marks the emergence of a real interest in family history and tradition and curiosity about the different roles in the family and in groups to which the Partner belongs. Partners become increasingly aware of and interested in the way their shared past experiences and potential future plans intersect with others. Eventually, Partners start developing true friendships and enduring links with others. This desire, and the accompanying skills, involve us in one degree or another for the remainder of our lives.

Participants

As in Level V, activities are designed for any number of participants. However the need for trust and mutual caring limits participants to those who have already established some degree of a caring bond.

Settings

Again, as in Level V, exercises are no longer dependent on a specific setting. However, the intimate nature of some of the exercises requires privacy in order to establish a sense of safety so that self-disclosure can occur. Relationships can continue over time and space, as Partners can be separated by many miles, over great periods of time, and still consider themselves intimate companions, eager to reconnect and quickly re-establish their shared bonds.

Language

Language is once again the critical dimension of Level VI. Here we see the development of a more sophisticated language of the Self, as Partners explore their innermost beliefs, dreams and fears.

Repair

The concept of "Repair" in Level VI now includes the concept of damage to the relationship. Relationships themselves are seen as crucial entities that have to be maintained and safeguarded. We recognize that, once damaged, relationships are difficult to repair and that we can unintentionally damage a relationship beyond repair if we are not careful.

Coaching Points

- Be careful to discuss issues of confidentiality and privacy of information. A major role of the Coach is to maintain a safe place to share personal feelings and information.

- Do not force or pressure anyone to disclose private information. This could have damaging consequences.

- Some partners will have a much harder time determining their own unique identity than in being curious about the identities of others.

STAGE 21: SHARED SELVES

Goals and Objectives

This first stage of our final level represents another major shift in relationships. Here we prepare Partners to share not only the product of their minds but the essence of who they are as people. In this stage, Partners share more intimate information that can make them feel quite vulnerable. Coaches must work hard to create an atmosphere of trust and confidentiality, so that Partners feel safe enough to make these types of self-disclosures. While there is an inherent risk in revealing your inner Self to others, there is also the benefit of intense closeness and bonding that results from mutual vulnerability.

Activity Summary

Stage 21 begins with Partners emphasizing the concept of "Personal Identity" and the different layers of the "onion" that constitute their personalities. The remainder of the stage explores ways in which Partners can safely share themselves with others. We look at methods of accepting and giving constructive feedback. Partners learn that the way others view them is not always consistent with their beliefs about how they are viewed.

Critical Tips

- Various exercises in Stage 21 are very private. A trained counselor or therapist may be the best person to conduct them.

- Remember to be careful to make sure that a group is ready to safely manage the self-disclosures of members.

- Spend as much time as needed on the concept of confidentiality within the group.

- Make sure to help Partners distinguish between their own core beliefs and the rules and principles that they have been trained to follow.

LEVEL VI, STAGE 21, ACTIVITY 135

Layers of Me

ACTIVITY HIGHLIGHTS
° Provide an understanding of the concept of "Unique Identity"
° Understanding the different layers of the Self

Summary:

We introduce the concept of the Self by using a concentric-circles diagram. The Self is like an onion. When you peel off one outer layer, there is another layer beneath. Partners get to explore the layers of Self and consider the "Public Self" they show to others in contrast to the "Private Self" that may be hidden from everyone.

Participants:

This activity is suitable for all groups and classes where there is a trained facilitator who can develop confidentiality and trust in the group.

Getting Ready:

Be careful to conduct this exercise in a group that already has a shared history and where all members can be trusted to respect the feelings of others. Prepare a "Circles Diagram" for each Partner, consisting of a series of rings with a small circle in the middle.

Coaches Instructions:

There are five steps to this exercise:

☐ STEP 1

Begin by discussing the concept of a Unique Self. Everyone has a Self that is different from everyone else. There are different layers to your Self. Provide each member with a Circles Diagram. It will serve as a reference point for distinguishing the outer Self that everyone may see from the inner Self that may not be shared with anyone. The innermost circle is labeled "My Private Self." The Private Self contains, amongst other things, the parts of us that we are most afraid to share with others, due to our fears that they might reject or laugh at us. This is the part of the Self you may share only with those you really trust. The next level is labeled "My Friends Self." This level is for the parts of you that are shared with pals and friends who have not yet reached the level of trust to share more intimate parts of you. The final, outer layer of the circle is labeled "My Public Self." This is reserved for the parts of you that you share with strangers and those you do not trust. Point out that the outermost layer may wind up having some elements that are the opposite from the innermost layer. For example, someone who is very sad inside may show the outside world that he is happy and always joking, because he doesn't want people to know how he really feels inside.

☐ STEP 2

Coaches should demonstrate the layers of Self by filling in one of the Circle Diagrams about themselves. They should use a standard list of areas of the Self that provide an initial framework. Sample items are listed below. The group should interview you about your placement of items.

☐ STEP 3

Next, you should provide a number of sample items. Partners decide individually and as a group at which level each item should be placed. Some of these sample items are also found below.

☐ STEP 4

Partners should attempt to place sample items from the first group in their individual circles. These can be shared with other group members. If you feel Partners are ready, they can make a preliminary attempt to place items from the second group in the different circles.

☐ STEP 5

As we move through the different exercises and explore more elements of identity, we would like Partners to routinely return to their diagrams and fill them in for themselves.

Variations:

If parents are willing, ask Partners to interview them and to construct the Self "Circles" for each parent. This is another unique opportunity to perceive parents as real people with their own feelings and needs.

Obstacles/Opportunities:

Be careful not to push for too much self-disclosure if the group is not ready to be trusted with intimate information. This is an excellent time to discuss the concept of confidentiality and how information shared in a group should remain in a group and should not be shared with anyone else.

Items for Circle Diagram:

° I am afraid of snakes.
° I like "Knock Knock" jokes.
° I believe in God.
° I am afraid I will go to hell.
° I still believe in Santa Claus.
° I would like to grow up to be like _____.
° I am a great baseball player.
° I am terrible at math.
° I get bored easily.
° I get overwhelmed in busy shopping malls.
° I worry about my parents dying.

21

Other areas to explore:

- Achievements.
- Interests.
- Opinions.
- Preferences.
- Religious beliefs.
- Fears.
- Dreams for the future.
- Enemies.

(You get the picture. Add your own!)

LEVEL VI, STAGE 21, ACTIVITY 136

Loneliness

ACTIVITY HIGHLIGHTS

- Understanding the meaning of loneliness
- Appreciation of friendships as an antidote to loneliness
- Practicing critical reflection skills

Summary:

For most of us the threat of loneliness motivates us to work hard to maintain emotional connections. Loneliness is not the same as being alone, or bored, or needing a partner to play a certain game that requires two people. Loneliness is about remembering times of being together and feeling sad at not being able to re-create those experiences at the present time. One of our most important findings is that some people with relationship problems have more trouble storing and retrieving – "re-constituting" – these Social Memories. As you are aware, we have been working on Social Memories. This exercise examines loneliness from a slightly more sophisticated perspective.

Participants:

This exercise can be done with a small group that has developed trust.

Getting Ready:

Participants should be able to remember and communicate significant Social Memories.

Coaching Instructions:

There are three steps to this activity:

☐ STEP 1   WHAT IF IT HAD NEVER HAPPENED?

Explain that loneliness is when you have a powerful memory about sharing something with a friend and you want to have the feeling again and you cannot. Ask each person to review their Journals and select their best memories with a friend. They can select up to three Social Memories. Now ask that they write a poem about the memory. Next ask that they compose a short story or poem about what it would feel like to never again have an experience with a friend like the one in the memory.

☐ STEP 2   THE LONELINESS SURVEY

There are ten questions that you can answer true or false to. Explain that this is not a test and there are no right and wrong answers. This is just a way of telling how you really feel. After taking the survey, try and use the questions as starting points for discussions about loneliness and friendship. You will find the survey at the end of this exercise description.

☐ STEP 3 THE ACTUAL EXPERIENCE OF LONELINESS

Construct role-plays where something really exciting has happened, such as getting a prize, or winning the lottery and you try to share the excitement with different people. Everyone you talk to is polite and says the right words, but nobody shares the emotion with you.

Variations:

Some Partners take their family's responsiveness for granted. There is a poignant scene in the book *There's A Boy In Here* (by Judy and Sean Barron) where the author recounts an episode during his teenage years when his father was so upset by the author's insensitivity that he did not speak a word to him for an entire week. The author recounts the painfulness of that week as a turning point in his life and his first experience of loneliness. If family members are willing and the partner gives his consent, they can practice not speaking to him for varying periods of time. The partner is not allowed to retreat to his room or electronics during that period, but must remain in the social setting to experience what it feels like to be lonely, even when you are in the midst of others.

Obstacles/Opportunities:

What do you do if someone who is always alone claims that he never feels lonely? If you believe that the person is really functioning at this high stage, then we should assume that this statement is a defense mechanism and the person might benefit from counseling to explore whether he still needs to hold onto this "safe" posture. On the other hand, the statement may reflect the fact that he may have developed many methods of relating to others, but has not developed sufficient "reasons" for relating and therefore we need to move back to a prior level.

The Loneliness Survey:

1.   There are times when I want to share something and there is nobody to share it with.

2.   I see other kids who have best friends and I wish I did.

21

3. There are lots of times I wish I had someone to play with, or talk to but there is nobody I can be with.

4. Many times I don't want to be alone, but I don't have a choice.

5. I see other kids laughing and smiling a lot with their pals and I wish I could be like them.

6. I wish that other kids would call me and invite me over to their houses, but it doesn't happen very much.

7. I feel sad when I have nobody my age to play with, or talk to.

8. I wish I had a friend who liked to do the same things that I did.

9. I wish I had a friend that picked me for a partner all the time.

10. I wish I had a friend who would always take my side and stick up for me.

11. I feel left out when I'm not included in conversations at work.

12. It would be nice if my co-workers invited me to go out with them after work.

13. I wish I could date somebody I find attractive.

14. Many times I wonder what it would be like to discuss how I really feel with my spouse.

15. I wish I were married.

LEVEL VI, STAGE 21, ACTIVITY 137

Beliefs

ACTIVITY HIGHLIGHTS
° Understanding beliefs that help to define your Personal Identity
° Respecting other people's beliefs even if different from your own

Summary:

This exercise helps Partners develop a sense of those personal beliefs that help define who they are. We return to the "Circles Diagram" as Partners define those beliefs that are most central to their identity.

Participants:

This activity is suitable for all groups and classes where there is a trained facilitator who can develop confidentiality and trust in the group.

Getting Ready:

Be careful to conduct this exercise in a group that already has a shared history and where members can be trusted to respect the feelings of others. For this exercise we are using the "Circles Diagram" and merging the second and third levels into one.

Coaching Instructions:

Define the term beliefs. A belief is a principle that helps us define how we live our lives. Some of our beliefs are more central to whom we are than others. This means that if we changed some of our beliefs our lives would be similar to the way they are now. However, altering other beliefs would have more profound effects. Present many examples of beliefs. We have provided another sample list below. Partners should discuss their beliefs about each of these areas. This is an important time to compare and contrast responses and to emphasize respecting Partners' rights to hold different beliefs and to communicate about those differences in a respectful manner. Each Partner should record his or her responses. Then Partners should attempt to place each belief somewhere in one of three concentric circles, representing how important that belief is to them. Point out to Partners that as beliefs move into the outer circles they become indistinguishable from the "opinions" they worked on in Level V.

Variations:

Practice holding respectful debates about differences in beliefs. It is more rewarding if Partners take positions in the debate that are the opposite of their actual beliefs.

Obstacles/Opportunities:

This is an important time to distinguish between holding your own beliefs and following a set of rules you have been trained to adhere to.

21

Sample Areas of Belief:

- How you should treat strangers.
- Your belief in God.
- Your belief in an afterlife.
- The importance of honesty.
- The importance of money.
- The importance of caring for others in need.
- Do you believe that if you try hard you will ultimately succeed?
- Do you believe that bad things ever happen to good people?
- Should you wait to buy things when they are on sale?
- Is there an absolute right and wrong and how can you know?
- Is there a correct way to express your emotions?
- Should men and women be treated equally in all areas?

LEVEL VI, STAGE 21, ACTIVITY 138

Strong and Weak

ACTIVITY HIGHLIGHTS

- Exploring and accepting Self Talk to cope with setbacks
- Distinguishing constructive feedback from destructive criticism
- Learning to give and accept constructive feedback

Summary:

One of the best things about having really good friends is that they are not afraid to tell us the truth about ourselves. If they truly care about us they know when not to hold back for our own good. They also know how to deliver the "medicine" in a manner that is honest but not hurtful. The articulation of honesty in this way is not something that we do with everyone, just with those with whom we feel we have moved into that inner circle of close relationships. In this exercise Partners learn how to manage the relationship of strengths and weaknesses. They work on both the self-management of areas of weakness and setbacks in performance, but also on how and when to give and take constructive feedback.

Participants:

This exercise is best conducted in the context of an ongoing group that has already developed a level of trust.

Getting Ready:

Make sure that Partners are familiar with the use of Self Talk for self-soothing and for planning their actions. Be aware that this is a rather long-term exercise, which will most likely be conducted over a period of several months.

Coaching Instructions:

This activity has eight steps:

☐ STEP 1

The exercise begins with Partners evaluating their areas of strength and competence. Each Partner constructs an "Achievements List," which outlines his areas of mastery and competence. This list can initially be placed on paper but, eventually, the inventory must be memorized so that it can be used when the Partner is faced with setbacks.

☐ STEP 2

Some of us have trouble accepting our achievements. We may over-estimate the degree of our achievement, "I received a 100 on the quiz today. I am a math whiz. I probably know more than the teacher." In contrast, we may diminish the value of an achievement by minimizing it, or "drowning" it in areas of weakness, "Yes I received a 100 on a test, but look at how many C's I've gotten in the past." Now Partners examine the ways that they respond to achievements. Practice both types of distortions using discussion and role-plays.

☐ STEP 3

The alternative to distorting our achievements is called making a "realistic appraisal." An appraisal is what we do when we want to determine the worth of something. Partners discuss how to make realistic appraisals for many different types of achievements and then work on using Self Talk to realistically appraise their achievements.

☐ STEP 4

Next, we move on to areas of difficulty. First we discuss why it is important to examine our difficulties, a term we use in place of "weakness." This is the only way that we can decide how to set our goals to improve. Partners construct an "Areas of Difficulty List" similar to the Achievements List. This list does not have to be memorized. Partners practice balancing their achievements with their difficulties. They choose one area of difficulty, state the difficulty and then immediately "balance" it by stating an equally important achievement. For example, "I have trouble writing neatly but I am a very good speller." We prefer that Partners spend a considerable amount of time making this "balancing" process an automatic habit.

☐ STEP 5

Now begin a discussion about why it is often hard to think or hear about our difficulties. We review the concept of Defensiveness and the role of Self Talk in either making us more defensive, or allowing us to explore these areas without upset. Next, Partners practice using Self Talk statements in relation to each of their listed

21

difficulties. They practice both over-generalizing and catastrophizing as well as realistically appraising and balancing the area of weakness.

☐ STEP 6

This phase involves learning to manage setbacks. Setbacks are defined as events that set us back a bit in our timetable for achieving our goals. We prefer the term setback to failure. We do not want to avoid or deny setbacks. However, we do not want to over-generalize or catastrophize them either. There are three important steps to managing a setback:

1.   First observe your stress level and, if you are having a stress reaction, take a break and use your preferred soothing methods.

2.   Realistically appraise the setback. Listen to your Self Talk and make sure that you are not catastrophizing or over-generalizing.

3.   Use your Achievements List to balance the setback.

☐ STEP 7

Now we move on to the communication of difficulties. First we focus on how to ask for and receive constructive criticism. It is much easier to handle criticism if it is solicited than unsolicited. However, we expect our really good friends to not always wait until we ask. Partners work on how to distinguish constructive from destructive criticism. Constructive feedback is specific and delivered within the context of general acceptance and approval. There is a message that the person values you and wants to share some information that they know is helpful to you. The information is not about who you are inside, but about some action that you are able to improve. Destructive feedback is delivered with the desire to hurt you or diminish you. There is no valuing message. The information is usually delivered in a general form of criticism. It is often directed at some "character flaw" that most of us would not be able to do anything about. Coaches provide examples of constructive and destructive feedback. Partners practice role-plays where they receive both types of feedback. The aim is to distinguish between them, as well as practicing the responses to both types. We respond to constructive feedback by thanking the person, becoming calm and considering what they are saying. We may also ask another trusted person to provide a "second opinion." We respond to destructive feedback by becoming calm and then dismissing the message as being aimed at hurting us. It is important to remember that most destructive feedback has a "grain of truth." So it may be hard at times to see that it is not helpful to accept it.

☐ STEP 8

The final phase of the exercise focuses on the delivery of constructive feedback. The key elements are, 1. to whom you should deliver the feedback, 2. when you should deliver it and 3. how you deliver it. We only provide constructive feedback to our closest friends. We make sure to wait until the person is calm. We watch their emotional reactions and their physical reactions, such as breathing, to determine whether they are calm enough. We always ask first if they want the feedback. We never deliver it without first getting permission. We always begin with a "softened startup." This means that we always begin the feedback with a positive supportive statement that affirms the person's strengths and abilities. When we provide the feedback, we are very specific. We avoid terms like "always" and "never" and we always end by emphasizing our confidence that the person can easily overcome the difficulty without much effort. After Partners understand all of these principles, begin role-plays in which Partners practice both delivering and receiving constructive feedback. Make sure to include characters in the role-plays who appear highly stressed and situations in which the character refuses the offered feedback. Also mix in some destructive criticism to make sure that Partners continue to see the distinction.

Variations:

Make sure that Partners record their difficulties and setbacks in their Circles Diagram. Keeping an Achievements and Setbacks Journal is an excellent tool for mastering this exercise. Once Partners have mastered this exercise, we can move on to how to deliver constructive feedback to yourself. The method is the same as if you are delivering it to a good friend. But, it is quite important for Partners to practice the delivery using a self-dialogue. How often do we all treat ourselves like our worst enemy rather than a loving friend?

Obstacles/Opportunities:

This is a great opportunity to help Partners who may suffer from depression. We know that depression is often greatly exacerbated by faulty self-statements, especially around achievements and setbacks. Learning to accept your successes and setbacks in a realistic manner is amazingly helpful in combating this disorder. People with depressive tendencies benefit greatly from maintaining an ongoing Achievements and Setbacks Journal once they learn methods of realistic appraisal.

LEVEL VI, STAGE 21, ACTIVITY 139

How do you see me?

ACTIVITY HIGHLIGHTS

° Learning how you are perceived by others

° Learning how to get an accurate picture of how others see you

Summary:

It is critical for Partners to develop a sense of themselves that is not a complete reflection of who the world tells them they are. But by the same token we cannot

21

downplay the importance of remaining open to the way in which others view us. It is not that one is more important than the other. They are both different aspects of our personalities. In this exercise, Partners contrast the way they believe they come across to others, with the perceptions of their peers.

Participants:

As with most of the exercises at this stage, we recommend a trained counselor and a group that has developed trust, confidentiality and mutual caring.

Getting Ready:

Materials include a number of copies of an "Adjective Checklist" describing different personality traits. Many versions of this are available. We have included a short sample checklist at the end of this exercise.

Coaching Instructions:

This activity has six steps:

☐ STEP 1

Explain the following to Partners, "We are going to look at the way other people see us. Do not be surprised if this differs from the way that we think they see us." Hand out an Adjective Checklist to each of the Partners. "Each word on the checklist represents a different aspect of personality. I want you to go through each item on the list and circle either the 1, 2 or 3 next to it. If you circle the '1' it means you think the word does not really describe the way other people see you. If you circle the '2' it means that you believe that some people may see you this way or they may see you a bit this way. A '3' means that you believe that other people will often see you in this way. Remember you are rating how you believe other people see you. Do not rate how you see yourself." Make sure that Partners place their names on the checklist. Allow Partners sufficient time to complete the checklist and ask them to hand their checklists to you once they are done.

☐ STEP 2

Now hand out sufficient blank checklists and ask them to rate the way that they see each of the Partners in the group. Make sure that they place the name of the person they are rating at the top of the sheet. When they are done, collect all the ratings. Make sure to keep them in a separate pile from the initial set.

☐ STEP 3

Now comes the tedious part. You must compute an average score from each of the ratings made by each of the group members, so that each Partner will have just one average rating to compare his own ratings to. The group can aid you in this if you wish. Once the averages are computed place them next to the ratings that each Partner made of how he thought others would see him.

☐ STEP 4

Now we finally get to the interesting part of the exercise. Hand back the single sheet containing the Partners' ratings of how they thought others see them with the actual "others" ratings next to each of their own ratings. Ask them to examine the ratings and evaluate how accurate they were. Ask them to note which areas had the biggest discrepancy (for example an item they rated as a "1" and others rated as a "3"). Ask them to look at how well they did overall. How many of the items were they accurate about and how many were they not?

☐ STEP 5

Now the group can discuss their perceptions. If they are willing they can ask the group about the items that most surprised them. This can be invaluable feedback.

☐ STEP 6

Partners can now discuss how difficult it may be to always know how others see you and ways that you may be able to obtain more accurate information, without interrogating the people around you. Good friends can be trusted to provide you with accurate feedback about how you are coming across to others.

Variations:

An important activity is to ask the Partners to fill out the checklist as they actually see themselves and then to compare this rating with the one they made about how they believe others see them. Some of the Partners will be similar in both ratings. Others will be quite different. This leads to the possibility of very interesting discussions of how much of yourself you should show the world.

Obstacles/Opportunities:

You can use the results of the exercise as an opportunity to set goals for those Partners wishing to alter their public "images." Remember to reassure Partners that this is not a test and the fact that their ratings were discrepant from the group evaluation is not a judgment about their ability, intelligence or anything else. It is quite common for this discrepancy to exist. On the other hand, it is important feedback for those members whose ratings were highly discrepant from the group. It means they do not accurately perceive how they are coming across to others and that it would be in their best interests to improve in this area.

How Others See Me Survey:

Instructions:

Circle either 1, 2 or 3 next to a different aspect of personality.

Description	My Perception 1 2 3	Average "others" rating 1 2 3	Difference
1. Happy go lucky	1 2 3	1 2 3	
2. Serious	1 2 3	1 2 3	
3. Nervous	1 2 3	1 2 3	
4. Peaceful	1 2 3	1 2 3	
5. Thoughtful	1 2 3	1 2 3	

21

6. Impulsive	1	2	3	1	2	3	
7. Emotional	1	2	3	1	2	3	
8. Quiet	1	2	3	1	2	3	
9. Talkative	1	2	3	1	2	3	
10. Compassionate	1	2	3	1	2	3	
11. Empathic	1	2	3	1	2	3	
12. Aloof	1	2	3	1	2	3	
13. Leader	1	2	3	1	2	3	
14. Follower	1	2	3	1	2	3	
15. Curious	1	2	3	1	2	3	
16. Forthright	1	2	3	1	2	3	
17. Hidden	1	2	3	1	2	3	
18. Fearful	1	2	3	1	2	3	
19. Courageous	1	2	3	1	2	3	
20. Powerful	1	2	3	1	2	3	
21. Helpless	1	2	3	1	2	3	
22. Self-absorbed	1	2	3	1	2	3	
23. Arrogant	1	2	3	1	2	3	
24. Warm	1	2	3	1	2	3	

LEVEL VI, STAGE 21, ACTIVITY 140

Private Me

ACTIVITY HIGHLIGHTS

° Learning to access and communicate safely about your innermost feelings

Summary:

In Level V we used poetry to help examine unique ideas and feelings. In this activity Partners use poetry to define their Unique Identities. One of the ways we determine our Unique Identity is by comparing and contrasting ourselves to others. Poems are an excellent device for this comparison process.

Participants:

This activity is suitable for any group or class size.

Getting Ready:

Partners should be familiar with the structured poetic frameworks we used in Level V. If they have not done these, we recommend beginning with Level V poetry activities first. As in Level V poems, choose the recording medium that best suits each Partner. Often, if we are working one-on-one, we will continue to do the keyboarding, while the Partner we are working with does the poetic work. This reduces the number of tasks he has to do and also provides him with immediate visual feedback of his efforts.

Coaching Instructions:

Partners are told that they are going to be writing poems that help them think about who they are. Partners are encouraged to use several different poetic frameworks for self-exploration. Following construction of poems we want Partners to return to their "Circles Diagram" and determine if there is any additional information to place in their two innermost circles. We have provided three formats. See if you can devise several more.

Like but not Like

I am like _____ because I _____

But I'm not like _____ because _____.

Who am I Really?

To my parents I am _____

And to my teacher I am _____

To strangers I'm _____

To my enemies I am _____

To my friends I am _____

To my sister/brother I am _____

But to myself I am _____.

People May Think

People may think I am _____

But really I am _____.

(Repeated four times)

Variations:

There are unlimited poetry and story-writing frameworks you can use for identity exploration. One variation is to explore another person's identity in more depth. You can use the format of "A Day in the Life of" to do this if you wish.

21

Obstacles/Opportunities:

Kenneth Koch's books provide an excellent introduction to using poetry for identity development. Readers will come away with many ideas for creating their own poetic formats. In this exercise, we do not yet encourage Partners to share their poems with the rest of the group. However, if you believe that the group has built up enough trust, you have the option of doing so.

LEVEL VI, STAGE 21, ACTIVITY 141

"Me" Executive Summary

ACTIVITY HIGHLIGHTS

° Describing your Personal Identity to another person
° Determining your special/unique qualities
° Learning to share what is most relevant about you

Summary:

Your Personal Identity is a highly complex thing. It is difficult for any of us to describe who we are, even given an infinite amount of time. However, it is extremely helpful to possess a sort of "Executive Summary" of yourself. For those of you not familiar with the term, an Executive Summary is typically a one-page document affixed to the front of a much larger business plan or proposal that provides the essence of the document to the company's CEO or president who is assumed to be too busy to read everything that crosses his or her desk. Most of us go through life treating other people as if we are busy CEOs. If they cannot produce for us a succinct and understandable Executive Summary of who they are and what they are about, we tend to pass them by and not take a deeper look at them. Of course the trick of a good Executive Summary is to make the reader curious and excited enough to want to read on. A boring recitation of the facts just will not do. This is really an exercise that summarizes all of the work that our Partners have done in this stage.

Participants:

This activity is suitable for any group or classroom setting.

Getting Ready:

Partners have the choice of including their condition in the Executive Summary. They will need to access their responses to all of the prior exercises in this stage in order to complete this activity.

Coaching Instructions:

Tell Partners that they will each be constructing a one-page summary of themselves. They will begin by reviewing each of the exercises they have completed in this stage and picking out several key points from each to include in their summary. The job is to pick out only the two or three most important points from each, so that the finished product can fit on a single typed page. Request Partners to break into smaller groups of up to four to help each other in making selections. Partners have to choose the most critical information about themselves from the following exercises:

- "Layers of Me"
- "Beliefs"
- "Private Me"

After they have made their selections and written their outlines, have each Partner read hers to the group. Allow the group to provide constructive feedback. However, the final decision of what is included should be left up to the Partner. At the close of the exercise, ask Partners to turn the outline into a one-page story. Help Partners to write their stories so that they would interest a reader enough to desire to get to know the Partner better.

Variations:

Ask Partners to write a one-page Executive Summary about one of their family members or best friends.

Obstacles/Opportunities:

This is a great opportunity for Partners to practice finding the most relevant information from a mass of data. It is also good practice for learning to summarize and synthesize information. It will also help immensely in conversations with new people.

21

STAGE 22: FAMILY ROOTS

Goals and Objectives

Partners have long been aware that they belong to families. The unique change reflected in Stage 22 is the budding awareness of family members as unique individuals with their own needs, dreams and fears. Along with this shift in perception, partners become aware of the family as a powerful, permanent entity. It is a system of many interlocking relationships that has a meaningful history and future to which we are inextricably connected. In this stage we explore the meaning of being a contributing member of both a nuclear and extended family. We especially focus on the growing responsibility of Partners to take their equal share in providing for the emotional needs of family members.

Activity Summary

The stage begins with several "Family Maps" exercises. Each asks Partners to examine their knowledge of the inner worlds of other family members. As the stage progresses, activities increasingly emphasize Partners' emotional responsibility towards family members.

Critical Tips

- Be sure that Partners recognize that their "Family Maps" must be regularly updated in order to be useful.

- Make sure that family members are providing accurate feedback to the Partner and are no longer "sugar-coating" their comments.

- In learning family history and constructing Family Maps, make sure that Partners stay focused on the larger picture – learning about their rich heritage and connections – rather than becoming caught up in fact finding and data collection.

- Teaching family members effective methods for productively managing their conflicts is a great way to place Partners in a competent role in their family.

LEVEL VI, STAGE 22, ACTIVITY 142

Family Maps 1.

ACTIVITY HIGHLIGHTS
° Viewing family members as real people with their own needs
° Caring about the "emotional worlds" of family members

Summary:
Some Partners seem unaware that their family members are real people with their own hopes, dreams, fears and separate lives. This exercise aims to teach our Partners to develop and maintain working "maps" of the internal worlds of their family members.

Participants:
This exercise is suitable for groups and classes.

Getting Ready:
To prepare for this exercise, have each Partner list the members of his or her nuclear family as well as other family members with whom they have frequent contact.

Coaching Instructions:
Remind Partners of the "Friends Map" exercises they all should have completed. Now, instead of mapping a friend, we are going to map our closest family members. Each Partner should begin by choosing a parent for their first map. After the parent has been chosen, have the Partner take a simple quiz to determine how much they already know about that Partner. After the parent takes the quiz, "score" it by interviewing the parent. The Partner's job is to obtain accurate information and record it on a page reserved for that family member. The process then continues for each family member. There are some sample "Family Maps" questions below. Feel free to add your own. Remember not to focus on facts or numbers but on the subjective experience of each family member. Substitute more relevant information for non-working parents, grandparents and younger siblings.

Variations:
Partners can construct "Family Maps" for all family members as well as for themselves. This allows for some very instructive comparing and contrasting.

Obstacles/Opportunities:
Make sure that Partners realize that they will change on a regular basis, so their maps must be kept updated.

Family Maps Quiz 1: My Father

1. Who is your father's best friend?

2. What is your father's favorite food?

3. What is your father's favorite type of music?

4. What is your dad's favorite TV show?

5. What does your father like best about his job?

6. What does your father dislike the most about his job?

7. What is the biggest stress in your dad's life?

8. What does your father like to do to relax?

9. Where does your father like to go for vacations?

10. Where would your dad like to live someday?

11. Who does your father go to when he needs help or advice?

LEVEL IV, STAGE 22, ACTIVITY 143

Family Maps 2.

ACTIVITY HIGHLIGHTS
° Learning to evaluate the effect of your actions on family members
° Recognizing the need for ongoing maintenance of good family relationships

Summary:

This exercise personalizes "Family Maps" by examining the relationship between the Partner and a family member. Partners are challenged to think about the need to work hard if they wish to maintain a close relationship with family members.

Getting Ready:

Partners should have completed Part I of the "Family Maps" activity.

Coaching Instructions:

Instruct Partners that now they are doing Part II of the "Family Maps" exercise. In this activity they will examine the feelings of their family members as they relate to the Partner. As in the prior exercise, have Partners choose a family member to begin with. Make sure it is a different family member than before. Now administer the "Family Maps Quiz 2" for that family member and proceed as in the prior activity. A sample "Family Maps Quiz 2" is at the end of this activity.

Variations:

Continue mapping all other family members. Again, it is quite instructive for Partners to compare and contrast the way that different family members view the

22

relationship with them, along with the different ways the family members would like the Partner to meet their needs.

Obstacles/Opportunities:

This is a great opportunity for Partners to become aware of the impact they have on other family members. It is also a good way for Partners to begin to discover the expectations that the family has for them.

Family Maps Quiz 2: My Mother and Me

1. What are three things that your mother would enjoy doing with you on a regular basis?

2. What are three things that your mother has done for you that most mothers might not do for their sons/daughters?

3. List the interests that you share with your mother.

4. What are five things that you do that can hurt your mother's feelings?

5. List three things you do that really irritate your mother.

6. What are three things you could do to help your mother?

7. What could you do to surprise your mother if she was feeling down?

8. How many times a week do you act in some way that makes your mother angry?

9. How often do you do something that makes your mom sad or tearful?

10. How often does your mom feel that you act like you care about her?

LEVEL VI, STAGE 22, ACTIVITY 144

Family Maps 3.

ACTIVITY HIGHLIGHTS

° Applying knowledge of family members to real-life ways of caring for them

Summary:

Now Partners get to apply their knowledge and see if their "Family Maps" are accurate. Their assignment is to choose a holiday or birthday present that would be uniquely appropriate for each family member.

Participants:

This is an excellent exercise for a group or class.

Getting Ready:

Partners should have some understanding of the value of money. If Partners have no ready recourse to money, you can easily satisfy other types of "gifts" such as commitments to do some type of chores or housework.

Coaching Instructions:

Each Partner uses their list of important family members. The assignment is to use their well-developed "Family Maps" to choose an appropriate gift for family members for either an upcoming holiday or a birthday. The present selected should fit an interest or preference of that person. It should be something that the person would really want and be excited about receiving. It should also be something that is within the means of the Partner to buy, if they save some money. Partners have to provide a specific rationale for each present. They have to then check out their ideas with the family member and report the results.

Variations:

An excellent follow-up exercise is to ask Partners to choose a vacation that everyone would enjoy, using the same format. Another excellent variation would be for Partners to actually save up their money and give the gifts they have selected.

Obstacles/Opportunities:

Family members who may have never before received a gift from this particular person have to pledge to be honest and not pretend to be excited by any idea a Partner has about what they would like.

22

LEVEL VI, STAGE 22, ACTIVITY 145

Family Appreciations

ACTIVITY HIGHLIGHTS
° Learn to regularly acknowledge the caring actions of family members
° Learn the value of communicating appreciation

Summary:

We all take our family members for granted to one extent or another, but this is particularly true for many of our Partners. People with these conditions often contribute greatly to the love and richness of the family, but they also draw heavily on the family's emotional and sometimes financial resources. The "Family Appreciations" exercise is one of several that teaches Partners how to make sure they are acknowledging the love and care that their family members provide for them.

Participants:

Suitable for groups of any size.

Getting Ready:

Partners should first have a good working understanding of the concept of appreciation. Appreciation is defined as communicating the value that you place upon what another person provides or gives to you.

Coaching Instructions:

This exercise has four steps:

☐ STEP 1

Partners begin the exercise by estimating the number of times per week they communicate their appreciation to different family members. They should provide examples of how they express appreciation.

☐ STEP 2

The next step is to role-play how to communicate an appreciation. Appreciations must be about highly specific things and not about general qualities such as "good" or "nice." An example would be, "I appreciate the way that you prepare breakfast for me every morning."

☐ STEP 3

After you are sure that all Partners know how to effectively deliver appreciation, ask them to construct an "Appreciation List" for each family member. They can choose from a sample list, or make one of their own.

☐ STEP 4

The final part of the exercise is to develop and carry out a plan for regularly communicating appreciations to family members. Partners use an "Appreciation Calendar" to plan their appreciations for the week.

Variations:

An excellent follow-up activity is to relate appreciations given to the treatment that the partners receive from family members. Partners can track the number of times they are appreciated in a week and then observe the change in their own receipt of appreciations as they provide them to others. Another important activity is to extend appreciations out from the family to other relationships such as teachers, co-workers and friends. We would like our Partners to recognize that just a little appreciation goes a long way.

Obstacles/Opportunities:

It is important for family members to actively model appreciations. They will quickly die out if they do not become a regular facet of family life. The dinner table is a great place to set up an appreciation ritual, as are regular family meetings.

Sample Appreciations:

I appreciate you for:
- Making my breakfast (lunch, dinner).
- Taking me to my favorite activities.
- Buying me surprise gifts.
- Helping me with my homework.
- Sharing your toys and games with me *(sibling)*.
- Letting me watch the TV show I want to watch, even though you don't really like it.
- Shooting baskets with me.
- Not punishing me after I have a meltdown.
- Taking me to the swimming pool.
- Telling me funny jokes that make me laugh.
- Spending time to have conversations with me.
- Teaching me how to _____.
- Giving me hugs.

22

LEVEL VI, STAGE 22, ACTIVITY 146

Family Stories

ACTIVITY HIGHLIGHTS
° Learning about the emotional history of your family
° Appreciating pivotal family events
° Developing family pride

Summary:

Shared memory is the ultimate emotional "glue" that binds us together. The same is true for family relationships. Any child that grows up without knowing the pivotal stories of how his family came to be as it is today will not fully value his family membership. In this exercise, Partners construct the beginnings of a family "Story Book" that hopefully will be enlarged and updated and shared regularly. Along with pivotal stories, Partners collect the humorous moments that we all like to share and laugh about at family gatherings ("Remember the time when _____").

Participants:

A group of any size can do this exercise.

Getting Ready:

Completion of previous family activities is necessary.

Coaching Instructions:

Partners are asked if they know any of their "pivotal" family stories. A pivotal story is defined as a "turning point" in a family member or in the functioning of the family as a unit. A sample of pivotal story topics is presented below. If Partners already know stories, they are asked to record them in "episode" format – a simple story-like narrative that is similar to the way in which one would relate a story to another person to keep her interested. The next assignment is for Partners to interview important family members and obtain their versions of the pivotal stories. The type of interviewing we want Partners to learn is different from an interrogation. Partners should practice asking a simple question, showing interest in the response and allowing the family member sufficient time to answer. Only then should the partner ask follow-up questions and these should be based upon the specifics of what the member has shared, rather than just moving on to the next question.

Variations:

After recording pivotal stories, Partners can turn to funny or silly stories. These can be collected from nuclear or extended family members. Another variation is to have Partners interview several different family members who were involved in the same episode. Record the different versions of the story and compare and contrast them.

Obstacles/Opportunities:

This is an opportunity to learn that there are multiple versions of any story.

Pivotal Story Sample Topics:

- The biggest crisis in my mother's life.
- Why we are no longer close with _____ *(a family member)*.
- How my parents met and decided to get married.
- How my grandparents came to live in _____.
- How people helped each other in a crisis.

Sample Interview Format:

- Tell me about how you and mom met?
- And what happened next?
- Did you know that you liked her right from the start?
- When did you decide she was the right one for you?

LEVEL VI, STAGE 22, ACTIVITY 147

Family Emotions Bank

ACTIVITY HIGHLIGHTS

- Learning the need for reciprocity
- Establishing a more equal give-and-take relationship with other family members
- Learning the damaging effect that negative actions can have on an emotional relationship
- Learning that only the affected person can judge the impact of your hurtful behavior

Summary:

There is no doubt that some of our Partners use a disproportionate share of the total family resources. If not placed in check, this tendency to use up finite resources can lead to resentment and burnout. This exercise requires Partners to begin tracking their "deposits" and "withdrawals" from the "Family Emotional Bank Account." In real-life there are two hard facts about emotional deposits and withdrawals. The first is that only the person who has been impacted by a withdrawal can judge how big the withdrawal has been and the second fact is that withdrawals have a much greater impact than deposits. In other words, it takes more than one deposit to make up for a withdrawal.

Participants:

Any group or class setting is appropriate. Family participation is essential.

22

Getting Ready:

Make sure that family members are willing to participate in the bank account system. This may require careful explanation that you are not trying to impose some "tit-for-tat" bookkeeping system on the family. In addition, some members may object that withdrawals must be compensated for by more than one deposit. Unfortunately, that is a fact of life for all of us. The difficulty of repair is an important reason why we work so hard not to hurt others in the first place.

Coaching Instructions:

This activity has two steps:

☐ STEP 1

Introduce the emotional bank account system to Partners. Explain the concept of deposits (actions that leave family members feeling better and more cared about) and withdrawals (actions that leave family members feeling stressed and/or angry). Make up a sample list of deposits and withdrawals. Pick one family member and ask Partners to rate how big a deposit or withdrawal each item on the list would be, using a one to three scale, where one is a small deposit/withdrawal and three is a large one. After ratings have been made, it is time for Partners to provide an un-rated copy of the list to the chosen family member and have them rate it. Have Partners compare both sets of ratings, focusing on the disparities. It is critical for Partners to gain the insight that they cannot necessarily evaluate the effect their behavior will have on another person. It is that person's subjective valuation of the action that is important, not what the "doer" believes. A particular family member can, in actuality, perceive something you believe may have minor irritating value as a major withdrawal.

☐ STEP 2

The next step is for Partners to keep track of their balances over the course of a week. No matter how the Partner has been behaving they can begin with a zero balance at the start of the week. The one important caveat in this activity is that withdrawals are calculated as twice the amount of points as deposits. Deposits can be either one, two or three emotional points. Withdrawals are two, four or six. To obtain their balances, Partners make their own daily ratings and compare them to a family member who has agreed to participate. The family member is instructed to only rate the way that he or she has been treated and not to include ratings based on treatment of other family members. At the end of the week, Partners compare their ratings to those of the family member and discuss discrepancies. If they wind up in debt for the week, they develop a plan to move into a positive balance.

Variations:

To be fair, it is best if families do this exercise with the entire family. Spouses can also do it with each other. For children who are behavior problems at home and who can appreciate this level of thinking, we advocate parents using the "bank balance" as a method of determining the child's privileges and especially their use of family resources such as drivers, money, electronics etc. Children learn that if they cannot keep a positive balance, with some credit in reserve (we all slip up and have bad days), then all of these resources remain off.

Obstacles/Opportunities:

The bank account system should not be initially used for rewards and punishment. Rather, in the beginning stages, it is just a means of providing information to Partners about their emotional bank balances.

22

STAGE 23: GROUP CONNECTIONS

Goals and Objectives

In this new group stage, Partners explore their group membership in terms of their interlocking roles and relationships. They study the group dynamics and deeper cultures of the groups they belong to. They decide in a more deliberate way how they want to function in groups.

Activity Summary

The stage begins with activities that sensitize Partners to the structure and meaning of the different groups in his life. Then we return to exploring Partners' personal goals and aspirations for functioning in group settings. Finally we explore the issue of the individual versus the group and teach Partners to consider how to balance the needs of the individual with the needs of the group.

Critical Tips

- The group that is working together on RDI activities represents a perfect unit from which to explore group functioning.

- Many of these activities are easily incorporated into a Social Studies, Psychology or Civics Middle School or High School curriculum.

- Make sure that you do not impose your own values onto group members.

LEVEL VI, STAGE 23, ACTIVITY 148

Group Diagrams

ACTIVITY HIGHLIGHTS
° Exploring your different group memberships
° Examining the relative importance of different groups

Summary:

We all belong to groups of one kind or another. Our group affiliations make up a significant part of our identity. This exercise asks our Partners to think about the groups to which they belong. It challenges them to consider the relative importance they place upon their membership in different groups and to compare their rankings with those of their peers.

Participants:

This activity is suitable for a group or class.

Getting Ready:

Partners should be familiar with the circle of closeness diagram used in the "Layers of Me" exercise.

Coaching Instructions:

There are three steps in this exercise:

☐ STEP 1

Partners begin by listing all of the groups that they belong to. Include grade, school class, church, teams, and any other organizations such as scouts in which they are members. They may also include their town or neighborhood, if they feel an affiliation with them. This is a good time for Partners to compare and contrast their different group memberships. You can make an overall list of all the groups that Partners belong to collectively.

☐ STEP 2

Now present Partners with a blank version of the same overlapping "Circles Diagram" they used in Stage 21. Instruct them to place all of the groups in either the innermost level (a group that is a big part of who I am and not easily replaced), the middle level (a group that might be enjoyable or interesting but could be given up without too much loss), or the outermost level (a group that has little or no importance).

☐ STEP 3

In the final phase, Partners discuss the reasons for their placements, as well as comparing and contrasting placements with other group members. Then they collaborate in generating a list of all the reasons they value the groups they belong to; the benefits they accrue from their group membership.

Variations:

A very interesting variation is for Partners to examine the way that the importance of different groups has changed as they have grown older. They can re-do the circles of importance diagram as they would have filled them out at a younger age and then discuss how their feelings and needs have changed or remained the same over time.

Obstacles/Opportunities:

Those Partners who do not feel a strong affiliation with any group – those for whom no group is listed in the innermost circle – present a potential obstacle. For these Partners, the activity becomes one of selecting a group that they would like to feel more affiliated with and planning ways of becoming a more committed member. Of course Partners first have to know why they would wish to become more involved.

LEVEL VI, STAGE 23, ACTVITY 149

Group Roles

ACTIVITY HIGHLIGHTS

- ° Awareness of the vastly different roles the same person can assume in different groups
- ° Methods for evaluating our performance in groups
- ° Setting goals to improve group functioning

Summary:

In this exercise, Partners get a chance to examine the many different roles they play in the groups they belong to. They have a chance to evaluate themselves as group members and to set goals to improve their group functioning.

Participants:

This activity will work better if done with a group that has a history of respecting the emotions of its members.

Getting Ready:

Partners should have completed the previous group activities.

Coaching Instructions:

This exercise has five steps:

23

☐ STEP 1

Partners go back to their group lists to review the groups they have placed in the innermost and middle levels. Next to each group they place the column headings "General Expectations," "Individual Expectations" and "Personal Contributions." Under the General Expectations column they describe the requirements that the group has for all of its members, such as attendance, dress, behavior and whatever specific actions are required. Under Individual Expectation, Partners list any specific jobs, duties and formal or informal roles they assume in that group. Under the Personal Contributions column they list any informal ways in which their presence in the group enriches the group as a whole or the lives of any of the group members (such as providing leadership, emotional support, wisdom, etc.).

☐ STEP 2

Partners make lists of their roles in the different groups they belong to. They compare and contrast the formal and informal roles they play in different groups. Of particular importance is examining how the same individual can function in vastly different ways in different group settings.

☐ STEP 3

Partners rate themselves on their performance in each area of their group functioning.

☐ STEP 4

Next, Partners discuss how important they believe they are to the group. What are the contributions they make to the well-being of the group? How do other group members feel about them? Would the group miss them if they left? What would they miss? How would their absence affect the group or any of the members?

☐ STEP 5

Based on the results of Steps 3 and 4, Partners set goals and make plans for improving their functioning in personally selected areas.

Variations:

Partners can examine how and why they have assumed certain roles in their groups. They may find that they are occupying roles that they are not entirely pleased with. They can discuss the roles that they wish to assume and make plans to reach their goals.

Obstacles/Opportunities:

For those Partners with a pessimistic bent, make sure that they rate the positive elements of their role performance as well as their shortcomings. This is an excellent opportunity for a bit of self-disclosure. Partners can discuss their difficulties in living up to certain group expectations. Coaches can point out that we all have areas in which we are not ideal group members. Partners can support each other in improving their group functioning.

Group Influence

ACTIVITY HIGHLIGHTS

° Awareness of the power groups exert to influence their members

° Learning ways of standing up to peer pressure

° Learning the "whens" and "hows" of appropriate assertiveness

Summary:

The focus of this activity is to help Partners preserve their sense of healthy entitlement as distinct individuals, despite their desire to be accepted as members of a group. All too often, our Partners, desperate for acceptance and friendship, are susceptible to the pull of peer and adult pressures. They may passively acquiesce and "go with the flow" rather than stand up for what they believe.

Participants:

This is an excellent group or classroom activity in dealing with peer pressure and in functioning in an assertive manner.

Getting Ready:

Partners should have completed all previous group activities.

Coaching Instructions:

Begin by discussing the concept of peer pressure. Groups can pressure individuals to take several different forms of action:

- Engaging in dangerous or illegal behavior.

- Acting cruelly to a group "outlier."

- Actions that, while not dangerous, illegal or harmful, do not correspond with the Partner's values and beliefs.

Partners should spend sufficient time identifying each of these three forms of pressure. Next, Partners participate in role-plays that illustrate each of these three forms of group pressure and examine the potential effect of different types of responses. Prior to role-plays, present a number of different options that Partners can use to respond to peer pressure. Responses can be categorized into two broad types: constructive and destructive responses.

Constructive – assertive – responses would include:

- Simply saying no in an assertive manner.

- Attempting to change the topic or provide an alternative activity.

- Attempting to influence the group to modify its course of action.

Destructive – aggressive – responses would include:

- Lecturing group members about the inappropriateness of their behavior.

- Threatening group members with punishment.

23

      - Physically trying to stop group members from taking a course of
action.

Partners will often need help in distinguishing between "assertive" and "aggressive" responses. The role-plays should be constructed to "stop the action" at the moment the Partner is faced with a need to respond to peer pressure. The group can then discuss alternative courses of action and their potential consequences. Partners should role-play both constructive and destructive types of responses and can discuss the potential effects of the actions.

Variations:

Bowing to pressure from peers is not the only difficulty in assertiveness faced by our Partners. Many report problems standing up to adult authority figures, even when they perceive that the adult has acted in an arbitrary, harmful manner. Partners can practice assertive responses with adults. We have provided two possible scenarios:

1.   You get a "C" on your report card and you really believe you deserve a better grade.

2.   Your teacher blames you for talking when it was really the kid sitting next to you. He denies it. You get in trouble.

Obstacles/Opportunities:

When working with teenagers, Coaches should be careful to take into account the real-life consequences of taking what would seem to be the "right" course of action in the adult world. Partners can understand the difference between the "right" thing to do in an ideal world and a response that may not be perfect but does not result in ostracism, or active harassment from the group.

LEVEL VI, STAGE 23, ACTIVITY 151

Group Problem Solving

ACTIVITY HIGHLIGHTS
° Learning methods of working effectively in problem-solving groups
° Learning to balance task demands with the emotional needs of co-workers

Summary:

This activity is an exercise in putting together and applying in context all the lessons our Partners have been learning about group functioning.

Participants:

This exercise is ideally suited for a class or ongoing group. It is an excellent way for all students to learn about collaborative work in groups.

Getting Ready:

Make sure that all Partners can both assert themselves when necessary and know when to back down and "go with the flow" for the good of the group.

Coaching Instructions:

Partners are divided into workgroups of four. They are given the task of constructing something together in a limited time frame and a limited materials budget (for example, six hours, divided into several meetings and $50 for materials). The construction project requires that each member take on one of four distinct roles:

1. An "Architect," responsible for the overall design of the structure.

2. An "Engineer," responsible for determining how the Architect's design will actually be constructed.

3. A "Contractor" who has to work with the Architect and Engineer and is responsible for procuring materials and constructing the finished product.

4. A "Human Relations Consultant" whose job it is to make sure that the end product does not take precedence over the feelings of group members and cohesiveness of the group. The HR Consultant has the ability to "stop the action" whenever he feels that the emotional state of the group is being endangered.

When it is time for construction, the Architect and Engineer continue to be involved both in their initial roles and as "Sub-contractors" taking on specific aspects of the construction as assigned by the Contractor. There are four additional steps to this exercise:

☐ STEP 1

Let Partners know that, aside from the HR person being able to stop the process, all other roles are equal and no one has any greater power than the other. Therefore they must work out their differences through discussion and negotiation. Prior to beginning the project, each team is assigned the task of developing their own unique structure. They must reach agreement on the format they will use for communication and the method they will use for making decisions and resolving conflicts. Finally, they must decide how they will respond if any of the Partners becomes unhappy with the process.

☐ STEP 2

Now the teams are ready for project development. Each workgroup decides the specific project they will undertake and the requirements for the end product. The final step before beginning is to determine who will occupy which of the four roles.

23

☐ STEP 3

Now the work groups begin their tasks. Coaches should "stop the action" of all groups frequently to illustrate problems that a specific group is struggling with. The Partners can collectively help a struggling group surmount its problem. Coaches should also "stop the action" to point out whether groups are operating successfully and smoothly.

☐ STEP 4

When all projects are complete, Partners come together and discuss the process of their work together. Partners contrast the different ways that the work groups chose to set up their structure and the pros and cons of each.

Variations:

Repeat a similar activity, but this time construct workgroups consisting of three Partners each. Try eliminating the HR Consultant role. Explore with the Partners whether eliminating the HR Consultant and also having an odd number of group members made the process easier or more difficult and why.

Divide Partners into groups of four or five members who are given the task to build a "tower" with interlocking blocks. Every round, the group must build a different tower according to a different set of requirements. But the task is more difficult than it seems: no talking is allowed. Instead, participants must depend on their non-verbal skills to communicate increasingly complicated specifications to the other members.

Obstacles/Opportunities:

This is a great opportunity for Partners to practice group dynamics in action. It also has the potential hazard for angry conflicts and for over-focusing on the product, to the detriment of the process and the feelings of Partners. Coaches should be constantly on the lookout for these problems and prepared to request that the HR Consultant "stop the action" at the first signs of them.

STAGE 24: INTIMATE RELATIONS

Goals and Objectives

Stage 24, our final stage, represents the culmination of what we think of as mature friendships. By the close of this Level, stimulating companionship remains important. However, exchanging intimacy becomes the crucial defining characteristic of close friendships. Friends have worked hard to develop and maintain a strong bond of trust and mutual concern. They know each other's fears, dreams, strengths and weaknesses and treat their friend's vulnerabilities with acceptance and respect. Each friend trusts the other's long-term commitment to the relationship. Partners view a relationship as something that exists apart from the moment, or from the individual's current actions. We perceive these relationships from a long-range perspective and believe they are critical fixtures in our present and future lives.

Activity Summary

We begin the stage with an exercise in differentiating levels of friendship. Partners learn to examine their friendships and determine which qualify as truly close friendships. Next, we address the concept of trust in much more depth. Partners learn to accurately define the concept and to evaluate their friendships in relation to the level in which the friend has earned their trust. They also evaluate their own trustworthiness. Then we move on to the everyday business of friendship maintenance and examine several methods of taking care of good friends. Finally, we explore close friendships as enduring entities with a rich history and a mutual expectation of a shared future.

Critical Tips

- Do not be surprised if after honest evaluation, some Partners determine that they do not have any close friends. Do not pretend otherwise if this is the case. Rather, help the Partner to determine how to pursue closer relationships.

- Partners who have been repeatedly hurt may be reluctant to trust one more time. Carefully teaching the Partner how to determine trustworthiness may lead them to be more willing to pursue more intimate relationships.

LEVEL VI, STAGE 24, ACTIVITY 152

Different Kinds of Friendship

ACTIVITY HIGHLIGHTS

° Distinguishing between different levels of friendship

° Understanding the different value of each type of relationship

° Classifying your relationships by their level of closeness

Summary:

By Stage 24 Partners realize that all friendships are not the same. There are people you can have fun with, but you may not share common interests with. The very person, who can be your Ally and stand up for you, may not be sensitive when you talk about a fear. Not everyone can keep a secret, or provide constructive feedback. This activity helps our Partners to identify different levels of friendship. We focus on three levels, which correspond to Level IV, V and VI respectively of our program.

Participants:

This activity is suitable for any group or class setting.

Getting Ready:

Partners should be familiar with the "different levels" concept from their work in Stage 21.

Coaching Instructions:

There are five steps to this activity:

☐ STEP 1

We are going to explore the different types of friends that everybody has. Discuss the three types of friends: Playmates, Pals and Close Friends. A description of each one is found at the end of this activity. Make sure that all Partners understand the key distinctions.

☐ STEP 2

Hand each Partner a copy of the "Different Kinds of Friends" table, provided at the end of this activity and make sure that they all understand how to use it. See if Partners can add any more items to the chart. We have left room for three but you can add as many as you would like.

☐ STEP 3

Now have Partners practice using the chart with different friends to determine in which category they would place them. Have them list all of their friends and use the chart to determine which category each would be in.

☐ STEP 4

Construct role-plays of interactions with friends and see if the group can agree on the correct classification of the friendship. Use the descriptions of the three types to create your role-play scenarios. We have provided a few examples but after a few trials it is very helpful if the group makes up its own role-play scenarios, if possible from real life experiences.

☐ STEP 5

Give Partners the assignment to be good "watchers" and determine whether their ratings are accurate. Over the next several weeks have them report their findings back to the group and revise their ratings if needed.

Variations:

Ask Partners to revisit past friendships and re-categorize these experiences. Do they remember thinking that someone was their friend and then later feeling rejected or betrayed? Was there someone who was more of a friend to them than they realized at the time?

Obstacles/Opportunities:

Some Partners may become upset at finding out that they do not have any close friends. Rather than pretend that they have, with disastrous consequences down the road, it is much better, at this more sophisticated stage, to provide constructive feedback and express your confidence that they will soon have real close friendships.

Three Different Kinds of Friends:

1. *Playmates:* People usually think of Playmates as only referring to small children, but we can have Playmates throughout our entire life. A Playmate is someone with whom we enjoy a common activity. A good Playmate does not try and control what you are doing. He does not cheat and when you are playing with him you have lots of fun, but Playmates are not going to be your Allies. You cannot trust them with highly personal information. You cannot share secrets with them. You may not want to know very much about each other. Still they are fun to be with sometimes.

2. *Pals:* The second type of friend is a Pal. Pals are always good Playmates and they are much more as well. Pals can be good Allies. They will be on your side if you need them. They are interested in many of the same things that you are. They can keep a secret, but they are not interested in the very personal things in your life. They may not pay attention well when you talk about your feelings. If they are very busy with something and you really need their help, they may not stop what they are doing to help you. They may not want to take the risk of upsetting you when you really need their constructive feedback. They will not share their most personal information with you, but they can be good friends up to a certain point.

24

3. *Close Friends:* Close Friends are usually good Playmates and good Pals and they are more besides. They want to know the personal things in your life and treat them with sensitivity and respect. They want to know how you feel and will share their feelings and personal things with you. They will always take the risk of upsetting you if they feel you really need constructive feedback. No matter how busy they are, they will stop and help you if you really need them.

"Different Kinds of Friends:"

What you should expect from this type of friend	Playmate	Pal	Close Friend
Fun to be with	Yes	Yes	Yes
Laughs at your jokes	Yes	Yes	Yes
Plays fair	Yes	Yes	Yes
Likes the same games	Yes	Yes	Yes
Shares common interests	Some	Yes	Yes
Can keep a secret	No	Yes	Yes
Will stand by you as an Ally	No	Yes	Yes
Interested in your ideas	No	Yes	Yes
Cares about your fellings	No	No	Yes
Will tell you the truth if you really need it	No	No	Yes
Will always stop to help you	No	No	Yes
Wants to share private things with you	No	No	Yes
More?			

Sample Friend Role-Plays:

- It is late at night and you have just woken up realizing that you have an important assignment due tomorrow at school that requires reading certain pages in a textbook. But you forgot to write the pages down. You call your friend's house, even though you know he is fast asleep.

- You have an embarrassing rash in a private part of your body and it really itches. You tell your friend about it.

- You are feeling sort of depressed and you don't really feel like things are going to get better. You tell your friend how you feel.

° A bigger guy keeps picking on you at school. You feel that if you had a friend who would stand by you, the bully would back down.

LEVEL VI, STAGE 24, ACTIVITY 153

Trust

ACTIVITY HIGHLIGHTS
° Understanding the concept of trust
° Learning the most effective methods to build trust
° Deciding who and how much you should trust
° Evaluating how trustworthy you are

Summary:

As we all know, trust is a critical concept in defining close personal friendships. We value our "trusted" friends and feel betrayed when someone we believed we could trust betrays us. But what is trust? Is it some elusive concept that can only be intuited? This exercise attempts to define trust for our Partners in an operational way. We provide a formula for gradually building trust with others and determining the level of trust you should be proficient in describing the different levels of Self, especially in regards to the Private versus Public Self.

Participants:

Suitable for a group that has a positive shared history.

Getting Ready:

Partners should be familiar with the "different levels" concept from a variety of previous activities. They should be able to clearly distinguish different types of friendships.

Coaching Instructions:

This is a six-step exercise:

☐ STEP 1

First we have to provide a working definition of trust. Trust is what makes close friendships work. When we have developed complete trust we know we can share anything with that person and it will be all right. We can always count on them. We know that they will never do anything intentionally to harm us. They always want to know what is on our mind. But, there are very few people we can develop complete trust with. There are many levels of trust and in each relationship we have

24

379

to determine how much trust we should have. Refer back to the three types of friendship and the levels of Self lists as illustrations.

☐ STEP 2

We have defined three crucial aspects of trust. They are safety, reliability and value. We have provided important questions at the end of the exercise description, to determine the level of trust in each one of these areas. Make sure that Partners understand all three areas. They can provide real life examples for each of these areas.

☐ STEP 3

How do we give and get trust in a new relationship? We like to teach Partners to build trust gradually. Ask Partners to reference their circles of me diagram. Discuss how to begin with outer levels and then gradually progress inward, to determine whether you can increase your level of trust.

☐ STEP 4

Now we want Partners to return to their list of friendships of all types and create a "Circles of Trust" diagram. This should directly relate to the different types of friends they have already determined.

☐ STEP 5

Now we turn to the question of to what degree our Partners should be trusted. Have Partners rate themselves with the trust questions. Ask them to discuss their findings as honestly as possible. This is a good place for constructive feedback from other group members. In what areas are they trustworthy? In which areas do they need to improve if they wish to be trustworthy?

☐ STEP 6

As a final step, ask Partners to track the building of trust in their relationships and report back regularly to the group on the trust status.

Variations:

We find it helpful to discuss the need for repair work when trust has been damaged. "I'm sorry," just will not cut it! Partners have to be prepared to accept that, purposely or not, when damage to trust has occurred it must be repaired. Unfortunately, the effort it takes to repair a damaged relationship is much greater than the effort it takes to damage it in the first place. Have the group discuss actions that might be more or less damaging and the levels and types of repair that might be necessary given the degree and type of damage done.

Obstacles/Opportunities:

This is an excellent opportunity to work on the concept of forgiveness. We all may inadvertently act in ways that damage other people's trust in us. One lapse of trust should not be the end of a relationship that has had a good track record of trust in the past. Discuss with Partners when to forgive and when not to.

Questions to ask about Trust:

Safety:

- ° Do they take what I share seriously?
- ° Do they maintain my confidentiality?
- ° Do they reciprocate and share themselves?
- ° Do they use personal information against me later?
- ° Are they honest without being cruel?
- ° Do they use the relationship as a threat?
- ° Do they judge me too harshly?

Reliability:

- ° Do they show up when they say they will?
- ° Do they live up to the commitments they make?
- ° Will they support me when I genuinely need them?

Value:

- ° Will they drop me when another friend is around?
- ° Do they take advantage of our relationship?
- ° Do they try and keep the emotional bank account equal?
- ° Do they think about what is important to me?
- ° Do they want to know my world?
- ° Do they genuinely feel excited by my successes?

LEVEL VI, STAGE 24, ACTIVITY 154

Friendship Maintenance

ACTIVITY HIGHLIGHTS

- ° Learning day-to-day actions that maintain close friendship
- ° Evaluating the quality of your "friendship maintenance"
- ° Examining friendships in relation to a "maintenance balance"

Summary:

Building trust is one important part of making and keeping close friends, but there is a second critical factor. This is the day-to-day actions that we must perform to keep the relationship in good repair. We call these "friendship maintenance" activities and this exercise focuses on defining, practicing and hopefully instilling them as habits.

24

Participants:

This activity is suitable for a group that has developed a degree of trust. A trained facilitator is quite helpful.

Getting Ready:

It is best if Partners have identified at least one relationship that both Coach and Partner agree qualifies as a potential close friendship.

Coaching Instructions:

This is a five-step activity:

☐ STEP 1

First, see if Partners can construct a list of the regular maintenance activities that close friendships require. When they have added all they can think of, discuss the items that have not been mentioned. We have listed sample items at the end of this activity.

☐ STEP 2

Make sure that Partners discuss and understand the reasons why it is worth working so hard to keep a close friendship.

☐ STEP 3

Now Partners examine whether they work hard enough at friendship maintenance to keep a close friendship. Partners evaluate themselves using the friendship maintenance activities. This can take several weeks as Partners leave the group and honestly examine their behavior.

☐ STEP 4

Partners evaluate their current friends and ask themselves whether they are doing most of the work to maintain the friendship. Friendship work must be a fifty–fifty deal for it to be successful.

☐ STEP 5

Ask Partners to set goals to improve their friendship maintenance. Try and maintain an ongoing feedback system, where Partners can return to the group and report their progress over a period of several months.

Variations:

Have Partners keep a Friendship Journal, where they can record the actions that they take to maintain their friendship. Videotape a role-play where Partners practice demonstrating good friendship maintenance. Then videotape a role-play where Partners demonstrate friendship turn-offs.

Obstacles/Opportunities:

Partners who have a long history of rejection may not initially agree that doing all the work is worth it. The Coach should acknowledge that the Partner has a right to feel this way. It is not paranoid or crazy. However, the Coach should reference back to all the new skills that the Partner has learned, including who and how to trust someone. Using these tools, Partners can pursue close relationships without as much risk of being hurt. However, even persons who are most skilled at relationships run the risk of being hurt from time to time.

Friendship Maintenance Activities:

- Keeping track of my emotional bank account to make sure I am not overdrawn.
- Forgiving my friend if he is sometimes overdrawn as long as in the long run we are fairly even.
- Making frequent contacts with no agenda except connecting.
- Giving him enough "space" so that he doesn't feel suffocated by the relationship. Allowing him to have other friends.
- Remembering events that are important to him.
- Trying to understand his emotions, even when he doesn't verbally share them.
- Lending him a new game or other object that you know he really likes even though you still really enjoy using it.
- Communicating appreciation for small things your friend does for you.

Friendship Turn-offs

- *Out of Sight, Out of Mind:* "Funny how I never think about you at all unless I see you."
- *Monopolizing:* "Don't even think about having any other friends but me."
- *Self-centeredness:* "I'll be your friend when I have the time, as long as you are there for me when I need you."
- *Mind-reading:* "I already know what you are thinking. I don't have to bother asking you."
- *Taking your friend for granted:* "What do you mean I never show you any appreciation. I thought because we were friends you would just know it."
- *Guilt trips:* "If you were really my friend you would ___ ."
- *Overuse:* "We do every single thing together."
- *Killing with kindness:* "I would never say anything but positive things about my friends. If they do something I don't like, I'll just stop thinking about it. That way, we never have to work out any conflicts."

24

Advanced Friend Maps

ACTIVITY HIGHLIGHTS
° Getting to know the inner world of a good friend
° Maintaining updated personal knowledge about your close friends

Summary:
As the title suggests, this is the more advanced form of the "Friendship Maps" activity we did in Stage 20, when we were exploring "mid-level" friendships. Now we are interested in "mapping" a more intimate terrain. Close friends maintain mental maps of their friend's personal worlds. In turn they expect to share the same information with a close friend. Along with trust and regular maintenance, keeping updated "Friendship Maps" is the third crucial step in having a close friendship.

Participants:
Partners must have at least one close friend to participate in this activity.

Getting Ready:
Review with Partners the "Friendship Maps" and "Family Maps" they have constructed in the past.

Coaching Instructions:
Explain to Partners that close friends maintain updated maps of each other's Personal Selves. After a discussion about the meaning of a "Personal Map" of your friend, proceed on to the following four steps:

☐ STEP 1

Choose a close friend whom you will be mapping.

☐ STEP 2

Try to make an initial map using the "Advanced Friendship Map Questions" listed at the end of this activity.

☐ STEP 3

Request that Partners spend several weeks trying to make sure their "Friendship Maps" are accurate and filling in any blank spots. Help Partners determine how they will obtain this information without their friend feeling interrogated.

☐ STEP 4

Work on keeping the maps updated. Each Partner should have an agreed upon method for making sure that his information remains accurate. Ask Partners to report to the group regularly concerning their efforts to maintain accurate maps and what they are learning as they go through this process.

Variations:
All close friends maintain their version of a "Friend Map," though it is rarely as structured as in this exercise. Ask Partners to determine as much as they can about

their close friend's "Map" of them. See if they can find out whether the friend knows as much about their world as a close friend should.

Obstacles/Opportunities:

Teenagers may balk at what looks like a "nerdy" interview of their friends. Make sure that if you get some flak about this that you agree completely. Assure Partners they are not to go out and try to obtain this information until, with the group's help, they have figured out a "cool" way to go about it.

Advanced Friendship Map Questions:

- ° Who are his enemies and adversaries?
- ° What do you know about his other close friends?
- ° What are his greatest fears?
- ° What are the biggest stresses he is dealing with?
- ° What is he most looking forward to in the near future?
- ° What are his biggest problems with family members?
- ° What are his secret dreams for the far future?
- ° What memory makes him the saddest?
- ° When does he feel the weakest?
- ° What is the best way to help him when he is upset?
- ° What is the best way to tell him something he needs to know, so that he will be able to really hear it?
- ° How can you tell when he needs private time and when he needs to be with you?
- ° What are the areas of difficulty that he is most ashamed of?
- ° What are the achievements he is most proud of?
- ° What are the personal attributes he would most like to change?

24

LEVEL VI, STAGE 24, ACTIVITY 156

Friends Forever

ACTIVITY HIGHLIGHTS
° Projecting a friendship into the future
° Appreciating the enduring qualities of a close relationship

Summary:

As you already know, we are as interested in "future memories" as we are in past ones. In this final exercise, our Partners consider what their friendship will be like at some point in the future, years from today.

Participants:

Partners should have at least one close friendship. We particularly like doing this exercise with Partners and their close friends together.

Getting Ready:

As in the previous exercise, there is really no preparation needed for this exercise, other than the Partners' readiness to appreciate this activity.

Coaching Instructions:

Ask Partners to choose some future time and talk about what they think their friendship will be like. Do they think they will still be able to remain friends? Will they live near one another? Will they be able to do things together? How will they remain close? Often Partners want to do this exercise in a humorous manner. We encourage this lightheartedness, because beneath it there is typically a great affection being expressed.

Variations:

If Partners wish, they can make a humorous video skit of a typical day in their lives "X" number of years from now, with the assumption that they still remain close friends. Another variation is to have Partners write an imaginary letter from the future to a close friend who they have not seen in many years.

Obstacles/Opportunities:

This is another opportunity to celebrate the "payoffs" gained from doing the hard work of developing and maintaining a close friendship. There is nothing so comforting as knowing that you have built a relationship foundation with someone that is so strong that nothing could break it apart.

Appendix A

The Relationship Development Questionnaire

Your responses to the following representative items should help you decide the proper volume to use. If you respond "Not Yet" to more than four items, or a combination of "Not Yet" and "Sometimes" to more than eight items in Level I or II, begin with Volume I.

	Typical	Sometimes	Not Yet
Level I: Novice			
Remains focused on your actions and words.			
Regularly observes others, even when involved in a different activity.			
Comforted by a glance and/or soothing words.			
Shares face-to-face expressions of enjoyment and excitement with you.			
Observes your non-verbal expression of disapproval and immediately stops his/her actions.			
Successfully carries out requested actions as your assistant.			
Carefully observes when requested to match your actions.			
Participates with enthusiasm when you introduce a new activity.			
Easily accepts your coaching to guide his/her actions.			
Transitions easily from one activity to another.			

Level II: Apprentice			
Observes your movements while walking together, to remain at your side.			
Shows enjoyment when you introduce novelty and variety into activities.			
Makes sure that you are ready, before starting a joint activity.			
Rapidly adapts, when you introduce changes to an activity.			
Obtains enjoyment from coordinating his/her actions with yours.			
Routinely takes actions to increase your enjoyment.			
Keeping peer partners happy is more important than controlling the interaction, or playing with a specific object.			
Enjoys synchronizing his actions with a peer for a common endpoint.			
Level III: Challenger			
Routinely cheers for and encourages others during competitive events.			
Quick to stop, or modify any action that confuses or bothers another person.			
Frequently checks to see if his/her communication is understood correctly.			
Keeps conversation topics coordinated with social partners.			
Tries to compromise when his/her desires are different from others.			
Successfully joins into ongoing activities with peer partners.			
Clearly shows that he/she is happy to see friends.			
Frequently makes his/her friends smile and laugh.			
Tries to find things to do that his/her friends will enjoy.			
Plays fair and does not cheat.			

Does not walk away in the middle of an activity.			
Makes sure that social partners can see objects just the way he/she does, for example, turns a picture around so that the other person can see it.			

Level IV: Voyager

Tries to understand your perspective, or point of view.			
Realizes your point of view can sometimes be more helpful than his/her own.			
Finds and accepts alternative problem-solving solutions when needed.			
Knows that different versions of the same activity can be equally valid.			
Makes peer partners feel important and comfortable.			
Accurately judges whether his/her actions or words are interrupting or enhancing a collaborative activity.			
Effectively joins into peer group activities, by using methods designed to gain entrance and acceptance into the group.			
Shows understanding when others make mistakes.			
Uses effective methods for coping with peer rejection.			
Uses effective methods to cope with teasing.			

Level V: Explorer

Actively attempts to solicit social partner's ideas and feelings.			
Successfully operates as a "Coach" with a less skilled partner.			
Communicates interest and appreciation for friends' feelings and ideas.			
Desires to know others' inner feelings and not superficial expressions of emotions.			
Determines if an action was accidental or deliberate, before reacting to it.			
Communicates with empathy when others are sad, scared or hurt.			
Conducts conversations mainly to learn about others' ideas and feelings.			

Non-verbally shows interest and acceptance during a conversation.			
Watches carefully to see if friends are confused or bored by conversation.			
Effectively manages conversational disagreements to prevent them from becoming arguments.			
Quick to act as an Ally whenever a friend requires assistance.			
Takes responsibility for inviting friends to the house and entertaining them.			
Communicates his/her complaints to friends, without criticism.			
Knows and frequently updates important information about friends such as interests, preferences, future plans and other relationships.			

Level VI: Partner

Shows respect for others' beliefs, even when different from his/hers.			
Willingly accepts constructive feedback.			
Knows how and when to deliver constructive feedback.			
Interested in obtaining information about how others see him.			
Maintains up-to-date knowledge of family members' feelings and lives.			
Finds meaningful ways to show caring and concern for family members.			
Values his/her membership in different groups other than the family.			
Works hard to maintain positive membership in groups.			
Appreciates different levels of friendship, from playmates to close friends.			
Uses effective methods for determining a friend's trustworthiness.			
Takes effective day-to-day actions to maintain close friendships.			

Appendix B

Progress Tracking Form

Use this form to set your initial objectives and also to track your progress. In the first column on the right place an "M," "W," "D" or "N" next to each item, along with the date, to indicate whether it has been mastered, it is partially or inconsistently in place or whether the skill needs to be developed. Choose your initial activities based upon the earliest in which you have placed a "W" or "D." Every few weeks return to this form and rate your progress along with the date.

Ratings Key

M = Mastered: 1. Performs the skill for the purpose of increasing the level of coordination, emotion sharing and mutual enjoyment with social partners. 2. Performs the skill independently over 80 per cent of the time. Initiates without help, prompts, or rewards. 3. Performs the skill at a frequency expected in typical development. 4. Initiates the skill with different adults and peers (where indicated) and in different, appropriate settings.

W = Working: 1. Performs the skill solely for the purpose of increasing the level of coordination, emotion sharing and mutual enjoyment with social partners. 2. Performs the skill independently less than 80 per cent but more than 20 per cent of the time. 3. Performs the skill in a majority of situations where appropriate, but at a frequency less than expected in typical development. 4. Does not frequently perform the skill with different adults and peers (where indicated) but does so in a variety of settings.

D = Developing: 1. Initiates the skill some of the time, to obtain some goal or reward that is unrelated to the social interaction. 2. Performs the skill independently less than 20 per cent of the time. 3. Does not yet initiate the skill with different people or in different settings.

N = Not Yet: Does not perform the skill. Or, performs the skill only to obtain some reward or goal, unrelated to increasing coordination and shared enjoyment of social partners (e.g. get a treat, getting to watch TV).

(This is an abbreviated version of the full RDI Progress Rating Form. Complete Forms can be purchased at our website, *www.connections center.com*)

Rating Periods: Date 1: _____   Date 2: _____
                      Date 3: _____   Date 4: _____
                      Date 5: _____

Rate each item with an M, W, D or N	1	2	3	4	5
Level I: Novice					
Stage 1: Attend					
1. Shows voluntary attentiveness to communication attempts.					
2. Stays focused on communicator's actions and facial expressions.					
3. Frequently initiates face-to-face emotion sharing.					
4. Communicates appreciation for the novel actions of social partners.					
5. Communicates for continuation of exciting actions.					
6. Enjoys acting as a participant in exciting adult-guided activities					
7. Routinely references adults for safety and security.					
Stage 2: Reference					
8. Monitors social partner's whereabouts, even when engaged in a competing activity.					
9. References non-verbal cues like head nods, headshakes, smiles and frowns to determine his actions.					
10. Follows the eye gaze of social partners to a common location.					
11. Communicates the desire to take an action and then visually checks for approval.					
12. Uses non-verbal gestures and facial expressions for simple problem solving and decision making.					
Stage 3: Regulate					
13. Accepts a limited activity role, when an adult requests that he function as an assistant.					
14. Engages in careful observation and modeling, when requested to match adult actions.					
15. Accepts the proper speed of effort as defined by an adult guide.					

16.	Varies the level of thoroughness in his work, based upon an adult's instructions.						
17.	Stays attentive and allows adults to guide actions while learning an activity.						
18.	Accurately references and follows a daily activities schedule.						
19.	Accepts insertion and removal of elements when using a schedule of activities.						
20.	Transitions fluidly from one activity to another.						
21.	Stops unfinished activities and transitions when requested without upset.						
22.	Recognizes and appropriately expresses six emotional expressions: proud, happy, frustrated, curious, sad, and angry, when requested to do so.						
23.	Ignores irrelevant information and focuses on important communication.						
	Stage 4: Coordinate						
24.	Coordinates role actions with a social partner.						
25.	Faces his partner, counts together and coordinates the joint release of two balls, timed so that each partner can catch the other's ball when they thow it to one another.						
26.	Synchronizes jointly pulling on a rope to create a comfortable back and forth motion with his partner.						
27.	Synchronizes coordinated hard and gentle actions with a social partner's guidance.						
28.	Synchronizes rhythms with a partner in order to drum together.						
29.	Synchronizes loud and soft actions with the guidance of a social partner.						
30.	Synchronizes fast and slow actions with the guidance of a social partner.						
31.	Matches simple patterns played by partners on a musical instrument.						
32.	Coordinates movement with a partner's guidance, to be equally close to and far away from one another.						
33.	Coordinates movements with a social partner's guidance, to face towards and away from one another.						

34.	Coordinates movements with a social partners guidance, to be face-to-face, side by side and facing away from one another.						
35.	Coordinates movements to be behind, ahead, or parallel to social partners.						
36.	Recognizes when he is in a state of connection versus disconnection with a social partner.						
37.	Collaborates with a social partner to introduce playful word combinations.						
38.	Coordinates with a social partner to remain on a topic.						

Level II: Apprentice

Stage 5: Variation

39.	Learns to make small changes in behavior to regulate joint actions with a partner.						
40.	Coordinates changes in degree of speed, to stay connected with a partner.						
41.	Rapidly adapts to small activity variations made by adult partners.						
42.	Adapts behavior to remain coordinated, after a social partner carefully introduces variations in the following elements:						
	a. Greater and shorter pause lengths.						
	b. Faster and slower actions.						
	c. Louder and softer rhythms on a drum or other instrument.						
	d. Harder and gentler actions.						
43.	Matches actions, to remain at your side while walking, or otherwise moving together.						
44.	Demonstrates an awareness of the effect on communication of moving too close and too far away from a social partner.						
45.	Understands that emotional changes occur in relative amounts or increments and not in an "all or none" fashion.						
46.	Understands that different events can trigger different degrees of emotional reactions.						

47.	Reacts as if the expression changes of his social partners are important.					
48.	Understands and uses the appropriate voice equivalents for simple emotional expressions.					
49.	Effectively perceives and values small degrees of improvement in his and others performance.					
Stage 6: Transformation						
50.	Enjoys the surprise of one activity transforming into another through a series of gradual changes.					
51.	Rapidly adapts and expresses enjoyment, when a social partner introduces new functions for familiar objects.					
52.	Enjoys and rapidly adapts to rule changes which transform familiar activities into new variants.					
53.	Demonstrates enjoyment and appreciation when the goal of an activity suddenly changes into its opposite.					
54.	Appreciates and uses humor in a non-scripted manner and enjoys the transformation of jokes from their original structure.					
55.	Appreciates the rapidity with which feelings can change in the same setting.					
56.	Changes in musical rhythm, volume and speed evoke different subjective reactions and emotions.					
Stage 7: Synchronization						
57.	Can translate simple instructions into Self Talk.					
58.	Uses Self Talk to plan immediate actions.					
59.	Uses Self Talk to narrate current actions.					
60.	Using Self Talk to evaluate the success of actions.					
61.	Makes rapid adjustments to remain coordinated with a partner when he observes, or hears that their drumming is not synchronized.					
62.	Enjoys the challenge of synchronizing actions with an unpredictable partner.					
63.	Synchronizes complementary roles with partners.					
64.	Uses his partner's cues and reactions as the critical elements for joke telling.					

65.	Enjoys acting as a Joke Team with a social partner, by synchronizing the delivery of simple two-line jokes.					
66.	Effectively uses the frameworks of "Telling and Telling," "Telling and Asking" and "Asking and Telling," to maintain true reciprocal conversations.					
67.	Bases his actions on anticipation of his partner's future actions.					
Stage 8: Duets						
68.	Functions effectively as a partner in a cooperative activity.					
69.	Keeping a peer partner happy is more important than controlling their interaction.					
70.	Routinely monitors and attempts to increase his peer partner's enjoyment level.					
71.	Effectively interprets and uses non-verbal facial expressions and gestures to communicate with a peer partner in simple collaborative activities.					
72.	Checks frequently to determine if his actions are coordinated with a peer partner's.					
73.	Demonstrates curiosity about his conversational partner's responses.					
74.	Plays word games with peer partners, in a playful, creative manner.					
Level III: Challenger						
Stage 9: Collaboration						
75.	Collaborates with a team to reach mutually agreed upon short-term objective.					
76.	Cooperates with peer partners to overcome shared challenges.					
77.	Uses partnership with peers to decrease anxiety and master mildly fearful settings.					
78.	Uses Self Instruction to regulate actions.					
79.	Uses Self Instruction to plan actions.					
80.	Reviews videotapes of prior activities and spots the need for corrective actions to function in a more coordinated manner with partners.					

81.	Successfully uses simple negotiation methods to reach a goal with a peer partner.					
82.	Maintains an emphasis on shared enjoyment with peer partners, even when faced with competitive goals.					
83.	Collaborates with a peer partner to find hidden objects using a map.					
Stage 10: Co-Creation						
84.	Communicates appreciation for and enjoyment of his partner's contributions to creative drumming compositions.					
85.	Creates enjoyable, unique songs through the joint efforts of peer partners.					
86.	Jointly contributes to creation of an artistically decorated model car, designed and constructed as a team effort.					
87.	Participates as part of a team to create inventive new games and role-plays.					
88.	Jointly creates humor that is based on wacky improvisation.					
89.	Jointly creates poetry based upon equal contributions of team-mates.					
90.	Engages in conjoint celebration of completed products following their creation.					
Stage 11: Improvisation						
91.	Enjoys improvising actions with peer partners, to create unexpected variations in familiar activities.					
92.	Enjoys improvising with peer partners to construct a new activity.					
93.	Uses flexible thinking to sharing in improvising new structures with partners.					
94.	Enjoys improvising new rules to familiar games with a partner.					
95.	Enjoys improvised drumming with a partner, to create unexpected variations in rhythms and composition.					
96.	Enjoys improvising familiar role-plays with partners to produce amusing, unexpected changes in the play.					

97.	Enjoys improvising joke formats with partners to produce hilarious changes in familiar jokes.						
98.	Enjoys improvising poetry formats with partners.						
99.	Demonstrates the ability to adapt rules as needed in order to enjoy improvised activities.						
100.	Communicates appreciations to social partner's contributions to joint activities.						
101.	Observes a partner to check for enjoyment or confusion after introducing changes.						
102.	Communicates clearly for acceptance of improvised changes ("How about this?")						
103.	Takes necessary repair actions when he observes his partner's confusion.						
104.	Rapidly discards variations that negatively impact his social partners.						
105.	Rapidly adapts to peer partner's ideas and contributions to joint activities						
Stage 12: Running Mates							
106.	Understands that emotional expressions emanate from internal feelings.						
107.	Meaningfully shares basic emotions with social partners.						
108.	Links feelings with simple causes.						
109.	Utilizes the different components of basic non-verbal expression needed to communicate the following emotions: sad, worried, angry, happy, curious, surprised and proud.						
110.	Understands the impact of body and physical position on communication effectiveness.						
111.	Understands the routine nature of communication breakdowns.						
112.	Checks for accuracy both in delivery and receipt of communications.						
113.	Keeps simple conversation topics coordinated with social partners.						
114.	Demonstrates the ability to engage in simple forms of ballroom dancing.						

115.	Regulates emotional reactions to losing. Can be a graceful loser.					
116.	Prioritizes maintaining a good relationship with his partner over winning.					
117.	Remains calm after making mistakes.					
118.	Acts in an understanding manner towards others' mistakes.					
119.	Uses simple, effective strategies for joining into peer activities.					
120.	Examines his behavior from a friend's point of view in determining his actions.					
121.	Finds ways to make visiting friends feel important and welcome.					
122.	Takes responsibility for determining which objects distract from attention to friends.					
123.	Understands and practices the basic elements of a beginning level friendship:					
	a. Clearly communicates that he is happy to see his friends.					
	b. Knows how to make his friends smile and laugh.					
	c. Tries to find things to do that his friend likes to do.					
	d. Does not act bossy/controlling.					
	e. Plays fair and does not cheat.					
	f. Does not walk away in the middle of an activity.					
	g. Acts like people are more important than things.					
	h. Cares more about a friend, than winning or getting your way.					

Level IV: Voyager

Stage 13: Perspective

124.	Carefully selects experiences and observations for later sharing with a friend.					
125.	Effectively uses Self Talk to narrate interactions.					
126.	Uses Self Talk to retain Social Memories for later sharing.					

127.	Takes actions to better understand his partner's perspective.					
128.	Recognizes that his partner's viewpoint can sometimes provide a more helpful perspective than his own.					
129.	Seeks to find commonalities between his own and peer partners actions.					
130.	Readily enacts the role of "social observer" and frequently observes peers interacting with one another.					
131.	Provides sufficient information to someone who is not present in a situation so they can share his perceptions.					
132.	Accurately and meaningfully describes a prior experience to a peer.					
133.	Understands the concept of strategy and seeks to determine and record simple strategies for future use.					
134.	Understands that partners may have learned rules in a different manner and may have different versions of the same activity that are equally valid to his.					
Stage 14: Imagination						
135.	Understands that his partner's emotional reactions to the same perceptual stimulus may be different than, but equally valid to, his own.					
136.	Learns to judge when his actions and words are interrupting versus enhancing a collaborative activity.					
137.	Understands that subjective reactions are naturally associated with perceptions.					
138.	Enjoys sharing imaginative reactions to perceptions.					
139.	Enjoys sharing and integrating subjective impressions with social partners while watching TV or movies together.					
140.	Actively seeks out social partner's imaginative enhancements and emotional reactions to compare and integrate with his own.					
141.	Contributes imaginative ideas and emotional reactions, as an equal partner, leaving ample room for others to add their unique impressions.					
142.	Communicates appreciation and enjoyment for social partners' imaginative enhancements, whether they are similar to, or discrepant from his.					

143.	Rapidly discards or modifies his imaginative contributions, when they are highly discrepant or cause discomfort to partners.					
144.	Communicates excitement for the product resulting from blending partner's imaginative additions with his own.					
145.	Thinks of humorous additions to shared perceptions that increase his peer partner's enjoyment.					
146.	Collaborates with social partners to reach consensus concerning discrepant perceptions.					
147.	Uses divergent thinking to generate alternative uses for objects and activities.					
148.	Functions effectively as part of a creative problem-solving team.					
Stage 15 Group Foundations						
149.	Integrates his individual efforts into a larger group theme, or composition.					
150.	Enjoys making contributions as part of a larger team effort.					
151.	Participates as a partner in a group creative process.					
152.	Participates as a partner in developing unique group games.					
153.	Uses the following strategies to join in with peers:					
	a. Observes to figure out the activity that social partners are engaged in.					
	b. Looks for a good moment to join into peer activities. Waits for a pause in the action, prior to approaching peers.					
	c. Uses complements as a method for being accepted into peer activities.					
	d. Quietly moves next to a potential partner.					
	e. Shows interest and enthusiasm.					
	f. Shows a desire to help or enhance their efforts.					
	g. Uses humor as an entrance method.					
	h. Persists when ignored – up to a point.					

	i.	Tries another strategy, if the first one doesn't work.					
	j.	Knows when it's time to move on and try again some other time.					
154.	Identifies himself as part of a group that he has participated in creating.						
155.	Has developed a sense of ownership as a member of a cohesive group.						
156.	Effectively negotiates with group members to reach consensus.						
Stage 16: Emotional Regulation							
157.	Accurately distinguishes between different levels of stress.						
158.	Knows when to stop and take a break, before he has a "meltdown."						
159.	Develops simple but effective coping mechanisms to reduce stress.						
160.	Recognizes that both parties in a conflict may be partly right and have a valid point of view.						
161.	Resolves simple peer conflicts effectively.						
162.	Integrates non-verbal and verbal emotional expressions.						
163.	Accurately understands and expresses 14 different emotions.						
164.	Uses several different media to represent feelings.						
165.	Has learned to realistically anticipate potential rejection.						
166.	Possesses tools for successfully coping with rejection.						
167.	Has learned and implements the seven skills needed for successfully inviting a friend to his house and be a good host:						
	a.	Pick the right person to invite.					
	b.	Coordinate with parents.					
	c.	Make the invitation.					
	d.	Choose the right date and time.					
	e.	Finalize plans with parents and friend.					

	f.	Place the date on a shared calendar.					
	g.	Prepare for the visit.					
168.		Takes personal responsibility for scheduling and preparing for social events.					
	Level V: Explorer						
	Stage 17: Ideas						
169.		Uses poetry as a medium to express and blend personal ideas.					
170.		A highlight of social interaction is blending ideas with partners, to create new integrated concepts.					
171.		Effectively communicates and shares ideas, without the need for an external stimulus to serve as an "anchor."					
172.		Actively attempts to solicit social partner's ideas and emotional reactions.					
173.		Works as a partner to integrate ideas and create new jointly invented stories.					
174.		Collaborates as an equal partner in complex role-plays, requiring improvising the thoughts and feelings of several characters.					
175.		Takes into account differences in the knowledge base between himself and social partners by "filling in gaps" during conversation and not assuming the partner will know personal information.					
176.		Modifies pacing and actions to provide effective assistance to someone who is less capable in a skill or activity than himself.					
177.		Successfully operates in a "coaching" position with a less skilled social partner.					
178.		Finds good solutions for problems that have no right or wrong answers.					
179.		Values partner's strategies even if different than his own.					
180.		Readily adopts alternative methods of problem solving contributed by other team members.					
181.		Enjoys solving hypothetical – "what if" – problems as a team.					
182.		Has a good working knowledge of his friends' personal interests, preferences and opinions.					

183.	Shares his personal interests, preferences and opinions in a manner interesting to friends.						
184.	Perceives emotions on a continuum of "shades" of feelings.						
185.	Distinguishes between "subjective" and "objective" information.						
186.	Validates the different opinions and views of social partners.						
Stage 18: What's Inside?							
187.	Understands that external emotional expressions may not be true reflections of internal states.						
188.	Recognizes that different "channels" of communication can convey contradictory information.						
189.	Expresses the desire to know social partners inner feelings and not accept superficial expressions of emotion.						
190.	Appreciates the difference between playful deception and lying or hurtful deception and knows the proper context for playful deception.						
191.	Communicates, "I am only joking" successfully (like winking) through non-verbal means, so social partners understand the playful context of his double meanings.						
192.	Distinguishes playful fables and stories from manipulative lies.						
193.	Distinguishes between emotional and factual memories.						
194.	Readily retrieves and communicates important personal memories.						
195.	Uses Social Memories as an important way to increase friendship bonds.						
196.	Regularly thinks about himself in past and future contexts.						
197.	Knows how to use Self Talk to prepare for a negative outcome.						
198.	Routinely prepares alternative contingency plans.						
199.	Analyzes and troubleshoots plans that did not work.						

200.	Develops realistic short-term goals.						
201.	Uses the support of friends to retain his motivation to persist towards goals.						
202.	Considers the intentions of someone along with their actions prior to responding.						
203.	Knows effective strategies to determine if an action was accidental or deliberate.						
204.	Effectively manages emotional reactions to teasing.						
205.	Uses constructive Self Talk to moderate the emotional effects of teasing.						
206.	Has learned the most effective responses to being teased.						
207.	Has learned to modify behaviors and other characteristics in order to decrease the likelihood of being teased.						
208.	Can put himself in another person's "shoes" by considering how it must feel to live their life, in contrast to his own.						
209.	Regularly demonstrates the use of five steps of empathy:						
	a. Step 1: Understand the other person's emotional reaction.						
	b. Step 2: Understand the experience that triggered the emotional reaction for them.						
	c. Step 3: Remember a similar emotional reaction that you had and a similar experience that happened to you.						
	d. Step 4: Communicate that you know the emotion they are feeling.						
	e. Step 5: Communicate that you have had a similar experience.						
Stage 19 Conversations							
210.	Understands the six different legitimate functions of conversations.						
211.	Understands the difference between authentic, reciprocal conversations and other verbal exchanges like Monologues, Interrogations, Lectures and Disconnected Dialogues.						

212.	Demonstrates effective methods to enhance ongoing conversations.						
213.	Effectively distinguishes between conversational enhancements and interruptions.						
214.	Is aware of the types of interruptions and topic changes that disrupt conversation.						
215.	Uses frequent self-monitoring to maintain conversational coherence.						
216.	Effectively uses eleven non-verbal skills for successful conversation:						
	a. Maintain a personal space that keeps your partner comfortable.						
	b. Provide a conversational space to allow your partner to contribute equally.						
	c. Communicate without words when you have something funny to say.						
	d. Communicate without words when you have something important to say.						
	e. Look expectantly to your partner after speaking, to indicate your interest in his response.						
	f. Use facial expressions, body orientation and voice to indicate your interest in what your partner is saying.						
	g. Use voice intonation, head nods and facial expression to indicate you are following what your partner is saying.						
	h. Express curiosity non-verbally while listening.						
	i. Express surprise non-verbally while listening.						
	j. Effectively communicate understanding and agreement without words.						
	k. Communicate respectfully, without words, when you tire of a topic and wish your partner would change the subject.						
217.	Views conversational breakdowns and repairs as normal parts of the communication process.						

218.	Takes responsibility for monitoring communication accuracy and repairing misunderstandings.					
219.	Demonstrates awareness of a number of common conversational "turn-offs."					
220.	Effectively reads non-verbal cues to determine if listeners are bored.					
221.	Uses three effective methods for communicating to a speaker that he/she is interesting:					
	a. Communicate interest directly.					
	b. Bring up a topic your partner has talked about.					
	c. Take an action to follow up on an interest of your partner.					
222.	Effectively manages disagreements to prevent them from becoming arguments.					
223.	Conducts mutually enjoyable discussions of different opinions.					
224.	Effectively uses seven essential steps for discussing differences without arguments:					
	a. Make sure you don't need to win.					
	b. Make sure you are not angry with your partner.					
	c. Don't make the discussion into a Monologue. Keep your statements short and give your partner lots of time to respond.					
	d. Use your non-verbal communication to show your partner that you are not upset and that you are having the discussion for enjoyment.					
	e. Make sure you take the time to understand your partner's position. Use the methods you learned in the misunderstanding activity to help you.					
	f. Make sure that your partner understands your position. Use the methods you learned in the misunderstanding activity to help you.					
	g. Communicate respect for your partner's opinion.					
225.	Maintains the primacy of a conversation while engaged in another activity.					

	Stage 20: Ally					
226.	Understands the concept of emotion regulation versus control.					
227.	Has modified destructive Self Talk that makes stress reactions worse.					
228.	Uses effective Self Talk to manage stress.					
229.	Determined his unique emotional triggers.					
230.	Uses effective self-soothing methods when stressed.					
231.	Knows how to view mistakes as learning opportunities.					
232.	Is aware of the different forms of negative Self Talk that escalate into bad reactions.					
233.	Uses constructive Self Talk skills when encountering mistakes and setbacks.					
234.	Develops realistic expectations for his and others performance.					
235.	Understands and has eliminated the six destructive elements of conflicts from his repertoire:					
	a. Personal criticism.					
	b. It has to be someone's fault.					
	c. Put-downs.					
	d. Contempt.					
	e. The silent treatment.					
	f. Aggression or threats (against objects or persons).					
236.	Uses constructive alternatives for productive conflicts:					
	a. Use "softened startup." Begin with a positive statement about your partner. Don't just plunge into the negative.					
	b. Briefly state your complaint without making it personal.					
	c. Keep it to as few words as possible.					
	d. Avoid any blame or personal criticism.					
	e. Avoid words like "Always" and "Never."					

	f. Make a specific request that is within your partner's power to provide.						
	g. Carefully listen to your partner's point of view and let him/her know you acknowledge that their position is valid.						
237.	Routinely repairs conflicts before they escalate.						
238.	Understands the various actions that can jeopardize or destroy a friendship.						
239.	Functions as an integral part of a team by using negotiation and compromise to reach common goals.						
240.	Utilizes knowledge about friend's likes, dislikes and interests to strengthen their mutual bond ("Johnny likes this candy. I'm going to save him a piece").						
241.	Understands the critical concept of friends as Allies.						
242.	Understands friendship as a mutual contract of support and concern.						
243.	Has a strong desire to develop and maintain friendships based on mutual alliance, joint interests and shared memories.						
244.	Uses critical friendship maintenance actions on a regular basis:						
	a. Find out your friend's interests.						
	b. Function as an Ally.						
	c. Show appreciation to a friend. Tell them what you like or admire about them.						
	d. Keep away from distractions when your friend comes over to visit.						
	e. Keep conflicts constructive.						
	f. Call your friend to show interest.						
	g. Learn about the things that are important to a friend like interests and problems.						
	h. Plan exciting shared experiences with a friend.						
	Level VI: Partner						
	Stage 21: Shared Selves						
245	Understands the concept of Personal Identity						
246	Understands the different layers of Personal Identity						

247.	Understands the meaning of loneliness.						
248.	Appreciates the value of friendships as an antidote to loneliness.						
249.	Is aware of the core beliefs that help to define his Personal Identity.						
250.	Shows respect for social partners' core beliefs even if different.						
251.	Willingly explores his personal strengths and weaknesses.						
252.	Distinguishes constructive feedback from destructive criticism.						
253.	Willingly requests and accepts constructive feedback.						
254.	Knows how and when to provide constructive feedback.						
255.	Constructively explores the personal meaning of his disorder.						
256.	Uses effective methods to obtain an accurate picture of how others see him.						
257.	Seeks out information about how he is perceived by others.						
258.	Appreciates the influence of key role models in his life.						
259.	Thinks of future success in terms of personal character.						
260.	Has learned to communicate safely about his innermost feelings.						
261.	Effectively describes key aspects of his Personal Identity.						
Stage 22: Family Roots							
262.	Views family members as real people with their own unique needs that are just as important as his own.						
263.	Maintains an up to date understanding of important events, feelings, preferences and stresses in the lives of family members.						
264.	Applies knowledge of family members to real-life ways of caring for them.						
265.	Evaluates the effect of his actions on family members feelings.						
266.	Recognizes the need for ongoing maintenance of good family relationships.						
267.	Regularly expresses appreciation for the caring actions of family members.						

268.	Appreciates the pivotal family events that have produced the family relationships of today.					
269.	Demonstrates empathy for and personal identification with parents.					
270.	Uses effective methods for constructively managing family conflict.					
271.	Effectively uses a shared family calendar to coordinate activities with other family members.					
272.	Desires to establish an equal, "give-and-take" relationship with other family members.					
Stage 23: Group Connections						
273.	Understands the relative importance of different groups in his life.					
274.	Can identify the formal structural elements of groups he belongs to.					
275.	Demonstrates ability to understand and analyze the informal group dynamics of groups he belongs to.					
276.	Displays sensitivity to the unique "culture" of each group he belongs to.					
277.	Can evaluate the emotional climate of a group he belongs to.					
278.	Is aware of the vastly different roles the same person can assume in different groups.					
279.	Is aware of the power groups can exert to influence their members.					
280.	Demonstrates effective methods to successfully counter group pressure.					
281.	Distinguishes between constructive and destructive methods of standing up to group pressure.					
282.	Determines when to compromise and give in for the sake of group functioning.					
283.	Balances task demands with the emotional needs of other group members when involved in a cooperative activity.					
Stage 24: Intimate Relations						
284.	Understands the distinctions inherent in three different levels of friendship: Playmates, Pals and Close Friends.					

286.	Knows that close friendships are based on a history of mutual trust, deep mutual concern and shared beliefs.						
287.	Understands the concept of trust.						
288.	Has learned the most effective methods to slowly build trust.						
289.	Uses effective methods for deciding who and how much you should trust.						
290.	Evaluates his own trustworthiness.						
291.	Takes eight effective day-to-day actions that maintain a close friendship.						
	a. Keeping track of our emotional bank account to make sure I am not overdrawn.						
	b. Forgiving my friend if he is sometimes overdrawn as long as in the long run we are fairly even.						
	c. Making frequent contacts with no agenda except connecting.						
	d. Giving him enough "space" so that he doesn't feel suffocated by the relationship. Allowing him to have other friends.						
	e. Remembering events that are important to him.						
	f. Trying to understand his emotions, even when he doesn't verbally share them.						
	g. Lending him a new game or other object that you know he really likes even though you still really enjoy using it.						
	h. Communicating appreciation for small things your friend does for you.						
292.	Examines his friendships in relation to a balance of "give-and-take."						
293.	Desires to get to know the inner world of a good friend.						
294.	Maintains updated personal knowledge about close friends.						
295.	Acknowledges and celebrates the importance of close friendship.						
296.	Projects his close friendships into the future and appreciates the enduring qualities of a close relationship.						

Appendix C

Index of Activities and Objectives

Activity	Objectives	Page No.
Level I: Novice		
Stage 1: Attend		
1. My Words are Important	1	41
2. I Lost my Voice	2	43
3. Unexpected Sounds and Actions	1, 2	44
4. Fast-Paced Activities	1–4	46
5. Beanbag Medley	1, 2, 3, 4, 5, 6	48
Stage 2: Reference		
6. Sneaky Pete	8	53
7. Follow my Eyes to the Prize	10	54
8. Locked Box	9, 11, 12	56
9. Was it Right or Wrong?	9, 11, 12	58
Stage 3: Regulate		
10. Transition	18, 19, 20	63
11. Incomplete Completion	21	65
12. Do What I Do, Not What I Say	23	67
Stage 4: Coordinate		
13. Role Actions	24	70
14. Two-Ball Toss	25	71
15. Ropes	26, 27	72
16. Drums	28, 29, 30	74
17. Patterns	31	75

	Activity	Objectives	Page No.
43.	Play on Words	74	136
Level III: Challenger			
Stage 9: Collaboration			
44.	Ball and Net	75	144
45.	Self Instruction	78, 79	145
46.	Replays	80	146
47.	Two-on-Two Soccer	82	147
48.	Map Reader and Scout	83	149
Stage 10: Co-Creation			
49.	Creative Rhythms	84, 90	152
50.	Creative Songs	85, 90	153
51.	Creative Games	87, 90	155
52.	Creative Role-Plays	87, 90	157
53.	Joke Factory	88, 90	158
54.	Poetry Factory	89, 90	161
Stage 11: Improvisation			
55.	Co-Variations	91	164
56.	Improvised Activities	92, 99–105	166
57.	Improvised Structures	93, 99–105	167
58.	Improvised Rules	94, 99–105	168
59.	Improvised Rhythms	95, 99–105	170
60.	Improvised Role-Plays	96, 99–105	171
61.	Improvised Jokes	97, 99–105	174
Stage 12: Running Mates			
62.	Emotions	106–108	179
63.	Talk without Words	109	181
64.	Can You Hear Me Now?	110	183
65.	Connected Conversations	113	184
66.	Learning How to Lose	115, 116	186

Appendix D
Topic Index for Activities

Topic Area	Activity
Accepting Help, Guidance and Instruction	1, 7, 8, 9, 10, 12, 13, 20, 21, 22, 104, 105
Behavior/Emotional Regulation	1, 10, 11, 12, 23–29, 33, 35, 38, 45, 46, 62, 64, 66, 67, 72, 76, 92, 94–97, 105, 106, 110, 117, 118, 119, 129–132
Change, Transition and Adaptation	4, 5, 6, 8–13, 20–23, 25–32, 35, 55–61, 105, 106, 116, 117
Collaboration and Cooperation	14, 15, 16, 17, 18, 20, 34, 36, 38, 39–42, 44, 46, 47, 48–61, 68, 73–79, 81–91, 93, 100–103, 105, 124, 126
Communication and Language Development	1,2,3, 7–10, 13, 18, 19, 23–26, 37, 43, 54, 62,64, 65, 71, 78, 81, 95, 96, 98, 99, 107–109, 111, 123, 126, 131, 132, 137
Competence	7, 8, 9, 10, 13, 14, 15, 16, 23, 24, 26, 27–29, 33, 34, 35, 38, 45, 46, 53, 54, 66, 68, 72, 76, 78, 97, 98, 99, 104, 105, 106, 116, 117, 128, 129, 130, 138, 139, 147, 154
Concern for others' feelings, beliefs, interests and opinions	42, 65, 69, 70, 71, 75, 77, 79–91, 98, 100–102, 107–111, 120, 121, 122, 127, 131–134, 137, 139, 142–145
Conflict Management: Communication, Negotiation and Compromise	47, 75, 79–81, 86–9, 93, 97, 105, 106, 118, 119, 126, 131, 150, 151
Conversation	19, 23–25, 36, 37, 42, 43, 53, 54–65, 71, 73–77, 79–85, 86–91, 94, 95, 100–103, 106–111, 122–128, 133
Coordinating Actions	4,5, 12–17, 20–22, 34, 35, 38–40, 44, 47

Creativity, Novelty and Imagination (personal and shared)	18, 20, 27–32, 34 36, 38–40 42, 43, 49–61, 73–4, 81–91, 96, 99–102, 106, 111, 116,127
Emotional Awareness: Emotional Expression, Understanding and Sharing	2, 24–26, 31, 32, 46, 54, 62, 80, 92, 94–96, 99, 110, 121, 129, 134–136, 138, 139
Empathy	111, 120, 121, 130, 133, 134, 136, 138
Executive Functions: Flexible Thinking, Problem Solving, Reflection, Planning and Anticipation	8, 9, 12, 17, 18, 23–33, 36, 38, 43, 45, 46, 48–61, 64, 66–69, 73–4, 76, 78, 79, 81–91, 93, 97, 98, 100, 101, 103–106, 111–117, 121, 129–131, 135, 139, 141
Family Participation	142–147
Friendship	42, 69, 70, 98, 107–109, 118, 121, 131–134, 136, 138, 139, 152–156
Group Participation	44, 47–52, 68, 72, 76, 77, 81, 86–91, 93, 100, 106, 148–151
Humor and Playfulness	18, 30, 31, 36, 43, 49–53, 61, 73–4, 80, 81, 86–91, 101, 102, 114, 115
Joint Attention: Sharing, Integrating and Contrasting perceptions and perspectives	7, 8, 9, 13, 38, 48, 69, 71–77, 79, 80, 81, 86–91
Non-Verbal Communication	2, 4,5, 7, 8, 9, 12, 13, 17, 23, 24, 25, 32, 41, 48, 63, 94, 125, 127
Pretense and Deception	112–115
Self-awareness, Self-evaluation and Identity Development	23–26, 32, 33, 45, 46, 54, 62, 66, 67, 69, 77, 92, 94, 96, 99, 105, 107–110, 116, 121, 129, 130, 134–141, 146, 150, 152, 153
Social Observation and Social Referencing	2–10, 12–17, 20–24, 38–41, 44, 47, 48, 63–65, 68, 72, 76, 81, 94, 103, 107–109, 111, 118,123, 125, 127, 134, 148, 149
Stress Management: frustration, anxiety, mistakes, winning/losing, unexpected/rapid changes, rejections, accidents and teasing	6, 9–12, 26–29, 33, 45, 46, 55–61, 66, 67, 78, 79, 92, 93, 95–97, 105, 110, 116–119, 129–131, 134
Theory of Mind: interest and appreciation for others' ideas, point of view, experiences, intentions and feelings	38, 42, 69, 71, 72, 75–77, 80–91, 98, 100–104, 106–115, 118, 120–123, 126, 127, 130–134, 137, 139–145

Appendix E:

Levels and Stages of the Complete RDI Program

Level I: Novice

Stage 1: Attend

Stage 2: Reference

Stage 3: Regulate

Stage 4: Coordinate

Level II: Apprentice

Stage 5: Variation

Stage 6: Transformation

Stage 7: Synchronization

Stage 8: Duets

Level III: Challenger

Stage 9: Collaboration

Stage 10: Co–Creation

Stage 11: Improvisation

Stage 12: Running Mates

Level IV: Voyager

Stage 13: Perspective

Stage 14: Imagination

Stage 15: Group Foundations

Stage 16: Emotion Regulation

Level V: Explorer

Stage 17: Ideas

Stage 18: What's Inside?

Stage 19: Conversations

Stage 20: Alliy

Level VI: Partner

Stage 21: Shared Selves

Stage 22: Family Roots

Stage 23: Group Connections

Stage 24: Intimate Relations

Further Reading

Attwood, T. (1998) *Asperger's Syndrome.* London: Jessica Kingsley Publishers.

Gutstein, S.E. (2001) *Autism/Aspergers: Solving the Relationship Puzzle.* Arlington, TX: Future Horizons.

Gutstein, S.E. and Sheely, R.K. (2002) *Relationship Development Intervention with Young Children: Social and Emotional Development Activities for Asperger Syndrome, Autism, PDD and NLD.* London: Jessica Kingsley Publishers.

Holliday Willey, L. (1999) *Pretending to be Normal: Living with Asperger's Syndrome.* London: Jessica Kingsley Publishers.

Jackson, L. (2002) *Freaks, Geeks and Asperger Syndrome.* London: Jessica Kingsley Publishers.

Koch, K. (1970) *Wishes, Lies and Dreams.* New York: Harper Perennial.

Koch, K. (1990) *Rose, Where Did You Get That Red?* New York: Vintage Books.

Koch, K. (1997) *I Never Told Anybody: Teaching Poetry Writing to Old People.* New York: Teachers & Writers.

Miller, A. and Eller-Miller, E. (1989) *From Ritual to Repertoire: A Cognitive-Developmental Systems Approach with Behavior-Disordered Children.* New York: Wiley.